L E A D I N G

BY D E S I G N

IKEA®

the story of Ingvar Kamprad & IKEA, the world's leading home furnishing company

Bertil Torekull

Translated by Joan Tate

HarperCollins*Publishers*

Originally published as Historian om IKEA by Wahlström & Widstrand, 1998.
Copyright © 1998 by Bertil Torekull

HarperCollins books may be purchased for educational, business, or sales promotional use. For information, please write: Special Markets Department, HarperCollins Publishers Inc., 10 East 53rd Street,
New York, NY 10022.

FIRST EDITION

Designed by Joel Avirom and Jason Snyder

Torekull, Bertil, 1931—
    Leading by design: the IKEA story / Bertil Torekull.
    p. cm.
    ISBN 0-06-111985-7
    1. Ikea A/S—History.   2. Furniture industry and trade—Sweden—History   I. Title.
HD9773.S84I48 1999
380.1'456841'009485—dc21

99 00 01 02 03 ❖/RRD 10 9 8 7 6 5 4 3 2 1

CONTENTS

PREFACE

At the time this preface is being written, seven years have passed since the original Swedish edition of *The IKEA Story* was published and started circulating around the world from China in The East to The United States in The West. Since the English language edition of 1999, the company has more than doubled in size as if untouched by the horrific events since then that profoundly shook the world economy. The wildly galloping information technology sector crashed with a bang louder than the stock market collapse of 1929, absurdly inflated values popped like balloons, and scandals of stock manipulation and corporate robberies in greedy short-sightedness were following each other in both the US and Europe. The terrorist attacks had severely wounded America and all of the international community. Add the War in Iraq and the continuous concern regarding the dollar, oil and the Chinese expansion.

Following a period of neo-liberalism bordering on jungle-capitalism, questions are once again asked in whose interest are the large corporations really working, towards whom is their loyalty directed. Again there is talk of the need for ethics and discussions about what a good capitalism looks like.

`From this perspective it is of interest to study the IKEA phenomenon, not to name the company a model student in the school of capitalism and not because of its strong survival during the recent economic turbulence. The company's performance might possibly show the difference between the seamy sides in the behavioral pattern of large publicly traded corporations on the one hand and an unlisted business empire that is directed by a deeply rooted and carefully monitored culture on the other hand. Where the stock market often prioritizes immediate profit, the family led business can instead follow its dictates regarding long-range interests and sustainable growth.

A new chapter in this updated edition exemplifies the company´s rapidly growing engagement in Russia. The story of IKEA and Moscow sometimes reads like a young first love. In adult memory parts of an early betrayal can still smart, but a glow remains smoldering, a new obsession erupts in maturity. Such are the rules of passion, and passion has always guided IKEA and its founder Ingvar Kamprad, even more so in my view as he ages—he is now 79 years old.

Since the early 1960's, he has dreamed of doing business with Russia, willingly helping to furnish the mighty, but industrially, economically and socially so backward country. At first the setbacks were formidable. The Soviet's rigid planned policy system collided with the creativity of the independent operator. A limited exchange, however, created an embryo for business, information, and friendship that later was shown to be valuable.

In the euphoria directly following the fall of Berlin Wall 1989 and the break-up of the Soviet Union, IKEA made its first serious attempt to get a foothold there. When it did not succeed, the retreat was as expensive and filled with pain as rich in lessons learned. Other continents were then given priority in the company's strategic planning; following Western Europe were first North America and later Asia and China. But finally with the successful opening of an IKEA-store outside Moscow in 2000, the founder's old vision of "furnishing Russia" began to be realized. IKEA entered into an epoch where human and commercial possibilities appear to be unlimited. The strategy of this campaign can be found in later pages of this book.

The question here is whether the Russian investment could have happened at all within conventional large corporations listed on the stock exchange. They would be vulnerable to the impatient shortsightedness of analysts and the business media's consistent demands for inflammatory information and climbing profits. The early not at all insignificant losses would surely appear as incompatible with stock value if IKEA had been a publicly traded company. There might have been talks about a fiasco, an abuse of stockholders´ funds, and a demand of renewal in both leadership and direction.

In short, the adventure would have been voted out. IKEA would have fallen like a rock on Wall Street and risked its good name and continued expansion in the US.

Ingvar Kamprad's—by FORBES mentioned as one of the world´s richest—followed a totally different direction, the opposite of shortsightedness. From separate starting points, he has seen both Russia and US as long-term possibilities that were allowed initially to be costly. In Russia not only did he perceive the opportunity to upgrade a badly decayed furniture industry to free market standards, but also that this would take time. It's not out of the question that we look at Russia in a not too distant future like a lately awakened European variation of tiger economy. The model could be Poland's economic miracle where IKEA started to build itself into a major player behind the iron curtain in the early 1960's.

However, Kamprad, who started IKEA as a young man of 17, hesitated when his young directors were pushing to establish the company in the US. The Americans did not "need" IKEA, he espoused a bit sullenly. They had "everything", one more furniture operator wouldn't change anything in a country made up of so many dissimilar states. Russia was a better choice. In its rapidly growing middle class he saw his dream-customers: people living in crowded conditions with a sudden hope of a better future who definitely "needed" IKEA to modernize life with inexpensive merchandise of excellent quality.

For America the approach would be quite different. It wasn't the low prices that made the public storm the first blue and yellow store near Philadelphia in 1985 but the appetite for modern design, the exotic feeling of being part of the light and stylish Nordic form. It has cost the organization a certain learning period to cultivate this chock of delight from the customers and formulate its very own more long-term credo. When IKEA USA now is celebrating 20 years, its Danish top executive Pernille Lopez repeats persistently that deep down this country "needs" IKEA as well as many other countries; even if in a more layered way.

Her argument may sound paradoxical but is logical and based on demographics. Most Americans do not earn decent middle class incomes but belong in society's lowest salary ranges. One fifth of the population earns at the most $9,000 per year, another fifth $18,000 and a similarly sized group, $36,000. Life is a tough battle for survival even in this country. For millions of Americans, a super low price (what IKEA calls "a breath-taking-price") is an equally strong buying incentive as for the Swede in the 60's, the German in the 70's, the Brit in the 80's and 90's and the Russian in the 2000's. That price plus that design plus that quality! And Swedish meatballs with lingonberries in the big restaurant or a simple hot dog by the checkout line…

In the USA a fortuitous circumstance has now evolved. After two decades, IKEA with about two billion dollars in US sales still captures only between one and two percent of this country's furniture and home decorating market. This is challenging the company's love for serious competition: Being the underdog is a wonderful entrepreneurial and creative feeling. Like a windmill the company likes to catch its power moving against the wind. Thus a long journey in this country has just begun.

IKEA remains an independent, foundation-owned company with a powerful culture within, mindful of simple virtues, thrift, and diligence pared with profitability and expansion. Even in the US, it has not needed to expose itself for the Wall Street or to publicly argue its smallest decisions in front of greedy stockholders or a critical group of market analysts. This gives peace of mind for decision-making, organic growth, and profits available to build tomorrow without publicly angry stockholders keeping their eye primarely on the next dividend and on shameless bonuses and options etc.

IKEA has—by the way—not been unaffected by strongly accelerating executive compensations across the whole Western world. The level is, however, comparatively and consciously modest.

So both US and Russia are good examples of economic earning capacity. In Kamprad's conviction it is better to remain outside the stock market. He allows time to produce the glowing profits in both these markets; they are still under tremendous growth.

In Russia the total number of stores (five today) will at least double during the next few years, in the US with 25 stores today IKEA will also grow fast. The hunt for good sites is on everywhere—Georgia, Illinois, New York, California, Texas, Massachusetts and Michigan etc.

This expansion is happening at a time of competition from chains like Costco and Target to name a few. They each profess to an ever more popular mantra that old borders of separate product lines exist only to be abolished. IKEA, pioneer in Europe as a furniture dealership with a restaurant and food shop (and today literally Sweden's no. 1 food exporter) is now coming up against fierce low-price-competitors selling primarily groceries, but offer cheap furniture as an extra bargain.

This challenge probably fits IKEA like hand in glove. The relatively closed corporate structure itself is the secret to being able to operate long-term but is only part of the explanation. Neither secrecy nor openness will guarantee good decisions. The theoretically open-for-scrutiny publicly traded US corporations, as well as those in the world, have made a host of wretched decisions in the financial crisis (type Andersen, Enron, WorldCom, Parmalat etc) that have not yet been healed. These events have been decided within a greedy and self-absorbed leadership group, who despite a formal transparency seems to be unavailable for accountability.

IKEA, with its single and unambiguous owner and with principles that the founder's spirit still fervently watches over, has made it easier to perform like the good capitalist regarding long-term planning, patience, and rebuilding of capital - let us officially call it: taking responsibility for the future.

If appalling options and bonus systems have created headlines on the stock market, IKEA has calmly marketed its own philosophy of humility and step-by-step created its special system for rewards and stimulation. Veterans in leadership roles have been offered co-partnership on a franchise basis as a successful even more frequency tried device.

Up to this point there are no indications that IKEA's choice of such more subtle but performance related incitement is worse than what has created so much misery in stock exchange corporations where boards and directorates helped themselves at the expense of stock holders and co-workers and also indirectly, the customers.

The absence of known scandals in the IKEA-sphere should perhaps not only be interpreted as a bonus of privacy but a sign as well that "Health speaks for itself". The learned corporate culture with its Japanese austerity and its roots in basic values like frugality, simplicity, and honesty live up to expectations into the global 2000's, and not only in fiscal terms.

Numbers comparing growth during the last few years speak volumes. The year 1998 IKEA's total sale was 50 billion Swedish Krona – the August 2005 accounts were around 130 billion. Then IKEA had 38 000 co-workers – today 90 000. The number of stores, combined having some 400 million visitors per year, have increased from 137 to more than 220 in now 33 countries including the 24 stores that are owned and run by franchisees outside the IKEA group. A dozen new stores are set to open during 2006 and the same numbers during the years to follow. Virgin markets like China are poised for a possible leap, and in others like Turkey, Japan, Portugal and Romania, the company is plowing unbroken fields right now. The classic IKEA catalogue prints about 150 million copies – an increase of tens of millions.

This rapid expansion, then, has occurred as if the company was unaffected by the international turbulence described above. This ought to be cause for reflection.

What can we learn from IKEA? For both established and future entrepreneurs, economists, and politicians, I see "The IKEA Story" as a manual from real life for what capitalism can achieve when built upon certain ethical base values. Combined with modern thinking regarding design, material, production, environment and logistics, these qualities seem to be valid irrespective of the many local markets with vastly differing structure or history.

When this edition is finished during summer of 2005, the founder Ingvar Kamprad has just returned from several major trips that took him to the US and Russia and a host of other countries within a short period of time. This is a program ambitious enough even for a young man. In his continuing enthusiastic involvement lies a value not available for usual analysis. The value will become manifest on the day he decides to step down.

Ultimately, the future will then be about how the company is able to handle its culture of independence and morality and how it will succeed in combining this with its joyous passion for growth. The readers will be left to judge whether this is a likely possibility.

Bertil Torekull
Brantevik, Sweden 2005

P.S. Like all major enterprises, IKEA is subjected to recurrent reorganizations and personnel changes. In the present book reflecting all of the company's history (Ingvar Kamprad's story of IKEA's remarkable creation), the names and numbers refer to the existing situation in 1998-1999. Thus they may differ from the data in the preface, the latest figures available. The IKEA group today is led by Anders Dahlvig as Chief Executive with Hans Gydell as second in command. In the foundation-owned INGKA Holding B.V., Ingvar Kamprad participates, as senior advisor while his eldest son Peter today is a board member. Hans-Göran Stennert, brother of Margaretha Kamprad, Ingvar's wife, is ruling Chairman of the Board. All three Kamprad sons Peter, Jonas and Mathias, are slated to play important roles in the leadership of a growing IKEA, unstated as yet in which positions. Sweden's role in the organization, in other words the connection to "the Swedish" and the concept "The IKEA Way", has rather strengthened lately concurrent with globalization.

PROLOGUE

In the Beginning Was the Moraine

Älmhult, Småland, Sweden, the World.

His earthly root, his spiritual biotope.

The statue in the market square is of Carl von Linné, the man who put a name to all the plants on earth, his back to the town hall as he gazes over at the large store on the other side of the railway. The founder of the store is a man whose legacy reaches all over the world.

In their common landscape, so harsh to the eye, not only flowers and ideas grew, but also companies.

The road from Älmhult to Pjätteryd church, then right toward Agunnaryd, is just as winding, hilly, and wooded as it was when his fore-fathers immigrated at the end of the nineteenth century. Seventeen kilometers further on is Elmtaryd, the farm where he grew up. Three houses around a yard, gravel paths, a flower bed in the middle. Outside the gate is the green shed that at first was the churn stand that became the cata-pult for his first childish dreams of becoming an industry giant.

The barn is empty, but the forest about it is as thick and dark about its mysterious pathways as it was when he first went to primary school. The silence is still more likely to be broken by the bark of a roebuck than the sound of a tractor or car.

It's a long way to the country where an empire was built.

Here, where he was born, the moraine rules: sandy, stony, gravelly heathland. Loneliness, silence, and reserve prevail, interrupted only once in a while by a pasture smiling behind the veil of a weeping birch. The cottages have always been small, survival has never been taken for granted, and the fields are stony.

In this stony clay silence, this harsh moraine and morality, the dream of IKEA first grew, for everything requires its special soil. This is the place where you can dig to find the full height and strength of the tree.

In the winter of 1999, as this edition is being completed, IKEA has about 44,000 workers and extends across a global network of 150 stores in thirty countries on four continents. Almost 100 million copies of the company's catalog will tempt more than 195 million people into its Swedish temples to buy goods worth more than $7.061 billion. Before the end of the year, five new stores will have appeared in various places, one of them in the busy city of Shanghai in China, 12,000 miles from the rural quiet of Elmtaryd—evidence of how far seeds can fly.

This is where the rough outline of the whole concept began to be written by a dyslexic boy on a farm. How can this be explained without also explaining where such talents come from, how success is born, how ideas break ground and confront their epoch or even help to create it?

At the start, it is on the moraine that the adult man based his business philosophy. Leaders of the future in this enterprise were to go on pilgrimages to the churn stand, the springboard to his thesis, as if to Mecca, to gaze at and contemplate, if not to worship. They were to touch the wood as if solemnly selling their souls to participate in a future realization of a myth, a saga, a legend, or simply hoping to fill their hands with strength from the actual source. Of what did that source consist?

Two empty hands, the myth says. He built an empire from nothing, the saga says.

But what are "two empty hands"?

What is really meant by "nothing"?

Do love and encouragement, innate energy, desire for revenge, imagination and curiosity, all count for nothing? What about fortunate circumstances and a handicap overcome? How can self-esteem, restlessness, and education be measured in known and unknown failures on the way?

And do not someone's meandering roots count, or the banal dream of being rich, or the vanity of one day showing your father and mother, and why not the whole world, what you could do, although no one had had any idea?

Of course they count.

The main character in this book grew up in a frugal but by no means poor home, among people who loved him. The background was dramatic, the people surrounding him recognizing his imaginativeness and joie de vivre and also providing him with exciting role models, though also some misleading ones. In this secure, loving environment he could test his ability to overcome instances of moderate opposition in an era that saw few obstacles and adored the idea of being part of the formation of what was called the "people's home," that is, the new Sweden.

This is not a book about a man starting out empty-handed. On the contrary, it is a book about a man with his hands full of resolute dreams, a heart tormented by inadequacy and self-pity, and a stubborn and inquisitive enterprise: a strange mixture of a social animal and an eccentric. The book is equally about a firm in which he realized and through which he lived out all these circumstances, for good or bad.

Objections may well arise to the idea of summarizing an outstanding and natural genius so simply, or the elevation of the work of an incorrigible capitalist, so restlessly obsessed by the lure of profit and power that he used a thousand tricks to endow his creation with eternal life.

Others will recognize themselves, for all of us bear within us the embryo of a miracle.

ROOTS OF A FURNITURE DEALER

Germans in the Forests of Småland

And from that shall his destiny come about.

—VILHELM MOBERG,
AUTHOR OF *THE EMIGRANTS*

A drama of life and death is being played out in the cold winter of 1897, in the dark forests surrounding Elmtaryd farm in Agunnaryd, twenty kilometers northwest of Älmhult. It is a drama of obscure forces—money, power, and ownership—a drama of unaccepted immigrants, and a misalliance between an illegitimate girl and an adventurous young man of good family.

It all began with mail order.

Achim Erdmann Kamprad and his wife Franziska landed in Trelleborg in south Sweden in 1896. He was barely thirty, she was four years younger, and with them were their two sons, Franz Feodor, three, and Erich Erwin, twelve months. Their firstborn had died in infancy in October 1892.

They now hurried to Småland, where Achim had purchased a forest property he had never seen through an advertisement in a German hunting magazine. For a family whose name was to become legendary in the mail-order trade, this was in keeping.

The young family had taken the train to Älmhult, where they were met by Karl Johansson from Möcklehult with a horse and cart. From there, they wound their way to the farm in the parish of Agunnaryd. Perhaps, on the way to their new home, the travelers were pleased to see the gleam reflected from some quiet lake, but most of all they must have felt the mysterious weight of the land and the solemnity of the silent pines. They knew not a word of Swedish, and their new neighbors were likely to be suspicious of these intruders. The Kamprads were undoubtedly challenging fate.

Achim threw himself into his new activities as owner of this home-stead of 449 hectares. He rapidly employed a coachman who faithfully waited with the barouche outside Ljungby town hotel, to which Achim liked to retreat now and again. Perhaps in his heart he had already given up; perhaps he learned quite early on to leave things to his strong and energetic wife, who seemed to manage most things.

The forest—timber—was his specialty, just as it had been his father's, a talent which, incidentally, was to continue down the line to both son and grandson and, God knows, perhaps to his great-grandsons as well. The problems of the large forest estate, however, overcame its owner. Considerable investment was required to put it in order, and while he probably made plans, his finances prevented him from carrying them out. Some of the neighbors tried to acquire the property when a whiff of the new owner's difficulties and possible insolvency spread its sour expectations around the district.

In the spring of 1897, Achim Kamprad's request for a vital loan was refused by the Agunnaryd Savings Bank. Desperate and filled with fore-boding for the future, he went back home to Elmtaryd and, according to legend, shot first his beloved hounds and then himself. Ironically, nearly thirty years later, his widow was to suffer a similar tragedy when her son Erich, young, weak, and overdependent on his mother, took his own life.

Six months after Achim's tragic death, his widow gave birth to her fourth child, a girl. Alone in a foreign country with her children, the young German woman had to unravel the tangled mess her husband had left behind him. Thanks to her great energy and a talent for management, she became a respected, almost feared employer, "the boss," her isolation in the district as great as her sturdy stubbornness.

Exiled in this new land, with no close friends, she found it difficult to show emotion. But when a vagrant came to her door, it was said she could be generosity itself. Her will, or rather her need to rule and control everything and everyone, has been testified to. Up to her death at the age of eighty, an aura of sternness, determination, and inaccessibility surrounded her harsh figure, as if she had never dared relent in such a hostile environment.

Why had she and her husband come to Sweden?

We know little of their motives. Perhaps Achim's mother, Sedonia, wanted to be rid of her good-for-nothing son and was behind it all. To her disappointment, her son had married beneath himself, and the awareness of his mother's disapproval may have been enough to tempt the young couple into exile.

Franziska was the illegitimate daughter of an innkeeper in Grunthal bei Olbernhau in Bohemia-Mähren, the fruit of her mother's unhappy love affair with a well-to-do and unfortunately married mining engineer. He bought himself free of the child by giving the mother money, with which she wisely bought an inn. Now in possession of a decent income, she married a customs officer with whom she was to have three more children.

Achim's mother, Sedonia, was already a noblewoman when she married the landowner Kamprad. Although her financial background was solid, she was not spared profound pain, for nine of her twelve children died young. Therefore, she must have felt an extra strong need for her surviving second son, Achim, to find a place in life, and the homestead in Sweden seemed the perfect opportunity.

Achim's suicide was an emotional disaster for his mother. Nevertheless, it was Sedonia who now took responsibility and intervened in the chaos that engulfed her lonely daughter-in-law. Sedonia not only ensured that there was money to keep the creditors in check; she herself traveled at the critical moment up to Elmtaryd to help Franziska, whom she unjustly and with slight contempt often referred to as "that stupid donkey." The children were provided with a tutor who taught them languages and mathematics before they were eventually sent to school in Lund.

When Sedonia died only three years after her son's tragic death, one of her German estates was inherited by Achim's three small children. It was sold, and Elmtaryd received yet another much-needed financial reinforcement. Seventy years later, her grandson would return the family name to its German native soil, conquer the market with his ideas, and build a house far grander than the *schloss* from which they had once originated.

This is only a brief summary of the drama of the Kamprad immigrants. Little is known of the innermost driving forces in people's lives, but perhaps this background might be added to the sum total of the triumphant journey by a Swedish businessman on his journey across the continent and all over the world.

This book is not just about a vulnerable family wrestling with the intractable (both mentally and physically) Swedish moraine. Nor is it about poverty. Mostly, it is about a family's return to its roots.

Occasionally, Franziska took her three children back to her home district in Bohemia-Mähren—while Elmtaryd was run by the foreman, Fritz Johansson, who acted as trustee to the fatherless children. When her elder son, Franz Feodor, was twenty-five, he took over the estate, still a bachelor. But Franziska was to watch over him like a hawk as long as she was alive. She reluctantly abdicated when Feodor married his heart's desire, Berta Nilsson, daughter of the owner of the best-known and largest local store. Franziska was cool toward her son's good-hearted and gifted wife. Solely to Ingvar Feodor, her grandson, did old Franziska show all the love, warmth, and weakness she had not dared let loose during her dramatic life as an undesired immigrant in the depths of the forests of Småland.

My Life on the Farm

> We taught him to dance to the gramophone
> beneath the thick foliage of the oaks down
> by the church. . . . He caught fish and crayfish
> and was adventurous and bold, stuffing the
> crayfish he'd just caught down the back of
> his long johns. He was like that.
>
> —I.-B. BAYLEY, INGVAR KAMPRAD'S COUSIN

My parents' first child, I was born in the White Cross Maternity Home in the parish of Pjätteryd on the boundaries of Älmhult. For the first years, we lived at Majtorp, a farm on the Ljungby road from Älmhult to Pjätteryd. My mother's father, the storekeeper in Älmhult, had given the farm to his daughter Berta, my mother, as a wedding present, just as he gave his other two daughters a small property each as a kind of early inheritance. The son was given the store.

In those years, Father cycled or drove a horse and cart the twenty kilometers between his father's farm, Elmtaryd, where my grandmother still reigned, and Majtorp. In 1933 we moved to Elmtaryd, which Father had formally taken over in 1918. Only twenty-five, he didn't really want to be a farmer at all, but his mother's word was law, and he became her obedient tool.

Similarly, Father's brother had also wanted to go out into the world but still lived on the farm. He had fallen in love with a bank cashier from Lund, but Grandmother said, "You're to stay at home," and so he did. He finally chose the same route as his father and shot himself in 1935. I was nine, and I remember what a gloomy atmosphere it created.

I loved my Uncle Erich. He was a great forestry man, a fisherman, and not least a good shot. Grandmother was no great cook, but she could roast the duck he brought home.

My mother, loved by everyone, showed good humor in the shadow of her mother-in-law. She was an amazing person to whom nothing was allowed to be impossible. I don't know what she thought, but just like my father, she went along with whatever Grandmother decided. It was the "old missis" and the "young missis," and everyone knew the difference in power.

She soon discovered the poor state of my father's business affairs, so she started a guest house, with his approval but not his enthusiasm. We rented rooms out to summer visitors, every room taken except my parents', into which we all squashed together. Mother also borrowed some rooms from Grandmother, and the guests paid a few kronor for full board, money that was truly needed.

So Mother was a heroine in silence. She contracted cancer before she was fifty and never really enjoyed being at last ruler of Elmtaryd; she died at the young age of fifty-three, when I was twenty-seven. A few years later, I started up a foundation for cancer research that bore her name and to which employees in Älmhult donate money every Christmas.

The very thought of it makes me weep.

When Mother was finally hospitalized, Father never left her side, staying there day and night. They loved each other.

We had a groom on the farm called Ture Andersson. His son Kalle and I were best friends. The greatest fun of all was to be allowed to stay overnight with him and his brothers and sister, all of whom slept on a large plush sofa, two in one direction and three in the other. Whenever I managed to get permission to stay overnight, I crept down there head to foot with the others; I thought that was great. I am a typical herd animal: I really only feel good when I'm with other people.

In other respects, I suppose I was slightly peculiar in that I started tremendously early doing business deals. My aunt helped me buy the first hundred boxes of matches from the eighty-eight-öre bazaar in Stockholm (nowadays Buttericks) in a large pack costing eighty-eight öre. My aunt didn't even accept payment for postage. Then I sold the boxes at two to three öre each, sometimes even five öre, so I was able to earn an öre or two in between. Talk about profit margins, but I still remember the lovely feeling. I can't have been more than five at the time.

Later on, I sold Christmas cards and wall hangings. I caught fish myself, then cycled around selling them. I picked lingonberries that were sent by bus to a buyer in Liatorp. When I was eleven, my main enterprise was garden seeds from J. P. Persson's firm in Nässjö. That was my first big deal, and I actually earned money from it. I was able to exchange my mother's old Hermes bicycle for a new blue Nordstjernan bike, a racing model. That was also when I bought myself a typewriter.

Perhaps I wasn't much of a farmer, but one summer a friend and I looked after the cowshed. My friend's name was Otto Ullman; he was a German-Jewish refugee child who came to us during the war and became one of my very best friends, and for a while also a colleague.

I am still proud that I'm able to milk a cow by hand and to mow a meadow with a scythe.

From that time, selling things became something of an obsession. It is not easy to know what might drive a boy more than the desire to earn money, the surprise that you could buy anything so cheaply and sell it for a little more. But I remember walking in the meadows with my father, Feodor, who had had training in forestry. I was ten, and we came to a place at which he said, "I'd like to make a forest track here, but it would cost too much." Then we were soon somewhere else, and again it was money that was lacking—to carry out Father's many plans.

I remember thinking: *If only I could help Father. Supposing I got some money so that I. . . .* To carry something out, you clearly had to have the means.

That's how I thought. On one occasion when I had taken on too much in my financial activities, I was allowed to borrow ninety kronor (eleven dollars) from Father. That was a lot of money at the time. On another occasion, Mr. Ekström, manager of the Skånska Bank in Liatorp, lent me five hundred kronor (sixty-three dollars—a fortune) on the strength of my blue eyes, and a bank draft was arranged so that I could purchase five hundred fountain pens from Paris.

This was essentially the only "real" loan I have taken out in my life. Trading was in my blood. My mother came from a leading trading family in Älmhult. Her father, my grandfather, was Carl Bernard Nilsson, who ran Älmhult's largest country store and was an ironmonger. Mother's brother Valter took over the store, and he was not such a good businessman, but he was a hunter, a Rotarian, a member of the chamber of commerce, and a sociable man who let me work as errand boy for a while.

C. B. Nilsson was a country store of the old kind with four or five assistants, the smell of herring and toffees and leather, and a large backyard where the horses were fed. Everything between heaven and earth could be bought there, even dynamite. I was nothing but a little lad running errands when I wanted to. Grandfather never made any demands on me, and sometimes I could spend whole days in the shop.

Grandfather had one great love on earth and that was me. He became my very best playmate. Those years I lived with two imaginary people, Kamfert and Schane, two Indians who shadowed me faithfully wherever I went and whatever I was doing. Then I had Grandfather with a capital G.

Together, we four built palaces and told tales. Together with me, he—a corpulent man—and Kamfert and Schane crawled under the table at dinner, and then all three of them would come out for a drive in the car. Grandfather knew the art of play and accepted my fantasy; nothing was impossible.

Unfortunately, he was just as kind in business life as he was in my invented world. He quite simply found it difficult to accept payment.

C. B. Nilsson no longer exists as a business, but by sheer chance IKEA in a sense took over. One day in the 1960s, when the time had come for Valter to close down, I bought the whole property and the site around it. We built the present inn on the foundations of the house.

Thanks to the purchase of that site—and others from the district council—we were able to continue to expand on the very spot where we once started IKEA, immediately opposite Älmhult station on the other side of the track. And thanks to that, somehow both families are represented with their roots in the enterprise—my mother's side as well as my father's. A furniture store now stands on the foundations of the country store, and furniture is made out of the trees in the forest.

Grandmother and Me

> It was the best of times and the very worst. It
> was a time of wisdom and of folly.
> —CHARLES DICKENS, *A TALE OF TWO CITIES*

My grandmother Franziska, or Fanny as they called her, influenced not only me but also the entire family to a great extent. She was a clever woman who had grown up in a simple home. Grandfather's family, which we have traced back to the eighteenth century, was more upper-class. Great-grandfather Zacharias August married a von Bärenstein, but the Kamprads themselves were not of the nobility. A question mark exists in the shape of an inherited sword, which I have kept, with the Order of the Garter from the Queen of England engraved on the handle: *honi soit qui mal y pense*.

No one knows where this weapon came from.

Once on a journey to Poland I found a gravestone with the name Kamprad on it. There are in fact Kamprads all over the place—a branch in Holland, another that came from Saxony to Odessa in the Ukraine. An elderly gentleman appeared once from Finland and wished to speak to me. His family spelled Kamprad with *dt* at the end. I have made no effort to find the most distant roots of the family, but my son Jonas has shown an interest in researching the matter.

My paternal grandfather's father was a qualified forester in a large province in Poland, and Grandfather also had training in forestry when he moved to Sweden. Others in the family were educated at a lyceum in Austria, where it was said no one was accepted if he did not have ancestors going back twelve to fourteen generations.

So the Kamprads were "gentry," and my grandmother certainly knew the difference between herself and "them." Her husband had fallen in love with a woman of a lower class and then, against the wishes of the family, wanted to marry her. I think that fact affected my father's mother all her life.

She had to fight to survive after Grandfather's violent death. Sedonia, Father's paternal grandmother, was a great support for a while and arranged for a tutor to teach all three children: my father; his brother, Erich; and his sister, Erna. For a while, Father went to a Catholic monastery school, which had a lasting effect on him. Later they all went to school in Lund, and Grandmother lived with them during that time.

Those difficult early times in Sweden affected my grandmother. Life had not turned out as she had thought it would. For the lack of a husband, she acted as master. Elmtaryd at the time had a groom and two laborers working on the farm: Ture Andersson, Hilding Sjöström, and Anders Collén. I remember the evening ritual when the milk was brought up from the cowshed in two or three pails and placed on Grandmother's bench in the kitchen of the big house she lived in until she died. She portioned out the milk, first to herself, then to our family, after that to the laborers and the groom, and finally to the crofters who lived nearby and bought milk from us. They thanked my grandmother politely, then went home.

Slaughtering took place two or three times a year, and Grandmother supervised the cutting up. The fresh meat, which Grandmother called *Weltfleisch*, was to be used at once. She made sure she and my aunt had a good piece, and the rest was salted down and left in a large pan in the cellar. In time, the meat turned a bluish green.

Grandmother had a curious habit of not allowing us to start eating the fresh meat until all the old meat had been consumed. Mother was often given the oldest bits. She would soak it for several days, perhaps weeks, to leach out the salt, but when we finally ate it, it was nevertheless always terribly salty.

There was a tension between Grandmother and my mother. Father was to a great extent his mother's son, and he helped her a great deal. Early every morning, he lit all the tiled stoves so that Grandmother would not be cold when she got up. She was a domineering person, regarded with great respect, but she liked me very much. In contrast to most of the others on the farm, I never suffered at all from her dictatorial temperament.

I remember one episode.

Mother kept chickens that ranged about quite freely. I was normally never punished by my parents, but I once got hold of a wretched chicken and wrung its neck. My father did not approve. He chased me across the farmyard, and I ran off while Grandmother stood on the kitchen steps slapping her knees and crying, "Hurry, hurry, Ingvar, hurry!!"

Father was only a few meters behind me when Grandmother grabbed me and shook her fist at him: "Don't you dare touch my little boy!"

So it is not strange that I was sympathetic toward my grandmother. Not only did she protect me from the outside world, but when I was only about five and began buying and selling things, she became my very special and most faithful customer. Regardless of whether she needed anything, she bought from me—not much, but always something. That gave me the courage to take the next step and go selling to the neighbors as well. When she died, we found a whole carton of things, pens and things of that kind, she had bought from her grandson.

In the early 1930s—I was nine at the most—Grandmother began telling me how bad things were for her relatives at home in what had been Sudetenland (Bohemia-Mähren), which by the Treaty of Versailles in 1919 had become Czech. I remember her crying at the thought. Every month she sent a parcel of clothes, and there was always a drive on the farm for old clothes. At the time it was also permitted to send a little food, including half a kilo of coffee. At the post office there was a list on which the contents of every parcel had to be specified.

My mother also sent parcels to our relatives, who clearly were having a very difficult time.

Grandmother became a great admirer of Hitler and his plans for a Greater Germany, in part because she felt more German than Swedish, or rather, she felt she was precisely the Sudeten German she had been at birth and certainly not Czech. Although she was a citizen in another country now, her heart was still with her own people, who had been exiled from their country. Before the First World War, when her children were small, she often went down to her south German homeland, while the rather rundown farm at home was looked after by the foreman.

After the First World War, a great deal changed. She could no longer go to Germany; her family were then living in Czechoslovakia. Grandmother described how the Germans who had stayed in Sudetenland were treated by their Czech masters, and I listened with empathy. Grandmother, who died in 1945 just after peace was declared following the Second World War, was never to know of the reconciliation today when Czechs and Germans represented by Vaclav Havel and Helmut Kohl asked forgiveness of each other for past injustices. Instead, she suffered with her fellow Germans. The happiest day of her life—she celebrated it with a coffee party for everyone in the vicinity—was and remained the day in 1938 when Hitler invaded Sudetenland and annexed what Germany had lost.

Father was also much influenced by Grandmother on these points. Politically, as a young man he had been keen on socialism, but in time he became increasingly conservative and nationalistic and a pronounced anti-Bolshevik. He also felt himself to be German, and he was just as upset by everything Grandmother's family was said to have gone through. He was very positive, if not as fanatical, in his admiration for Hitler, who had "saved" the Sudeten Germans. Who could dislike a man who wanted to unite Germans with Germans?

In the district, many people have regarded Father as pure Nazi, or *nasse*, as they were called behind their backs. I can understand that, but I don't think he ever became a member of either the Lindholmers—the Swedish Nazi Party, named after Sven-Olov Lindholm—or the Neo-Swedes Party. However, the difference between being a sympathizer and joining a party is a very fine line.

I was a child who loved both my stern grandmother and my good father. I listened to their stories, and of course I was indoctrinated, "pro-Germanized."

A lot of propaganda came to the farm from Germany: glossy pictures of happy, handsome young people in uniform, sitting around campfires, and the words said they were on their way to doing great works. Grandmother showed me a colorfully illustrated magazine called the *Signal*. It also showed how wonderful things were for young people. My childish reaction was, of course, that it was great that Uncle Hitler was doing so much for Grandmother's relatives, particularly for children and young people.

I was perhaps more easily influenced than most. Ceremonies and such often move me. I remember how solemn it was when Uncle Erich, the one who eventually shot himself, hoisted the flag on the farm on high days and holidays. I was always near tears. It was the same when we sang the national anthem at school. I still have the same characteristic: call it a kind of profound sentimentality or tearfulness. A memory appears from adult days, probably as late as the 1980s. My very good friend and confidant, and IKEA's accountant of many years, Sigurd Löfgren, was with me in the basement of the office in Humlebæk in Denmark, which we had turned into a recreation room. Sigurd was reciting a poem by Dan Andersson, the Swedish romantic poet, and we were holding hands, I all the time fighting against those eternal tears.

The close contact I had with Grandmother turned out, I can

say now, to be fateful. In fact, it gave birth to a way of thinking that was to have unexpected consequences in my life. Long after the political aberrations of my childhood and teens, with their overtones of Nazism and fascism, and decades after I had at last awakened from a youthful ingenuousness, in the maturity of my old age, I was made to pay for this German influence.

From that point of view, perhaps no one has played such a great and sorrowful part in my life as old Grossmutter Fanny. She who liked me so much.

THE
ENTREPRENEUR

How I Became a Furniture Dealer

Young man, you'll never become a businessman.
—GUNNAR JANSSON

Mother grew worried when I brought home so many things to sell. People won't buy all those pencils and rubbers! But there were people living in every house at the time, and I stubbornly went on and on about it, and if I had decided in my own mind to do something, then I would do it.

In my last year at middle school, my first rather childish business began increasingly to look like a real firm. Under my bed at the school boardinghouse in Osby, I always had a brown cardboard box full of belts, wallets, watches, and pens.

I was seventeen in the spring of 1943 and wanted to start my own firm before going to the School of Commerce in Göteborg, but as a minor I had to have permission from my main guardian Mr. (Uncle) Ernst. (By Swedish law, every child has a guardian outside the family, normally a respected local citizen.) I cycled the six kilometers up to Agunnaryd village and explained to Uncle Ernst that I was going to start up a firm. He found that rather difficult to understand. But he stopped harrowing his field and went into the kitchen to sit down to talk to me, asking, "But what's ye goin' to do wi' that, dear boy?"

I explained as best I could, and he signed a paper, which I sent to the county council with a ten-kronor note. Thus was the trading firm Ikéa Agunnaryd founded amid the aroma of coffee in Uncle Ernst's kitchen. I is for Ingvar, K for Kamprad, E for Elmtaryd, and A for Agunnaryd.

My time as a student at the School of Commerce in Göteborg was a turning point in several respects. One of my teachers, the professor of national economy, Ivar Sundbom, aroused my interest in wider contexts. That was when I began to understand certain things; from this time, distribution became an idée fixe. Solving the question of how in the simplest and cheapest way to convey goods from the factory to the customer was fundamental if one were to become a good businessman.

In the school library I found trade papers with advertisements for exports and imports, and in halting English I wrote to a foreign manufacturer, whose general agent for pens I then became. Direct import was a way of fixing the lowest possible price.

In Göteborg I went into a shoe shop and saw the old-fashioned way they had of selling anything. White cardboard boxes stacked on shelves going right up to the ceiling. They had ladders they had to keep going up and down to fetch brown and black shoes. That couldn't be rational, and it wasted money.

Fountain pens were the first major element in the stock I was now building up in my firm. I could import five hundred at a time at a very low price. Then I took the train to various places in south Sweden, went into tobacconists at home around Älmhult, and I also advertised my goods for mail order. Brio in Osby bought some. I imported cigarette lighters from Switzerland, while ballpoints, a Hungarian invention, came in later and at first cost all the money in the world—up to sixty kronor (about seven dollars) each. They sold badly until the price fell, and then I dispatched thousands of ballpoints by mail order.

In 1945, when as a clerk I went into the office of the Forest Owners' Association, the finance manager allowed me to sell files to my employer. This meant hundreds of files. They came by rail to Växjö, so I borrowed a cart and took them home. I think I sold them for ninety öre each and had paid sixty-five for them. With a salary of one hundred fifty kronor, and at a time when three meals a day cost eighty kronor a month, those files made a profit that turned out to be greater than my fixed salary.

A year later, after a spell at the Forest Owners' factory in Hultsfred, where they made timber houses, I did my national service with the Kronoberg Regiment in Växjö. The colonel gave me extra night leave, so I was able to rent an office with a telephone in the basement of a small house. I had more mail than the colonel himself.

In 1948 I advertised furniture for the first time. Up until then I had sold minor wares: Christmas cards, seeds, fountain pens, wallets, picture frames, table runners, watches, jewelry, nylon stockings—that kind of thing. But Gunnars Fabriker in Alvesta, who was my toughest competitor, had long sold furniture in Råshult. I read its advertisements in the agricultural society's paper, which Father took, and I decided to try the same route.

At the time there were a number of small furniture makers around Lake Möckeln where we lived, so the step in that direction was easy to take.

I tried advertising an armless nursing chair from Liatorp, another from Lundberg's upholstered furniture in Möckeln, and a coffee table from Öljehult. The armless chair was called Ruth; I found remembering the order numbers of goods difficult, so giving names to furniture later became natural for IKEA.

The response was unambiguous. We sold a huge amount of this "test furniture." In the little brochure—*Ikéa News*—that I began to publish and send to customers, I added a sofa bed from Elf's Furniture in Älmhult, and I also remember a cut-glass chandelier from Örsjö on the border of Blekinge-Småland. Everything went.

That was how the business started. People ordered on a form from us, and the factories delivered. Minor wares were still being packed on the farm; then Gustaf Fredriksson came with the milk bus at ten to seven every morning to take them on to the railway station. Furniture began to take over more and more, and evenings were passed cutting up material for upholstery. I bought the materials from firms such as Gösta Svensson in Göteborg and the spinning and weaving factory in Karlstad.

Ikéa (we still spelled it lower-cased) could now no longer remain a one-man firm; it wasn't enough to have Mother and

Father and others helping me in the business, packing goods, and so on. In 1948 I appointed my very first employee, Ernst Ekström, who stayed with me for heaven knows how many years and did all the accounts. Two years later the firm had grown to a staff of seven or eight, among them a fantastic housekeeper who cooked for us all.

So, by chance, the furniture trade—which I entered in an attempt to imitate competitors as soon as possible—decided my destiny. No other event in life pleases me more than the fact that I ended up there. My interest at first was purely commercial: selling as much decent furniture as I could as cheaply as possible. Not until the first complaints started coming in did I realize that it was quality that was lacking. One day that would force me to draw certain conclusions and choose another way.

I had made contact a few years previously with my nearest competitors—Gunnars in Alvesta—and that taught me something for life. As a cadet at the Karlberg army school, I had continued to do business. I acquired a small hovel of an office in the Old City in Stockholm and was making real progress as general agent for a large firm that manufactured fountain pens and ballpoints, La Société Evergood in Paris. Among my customers was "the Pen Specialist," from which grew the successful firm Hennes & Mauritz. Stefan, the son of the creator, Erling Persson, is now on the board of IKEA.

At the time I also sold watches to various watchmakers in Stockholm. Importing was banned, but Gunnars in Alvesta had promised me I could buy from their stock, so I went down there.

Gunnar Jansson was a man in his fifties, and he offered me about a score or so of watches for fifty-five kronor (almost seven dollars) each. I couldn't afford that, I said, and somewhat immodestly appealed to his sympathy: I was young and very much wanted to become a businessman like him and needed all the help I could get. He weakened and said, "All right, boy, you can have them for fifty-two kronor instead."

"That won't leave much over," I said, "but it's a deal."

Taking his fat cigar out of his mouth, Gunnar then said: "Young man, you'll never become a businessman. If you say, to start with, that you can pay fifty when I say fifty-five, then you can't accept fifty-two without first having tried offering fifty kronor fifty öre. One thing you have to learn in business is that ten öre on a price can mean everything."

"I promise I'll never forget that," I said politely, and I've kept that promise ever since. Still today, at the open market where we live in Switzerland, I have a habit of taking the opportunity just before they are packing up to ask if I may buy a little more cheaply. My wife gets pretty tired of this.

But on the train home that day, I very much regretted that I hadn't at least tried a counteroffer of fifty-one kronor.

Gunnars was big on mail order. It moved later to Nässjö and from there to Linköping, but it had problems with the transition. Gunnar registered himself in Lichtenstein, where he died.

Starting in 1949, I occasionally sent out a supplement with the edition of the farmers' national weekly paper. In it I wrote somewhat grandiosely a kind of appeal with the headline: "To the People of the Countryside." That entailed 285,000 copies; for the first time I was aiming at a mass audience, which I later called "the many."

The following is some of what I put in my appeal:

You must have noticed that it is not easy to make ends meet. Why is this? You yourself produce goods of various kinds (milk, grain, potatoes, etc.), and I suppose you do not receive too much payment for them. No, I'm sure you don't. And yet everything is so fantastically expensive.

To a great extent this is due to the middlemen. Compare what you receive for a kilo of pork with what the shops ask for it. . . . In several areas it is unfortunately true that goods that may cost, say, one krona to manufacture, cost five, six, or more to buy.

In this price list we have taken a step in the right direction by offering you goods at the same prices your dealer buys for, in some cases even lower.

I stated the case for direct purchase with no middlemen, and the brochure showed among many other items a little furniture, a chest of drawers in elm veneer, a pedestal table that could be raised and lowered, a combined chair/ladder, and some solid bookcases.

This mass-distributed supplement was not unlike the sales paper *Ikéa News* that I had published earlier and called the organ for the Import-Ikéa sales organization (the organization was me). *Ikéa News* offered in the 1949–50 edition, as its main item, the fountain pen called Admiral Osmia (retail price 28 kronor, wholesale price 11.20 for at least ten). At the top it said: "Doctors Scientists Armed Services Farmers Foresters Seamen Schoolchildren—*Everyone* needs the pen sensation of 1948."

While *Ikéa News* turned to retailing, my "appeal" was aimed at the general public—in this case, people living in the country. It consisted, it could be said, of the birth of the idea that very shortly was to develop into our very first catalog in 1951, the catalog that today, half a century later, is distributed all over the world.

In the spring of 1951, I made what was perhaps the most important appointment my company has ever made, although I did not realize it at the time. After an interview lasting a day and a half—at first we sat talking in the garden, then we went into the kitchen and stayed there all night—Sven Göte Hansson became an office clerk with Ikéa. Only two years later he became head of the newly opened furniture exhibition in Älmhult and, during the pioneer days, a member of the small management group that decided everything. He was, for instance, the great expert on setting prices.

Sven Göte came into my life at a time when Ikéa was very much at a crossroads. Competition in mail order had become almost unendurable, a fact that one simple example can illustrate. The Mellby ironing board was manufactured by Harbo/Åsljunga and sold by us one season to the customer for 23 kronor. Then Gunnars lowered its price to 22.50, we followed with 22 kronor, and the spiral continued.

Step by step, this price war affected the quality of the ironing board, which became simpler and simpler, but also worse and worse. The same applied to furniture. Complaints started to mount, and I could see how things were going: the mail-order trade was risking an increasingly bad reputation, and in the long run Ikéa could not survive in that way. The core problem with mail order was that the customers themselves could not touch the goods but had to rely on descriptions in the advertisement or catalog. Consumer protection was poorly developed, and it was easy to cheat.

We were faced with a momentous decision: to allow Ikéa to die or to find a new way of maintaining the trust of the customer and still make money.

Out of long talks through the night with Sven Göte about how we were to get out of this vicious circle—lower price, worse quality—the idea grew of trying a permanent display or exhibition of our furniture. People could go to the display, see the furniture for themselves, and compare the quality at different price levels.

In the middle of all this, Albin Lagerblad's joinery in Älmhult was to close. For what I thought was the tremendous sum of 13,000 kronor ($1,625), I bought the entire shabby building. Compared with that price, a modern department store today can cost up to a quarter of a billion kronor. The decision was logical.

In the spring of 1952, *Ikéa News* came out in its last edition distributed as a supplement, and we had a sale of our entire stock of minor wares (though I have a dozen or so dried-out fountain pens and a few hundred Christmas cards at home in my cellar should anyone wish to have them). We informed our customers that in the future we would sell only furniture and domestic articles. Using a form on the back of the brochure, people could order the first real furniture catalog.

That was how I became a furniture dealer.

In the autumn of 1952, we completed the catalog, which came out in time for the opening of the furniture exhibition on March 18, 1953. The main item was an armchair called MK. I still have it in the parlor on the farm outside Älmhult.

We had cleared out all the rubbish at Lagerblad's, scraped off all the old lime, put in new windows, and nailed masonite boards to the walls. We then displayed our furniture on two levels. We could now at last show those cheap ironing boards alongside those that cost five kronor more and were of good quality. And people did just what we had hoped: they wisely chose the more expensive ironing board.

At that moment, the basis of the modern IKEA concept was created, and in principle it still applies: first and foremost, use a catalog to tempt people to come to an exhibition, which today is our store. "Come and see us in Älmhult and convince yourself that . . ." we wrote on the back of the first catalog.

Second, we provided a large building in which, catalog in hand, customers could walk around and see simple interiors for themselves, touch the furniture they wanted to buy, and then write out an order, which would be put into effect by mail via the factories.

Mail order and furniture store in one. As far as I knew, that business idea had not been put into practice anywhere else. We were the first. It was actually the invention of both Sven Göte and myself.

Success was immediate, and it created the embryo and resources for the store we created five years later. But I have never been so scared in my whole life as when we opened and I saw the line outside Lagerblad's: there were at least one thousand people there. I couldn't believe my eyes. On the upper floor of the factory, we had arranged coffee and buns alongside the furniture, and we didn't know whether the floor would hold or—even more important—whether we would be able to supply enough buns. That was precarious, as we had promised coffee and buns to those who came to the opening.

But the floor held, and the buns were swiftly baked. I remember the time afterward as one long rush of constant and joyous work: on the weekends crowds of people besieging our furniture exhibition, at night writing out consignment notes and invoices in the tiny office where we all sat around the same table. Tens of thousands of people those first years were to go on a pilgrimage to remote Älmhult from all over Sweden. Some had seen us for the first time at exhibitions in Stockholm, Göteborg, and elsewhere, but most had learned of us through the free catalog that had gone out to our little list of customers in an edition of scarcely one hundred thousand copies.

Although life in the country was coming to an end—the famous churn stand was suddenly empty—Ikéa was taking shape as a "real" firm. Many of our unwritten laws were already "written" by this time. It could be said that we simply transferred the family spirit from Elmtaryd: helpfulness, thrift, and a strong sense of responsibility.

I remember one small episode. One morning I found that our cashier had forgotten about a roll of postage stamps on the table. I was extremely annoyed. I calculated how much the stamps were worth and put the corresponding sum of money—perhaps fifteen kronor (today about two hundred)—on the table. Then, red in the face, she came and told me someone had put money on the table for stamps she had forgotten to lock up.

She has never forgotten that. It was a lesson in what things are worth. It was easier to see when money lay there and not the stamps. To this day at IKEA we try to translate everything into a clear price and state it. Our advertising brochures have, on the front or back, information on what they cost to compile, often with an indication that it is, in the end, the customer who has to pay for whatever we waste.

The cost awareness that was to be IKEA's anthem was born in this renovated joinery. We saved on string (we actually tied bits together) and paper and boxes. But something else was born during this first pioneer stage: offering coffee and buns. It could be said that they became our now quite famous restaurants, which turn over a total of 1.6 billion kronor. They are in our stores for the same reason that we offered coffee and buns in Älmhult: no good business is done on an empty stomach. At that time in Sweden no one dared say that a drink in combination with a deal also gives a buzz. But we now have a license that allows people to buy schnapps at the checkout. Times change.

In Älmhult the question of food became acute for special reasons. People were coming from all over the country. Ikéa had become Älmhult's tourist attraction, even a tiny bit more popular than the famous Linné birthplace. Traveling was expensive, but we arranged a discount with Swedish Railways, and those who furnished their entire home with us—we called them setting-up-house customers—for a while were offered dinner at the New Hotel in Älmhult.

Gradually the pressure on Älmhult grew even greater, and it wasn't long before, apart from the restaurant, we also had an inn on the site, with a hotel and a pool. My grandfather would have been amazed, for the place was his old country store.

Thus, sometimes some fairly simple observations and some modest improvisations led to major decisions. Step by step, we were building our future philosophy, which would turn out to be valid in international contexts.

The Family as Firm, the Firm as a Family

> Life at Elmtaryd was work, a tremendous
> amount of work. We had dinner at six. The
> telephone closed at seven; then we could
> neither accept nor make calls. Then we went
> on working as long as there was something to
> do because anyhow you didn't have anything
> else to do. On Sundays we went fishing and
> picking wild mushrooms. . . . Ingvar taught me
> that. . . . We were alike, . . . I was thrifty too,
> even more than he was, . . . That might be a
> reason why we found each other.
>
> —SVEN GÖTE HANSSON

Whenever Ingvar Kamprad today talks to the firm's employees, it is a father talking to his children and grandchildren. "Dear IKEA family, a great hug to you all"—that is how he introduces his Christmas message. "Then I couldn't stop the tears"—that is how a letter in the in-house magazine starts in which he thanks his employees for their support through tough times.

Few well-known businessmen communicate so directly, so intimately with their employees. In Sweden the days of patronage have long since gone. At IKEA, alongside Hennes & Mauritz, our most modern large companies, patriarchy flourishes to the full. There are moments when Ingvar resembles some venerable African freedom fighter who, with a mixture of humility in the face of the responsibility and the obvious pride of leadership, confronts his people after the liberation. There are emotions, tears, laughter, memories, reprovals—and scoldings when the family for some awful reason has left the narrow path of thrift and "not turned out the light behind them" in the hall.

Thus, he behaves in a way that is not typical of the times; paradoxically, anachronism is his strength. Talk of a special management style is a false trail. This is not something Kamprad has learned; it is simply who he is. He quite literally sees his company as a kind of family and himself as the father.

How did that come about?

It is hard to imagine a person more dependent on his family. It is all about a feeling that goes far beyond the inner circle of kin; Ingvar Kamprad is at every moment prepared to integrate outsiders into the family. Presumably to his wife's despair, he loves spontaneously inviting people back for a meal even when other things have been planned. Breaking bread with others is all part of his delight and inclination.

He became a young businessman in the shelter of his family while his contemporaries were hanging around the dance floors. His first customers were his close relatives: mother, father, grandmother, aunts on both sides of the family. Thanks to that inner circle, he could always rely on a helping hand as the business grew, if a mail-order parcel needed packing quickly or the telephone needed to be answered or there were complaints to note down. His home became his office, and the office his home. The farmhouse was cleared so that the boy, not the farm, could expand, his father keeping the daily accounts and becoming chairman of the board and his mother making the coffee.

The family became his firm, so it is not strange that in the future he always regarded the firm as his family.

With this philosophy, he also created the outstanding metaphor for his leadership, the one that includes mutual helpfulness, loyalty, solidarity, simplicity in way of life, and principles such as "clean up after yourself" and "never take more than you can eat." The first employees were drawn into this intimacy as a matter of course. When Sven Göte Hansson, the legendary IKEA pioneer, came to Elmtaryd, he at once became a member of the family. This is what he says:

> I was employed in the office in the summer of 1952. It was just mail order then. There was already another clerk there. We worked in the farmhouse but lived across the road in the tenant house where two rooms had been fixed up in the attic—one for me and one for him.
>
> Otherwise, apart from Ingvar and his wife and a housekeeper . . . we were Feodor the father, Berta the mother, who lived in the stone house. There was no need for any free time. We worked in the evenings as long as there were things to do.

In a photograph in the *Aftonbladet* in 1957, Ingvar is standing in front of his staff, about seventy people just about to leave for Mallorca at the invitation of the firm. He is to lead one contingent himself for a fortnight while the others keep things going at home in Älmhult. Then his wife Kerstin is to fly down with those who stayed at home, and the plane will bring back the first group. It's a mother-father-children outing. One day the photograph, quite rightly, was to go into the family album.

It appears contradictory that this profoundly family-bound man often neglected his own family for the sake of the firm. One of his favorite expressions in those early pioneer days was: "Once we've done this, it'll be better." "Didn't you say that once we'd done that, it'd be better?" his wife would then remind him, but "better" it never became. There were always new things that he had to do before things would be better.

It was to be one of Ingvar's great sorrows and the cause of some soul-searching that business made him neglect his three sons as they grew up. He has done everything to make up for it since, but everyone with children knows that childhood does not allow itself to be reconquered.

While his father, Feodor, was a more formal man and thought everyone should address Ingvar as "the Chief," the son behaved precisely the opposite way. His unpretentiousness became the example, and later on it never paid to have any special pretensions. Those who tried did not survive long and left of their own accord. As Sven Göte expressed it: "Ingvar seemed to become simpler and simpler. . . . Informal clothing was introduced late in the 1960s. I still remember the strange feeling of going to work for the first time in a polo-necked jersey and no tie. The personal use of *du* in speech was carried through via a memo from Ingvar. We were not at all the first in that field, and some of the management were against it."

At first all the employees knew each other and were pulling in the same direction. Many of those pioneers benefited greatly from working in IKEA and in time achieved positions they would otherwise never have risen to. All of them had learned the hard way; hardly any had a college education.

The firm as family became Ingvar's great pride. In the name of the family, the IKEA spirit was created, something that later was to become the subject of a doctoral thesis and of profound analyses by Harvard professors.

The transition from the closeness of Elmtaryd to the less intimate atmosphere of a large company was difficult for the founder. Essentially, he has never really accepted it, and at heart he regards his employees as children, siblings, and other relatives, although their numbers are now approaching forty thousand.

The adjustment to the new reality occurred gradually, and at first no one not noticed it at all. The step from Elmtaryd in Agunnaryd to the old joinery in Älmhult was a big one, but the family still lived on the farm; Ingvar's first wife preferred not to go with him into town after their adopted daughter came into their lives.

In the 1955 catalog, the postal address for all correspondence was still Agunnaryd, and the telephone to Ikéa, as it was still spelled, was still over "Elmtåsa." At first there was only one line to Ikéa—Tjurköby, number 6B—with extensions. On the business letter heading it said "Extension Store and Extension Management," but the telephone was the same.

In an old Studebaker to start with, then a Citroën and later a white Porsche, Ingvar commuted the twenty kilometers at about six every morning and then went back home again in the evening. But essentially, in his heart, he still lived at Elmtaryd. As he himself describes it:

> When I talk about the IKEA family, it is life in the country—the time when Ikéa had not yet become IKEA—that guides me. My ideas on fellowship were born there, on our dependence on each other, and we lived our own message there in a surveyable microworld.
>
> That first wonderful time of strong working fellowship with a circle of individuals, all of whom I knew personally, made me dream foolish dreams of it always remaining the same. I nourished a false belief that it would be possible to preserve the total "us" feeling even when we grew large. So for the trade union organizations we were a large black blob on the agenda, or a white spot on

the map; at IKEA neither the LO [Trade Union Council] nor SAF [Employers' Federation] intervened in our activities. But it was a severe miscalculation on my part and a very great disappointment that it was not possible to stay that way.

One day at the end of the 1950s I was summoned to a large meeting down at the store. Many of my colleagues had assembled, and they asked me whether I thought they should join the union. I was put in a great quandary and replied that that didn't really fit in with our situation within IKEA. On the other hand, I had no really good alternative. If my colleagues joined the union, then my management and I would have to join the employers' federation, for those were the rules of the game.

So they made their decision and joined the union, and IKEA joined the employers' federation. Naturally, that depressed me, but conflicts have been few. What has irritated me most have been things such as centrally decided bans on overtime. A union man came one day and said to me: "Ingvar, you have to know that we in the union have three hells. One consists of all those malcontents who are nearly always overpaid in relation to what they achieve. The second hell is central organizations who send out remittances and ask us to comment on the most peculiar things, such as the question of tax on leisure boats. What the hell has that got to do with us?

"The third hell is wage negotiations. We sit there haggling all through the nights, a chasm between us, and we get nowhere, but then one day it's all over and we all shake hands, and then at least that hell is over anyhow. The other two are permanent."

I myself once took part in a delegation that was to negotiate in Stockholm. Then I realized that I was too much of an "us" person to be able to participate in that kind of game. I can only understand with my brain that unions are something natural and perhaps good. As long as they are not militant, they work for the good of the company and the good of everyone.

The days of the family idyll have passed. The IKEA spirit

still lives on, but in another way. But those days at the beginning on the farm at home when IKEA really was a family—that remains my very best memory.

Today the spirit of the IKEA family still lives in the business concept taught in the training program called the IKEA Way. It is practiced, according to the promise participants make at the end of the seminar, in everyday life as well; wherever Ikeans go in the world, they will be looked after. "It's the extended family working," says the young head of the travel section, Ann Christine Hallström.

Also included in the "family" is the consumers club, whose members buy at discounted prices; it regularly makes special offers in several countries. The eight hundred thousand Swedes who are IKEA's especially devoted core customers receive the magazine *Family* three times a year. This is, of course, fundamentally a commercial story, but it is based on the business philosophy that makes meaningful phrases such as "cares about," "helps out," "being together," and "everyone is equally important."

The family as firm, the firm as family.

No One Has Had as Many Fiascoes as I've Had

Only those who are asleep make no mistakes.
—INGVAR KAMPRAD

I still feel enormous delight in doing business. An even greater joy is having business ideas and convincing others that they are possible to achieve. Perhaps I have acquired that from my mother's side. Perhaps it is ultimately this that keeps me and the actual business going, a special feeling of pleasure, a kind of keenness not to miss a chance, that makes me never able to stop thinking about whether something could perhaps be a deal. I can feel the same urge in a secondhand market.

But best of all are the victories in which there are no losers. Unfortunately, I have not been able to avoid severe losses. Both fiascoes and triumphs have marked the history of the firm.

The best deal I ever made as a young businessman was when I imported five hundred fountain pens from Paris for one krona each, including freight and customs. When I sold them to a Swedish watch and pen firm, I received four and a half kronor for them. That happened in the shadow of import restrictions: a license was required. The return on the deal was extremely good, an enormous margin. Imagine, five hundred times three and a half in one fell swoop.

That whetted my business appetite.

Soon afterward I made what was perhaps my stupidest deal, the first of many fiascoes. I was cheated by an Austrian businessman in Göteborg, who started the firm Ballograf and whom I contacted through an advertisement. He showed me a simple but good ballpoint pen he wanted to sell for two and a half kronor, which was sensational: the nearest competitor sold for between ten and fifteen kronor. I ordered a few thousand and advertised them at 3.95 kronor—even that price was sensational.

Eventually five hundred or so orders arrived, and I went up to Göteborg with the money in my hand to fetch the pens. Then my supplier explained. I can still remember his broken Swedish as he apologized and said there had been a big mistake and he couldn't at all supply them at two and a half kronor, but for four kronor—that is, five öre above my price.

My despair was great. We had shaken hands on the deal, and I appealed to him to help me.

But no!

Tearfully, I boarded the train home with a couple of hundred pens I had been forced to buy at the new price, which I sent off to those who had ordered first.

I saved face that time by sending out a somewhat different pen to my other customers, but afterward I was almost cleaned out. Then I hit the next setback. I had bought and advertised a consignment of jungle oil from a chemical firm, but the consignment never arrived.

Again, I had to find a solution. I wept a lot, as I couldn't bear adversities. Actually, I often fail to look at things from the bright side.

The sad thing is that I didn't learn much from these early failures. On the contrary, I kept repeating them. Father always said, "You're too gullible, Ingvar. Nothing will come of you."

And that is still true. For a long time I found it difficult not to believe people. Now that I am older, I have become slightly more crafty and guarded toward people in general. On the other hand, toward colleagues I am usually 100 percent trusting. But nowadays I say to them all (thinking about my pen supplier in Göteborg): don't make verbal agreements. Don't rely only on a handshake. Make sure everything is down in writing.

In addition: no lawyer in the world can help you out on a bad deal sealed with a handshake.

My fiascoes have continued throughout my life.

My involvement as part owner of a television factory— brand name Prinsen—in Helsingborg was perhaps the worst of all. That was in the 1960s, and it cost IKEA 25 to 30 percent of the firm's assets at the time—or, in today's figures, 30 to 50 million kronor ($3.75 to 6.25 million) over a period of five years. I had put the husband of a relative in management, but both he and the managing director of the firm were more interested in flying airplanes. The unforgivable part of the fiasco is that I saw the way things were going but did not have the courage to make the decision to settle the matter in time.

After that, the main principle was created that IKEA was never to buy from IKEA. Others are to produce for us. We are in principle not to own industries; ownership at once entails extra responsibilities, not just to sell but also to provide backup. But there have been many exceptions to that rule, some of them deplorable.

Now, in the 1990s, investment in Russia is a prime example of my talent for fiascoes. Jan Aulin, who was behind our great investment in Europe, and his colleagues had made advance investigations into how we could rent forestland in the Urals and run a sawmill, thus securing our timber needs for a long period of time. So we leased one hundred thousand hectares with the felling rights for ninety-nine years—not a bad little woodland to look after for a whole century.

We bought and dismantled a Swedish sawmill, set it up again in Russia, appointed a forester as project manager, and started up. In the background were the Japanese, who had come from the other direction, ruthlessly clear-felling with no thought of replanting. The idea was that we would demonstrate a rational model of both ecological responsibility and Swedish technical know-how. Then, in addition to sawmills, we were later to build factories to refine the raw material for our furniture.

There was nothing wrong with our plans. Our own heavy-handedness, however, combined with elements of the Russian Mafia and endless Soviet-type bureaucracy to make everything go wrong. The slightly adjusted loss in our financial report came to 60 million kronor ($7.5 million). But including everything we had invested in the way of time and people, the fiasco certainly amounted to 100 to 125 million kronor ($12.5 to 15.5 million).

As an individual disaster, this is probably the worst example, but in Romania we made another miss that cost us nearly 50 million ($6.25 million). We invested in the modernization of a factory in Codlea, with environmental sensitivity and Western management. Amid frequent criticism (and some praise), our effort to increase production to a rational level failed. We had no ownership but had acquired shares as security. They now became worthless.

Altogether, IKEA has lost many hundreds of millions on projects of this kind for which my responsibility has been considerable: half a billion would be a conservative estimate. In Thailand we built a large chair factory together with a local partner; that is another disaster we are still buying our way out of today. In Malaysia too there was a catastrophe with a local conglomerate, a furniture factory. The final bill is not yet settled but unfortunately will be considerable. Such are my fiascoes; the list could be even longer. I have not mentioned purely personal failures, such as unfortunate appointments of people who later cruelly betrayed us or breakdowns of love and friendship. On both a personal and a business level, my connection with the Nazi Lindholmers and the Neo-Swedish movement was the fiasco that has been given the greatest publicity.

For several difficult weeks in the autumn of 1994 and then again in the spring of 1998, the ground beneath me began to rock.

That's What It Was Like

> As the German Reich, under purposeful leader-
> ship, has restored her position as a major
> power . . . the time is considered ripe to real-
> ize her foreign policy program. . . . Secured by
> her alliance with a rearmed Italy under the
> forceful leadership of Mussolini, without firing
> a shot, Germany was able to occupy . . . the
> German-speaking parts of Czechoslovakia.
>
> —STOCKHOLM ENSKILDA BANK
> ANNUAL REPORT, MARCH 1939

Perhaps we are all in some way born in times of upheaval; perhaps it is everyone's condition that nothing is obvious, that the only guarantee in life is its uncertainty. But for some people, it is just that unrest, that change and shift in prevailing systems, that enables them to realize their dreams. In the actual time of upheaval, they see possibilities and build new worlds for themselves, blind to their own foolishness. In their lack of certainty, they see their best chances and swiftly seize them.

That applies to individuals as well as companies, for behind every expanding firm, there is always one or more individuals.

Perhaps it could be said that the main character in this book was born at the right moment. Perhaps it could be said that his firm is a product of the happily hectic restlessness of the day, a child of violent social and economic pressures during a time of change.

In Europe the period between 1914 and 1945 produced great tragic upheavals equal to the unprecedented material developments of the period after the Second World War. Different cultures collided violently and then were reconciled; racial ideologies flourished, only to disappear into oblivion later. In the 1930s, postwar Sweden very much wanted to suppress the fact that it was a country that had turned its face and sought cultural roots in the Germanic. Enthusiasm for Germany was considerable, and not until today have we begun to acquire full knowledge of the covert association of Swedish government, industry, organizations, and leading financiers with the Nazis.

It was not only the old grandmother and her son, the farmer, in Elmtaryd who saw Hitler as a benefactor. The nation began to change its tune, however, at the turn of Stalingrad and North Africa, then very swiftly after the war. With its face turned to the West, Sweden became the most Americanized country in Europe; American culture led and inspired Swedish cultural and commercial life, and schoolchildren happily exchanged their German grammar books for the more supple English of films and entertainment.

Obvious as this cultural and economic turn is, it is equally clear that almost no country in the world had a greater chance than Sweden of making this modern transformation. Protected from two world wars, the country was ethnically and culturally homogenous; extremism and social unrest were as good as unknown. Sweden faced peace with an untouched production apparatus at a time when most factories on the Continent were in ruins.

Ingvar Feodor Kamprad was born in 1926, a few years before the Great Depression of the early 1930s. The little boy heard talk very early on about the miracle man, Ivar Kreuger. He grew up in a considerate and secure environment marked by the jog trot of agriculture, the smell of horse manure, the idyllic economy of a country store. When he first found the courage to turn to a larger public, to sell his goods by making his first *concentration of strength*—words he came to love—it was to the people of the countryside he appealed, and he did so for one simple, logical reason.

This was the customer circle he knew. He knew its needs for udder ointment and corsets, timepieces, double ottomans and ready-made ties, for he himself was a worker in this simple reality. So far he was still largely a grandiose peddler, though he had an inkling that the revolution in trade was waiting just around the corner. Pictured on his first brochure is a truck roaring past, an airplane, and a merchant ship on its way to an unknown destination.

As a boy he saw little of the specter of unemployment, for in the countryside, life was one of bare necessity and what the town did was the town's business. But gradually the fruits of an active stabilization policy fell on the whole population during the 1930s, making the wheels turn faster and faster. More and more roads were built, and more and more individual homes, "child-rich houses," were built. Urbanization was still in its cradle, but industry had begun to take hold, and investment in building houses increased greatly from 1933 onward. It was not until Ingvar Kamprad was a fairly mature and aware businessman of twenty-five, however, in the 1950s, that the expansion took off. With the Korean inflation behind him, he could not have chosen a better moment to stand in the great Swedish market square with his remarkable business idea.

Devaluation in 1949 by a whole 30 percent gave a gigantic push to an export industry that was not destroyed by war; from 1950 to the early 1970s, Sweden's gross national product grew on an average of almost 4 percent per year, not falling below 2 percent in any one year. Between 1960 and 1965, the pace of increase was almost 6 percent. From then on the Swedish model was confirmed, peace reigned in the labor market, and unemployment was a bitter but increasingly forgotten memory. The government, however, stayed eternally the same, in principle social democratic.

This was the happy period of democratic government, the realization of dreams. Everything was going well for Sweden, and the world was crying out for its goods and ideas. It also turned out that Ingvar

Kamprad was not the only businessman to understand the possibilities of aiming at a mass market. On the contrary, there were already quite a few businessmen in the cut-rate market.

This was the time to reap the benefits of the reforms, the record years knocking at the door. As a result of modernization, Sweden became the most advanced peaceful country in the world. During the 1960s alone, the number of cars increased from one million to twice that number. The countryside was quickly depopulated. It no longer paid for the young businessman in Älmhult to talk to people who sold pork; now his customers were the many newly rootless people, young and full of energy, seeking somewhere to live, townspeople needing to furnish their homes as cheaply as possible.

During the 1950s alone, fifty thousand farms closed down; that number doubled in the following decade. In thirty years, employment in agriculture was reduced by 75 percent, and the suburbs grew as if sprouting out of the ground outside the cities.

The building program that came to have such an enormous influence on IKEA—or rather, the need for IKEA—broke all records. During the first twenty years after the end of the war, one million new apartments were built. When IKEA opened in the mid-1960s in the Stockholm region, the environment was archetypal postwar Swedish. At the same time that the store on Kungens kurva (King's Bend) was being built in the mud, a whole suburb, complemented by a shopping center, appeared on the slope across the way, with tens of thousands of potential consumers hungry for material goods.

Subventions and loans increased the pace; social housing initiatives followed one after another. Housing benefits had existed ever since the mid-1930s, but now area housing commissions were created, and in 1954 the housing authority started publishing a standards publication called *Good Housing*. *Good Housing* set the regulations for minimum living space and thoroughly outlined the requirements for every room and every part of a dwelling: utility room, kitchen, hall, and so on.

The idea of the "people's home" enfolded everything and everyone into its regulated embrace. The state gave advice on furniture, on life, on health. Discussions were held on how the country was to maintain its level of consumption at a time of a downturn in trade; items of furniture—beds, chairs, and tables—were considered the most important goods. The benefit system evolved, and as long as the country did not borrow for growth, it was part and parcel of the actual dynamic model.

Whatever all this did to Swedish society and its citizens, industry and business life profited from the development through uninterrupted rationalization. In the eyes of enterprise, politics was more ambivalent. During this postwar period, the holy fraternity of large unions, large firms, and the state was confirmed, with laws, decrees, and wage conditions adjusted accordingly. But it was also during this period that the model for small businesses materialized in Gnosjö in Småland; a symbolic ideal took shape, and it was still fairly easy to establish a firm.

Before the social security system was extended and job security perfected, and before the debate on enterprise as a parasite infected political talk, a large number of speculative new companies managed to thrive. Many entrepreneurs managed to get rich from selling profitable companies while heavily burdened by a wealth tax calculated on working capital.

Yet it is still astonishing what a rich flora blossomed in Sweden after the Second World War, a multitude of dynamic family-owned companies such as Tetra Pak and Hennes & Mauritz.

All of them were relatives of Ingvar Kamprad's mail-order firm. Many of them at first grew strong in their local environment, where they controlled the entire commercial infrastructure, then afterward took the first step out into the wide world and life beyond Älmhult, Liatorp, and Elmtaryd. All of them had a story to tell about how they had once been small and had to become large, how they had gone from almost poverty-stricken circumstances to sophisticated business success, honor, and wealth. They were the enterprising breakaway kings of the "people's home."

That was what it was like when IKEA was born.

The company quite simply was in step with an accelerating development. Without the housing program, without the democratic reforms, without the urbanization and expansion of cars and roads, without the growing number of women at work, without social reforms within home and family and housing, without the increasing strength of consumer lobbying groups, it is hard to see how IKEA could have grown so strong so quickly, gaining wide acceptance with so little resistance.

Against this background, the entrepreneur Kamprad was able to act. With his usual business sense, he and his firm adopted the virtues and vices of the day: in step with the times, he seized the *du* reform of informal speech; he made trade descriptions his own; he extracted from the concept of the "people's home" what was purely material and created "democratic design"; he exploited what was Scandinavian and Nordic; and he transformed IKEA into a standard concept, indeed, a household word.

And out of the Småland moraine, unhesitatingly and with the energy of a preacher, he took the virtues that are to take the company on into the future: simplicity, thrift, humility, energy, shrewdness, obstinacy, and "craftiness," that is, the ability both to be content with the resources one has and to find ways out of tight spots.

The new things Ingvar Kamprad planted were grown in the same soil that had seen other ventures die. But the soil was prepared in a new way, the flowers had different colors, and the scents had changed.

The good Linné would have had his hands full putting names to the multifold developments that were beginning to sprout from that ground.

THE TROUBLESOME CAPITALIST

Boycott, Divorce, and Success

At the beginning of the 1960s, a Norwegian consultant, Hans Bernhard Nielsen, came to help us rationalize a little at Älmhult. On the evening of his first day, he came into the office and said he wanted to give up the assignment. He explained why. If anyone had asked him whether it was possible for a store in such a godforsaken dump to work, he would have issued a serious warning at the very thought. It would not.

"But," he said, "damn it all, it's working. In other words, I have no advice to offer you. I'm going home."

He went back to Norway. The beauty of this is that I didn't have to pay even for that first day. In their prospectus, the consultancy firm of Vercosen offered a day's free consultation.

Step by step, the IKEA recipe began to be prepared over five turbulent years at the old Lagerblad's joinery in Älmhult. A renovated two-story wooden building with masonite panels originally covering the once whitewashed walls gradually became the superb laboratory for everything new that was to be created. A workshop was formed for learning to build the perfect selling machine with the help of a catalog, business sense, and the underdog's obsession with always doing the opposite of what others were doing.

When the first store was opened in Älmhult in 1958, the company seemed to have taken the step up into furniture high school. "How shall we fill all this?" said Ingvar Kamprad and the future manager of the store, Sven Göte Hansson, gazing with some despair at the empty 6,700 square meters that were, a few days later, to become the largest furniture exhibition in the world.

It was only fifteen years since the churn stand had served as a distribution warehouse, and five years since Albin Lagerblad had sold his building for 13,000 kronor ($1,625) to IKEA. Building the store cost 600,000 kronor ($75,000), for by now the firm was on its way to becoming a major company. The first million in sales flew by, soaring like a rocket, with the turnover in 1954 reaching three million, then doubling that figure the following year. But in 1956 there were still only about thirty employees; it was possible to know every one of them personally.

The family had grown so that the walls were bulging, but the principle of closeness was still functioning. Hundreds of thousands of Swedes had visited the first furniture exhibition in the old joinery, and in 1955 half a million copies of the catalog had gone out, with "Ikéa" still spelled with an accent mark and the address given as Agunnaryd, for that was where the owner lived on his family farm.

Major life events sometimes tend to occur at the same time. Privately, life also changed radically for Ingvar Kamprad over these years. His mother died of cancer in 1956, and after his marriage to Kerstin Wadling fell apart in 1960, he missed his adopted daughter, whom his father, Feodor, had carried around and proudly introduced as "the one who is to take over after Ingvar."

We had married young. My wife worked at Swedish Radio as a secretary to Lars Madsén and in the evenings for Povel Ramel. We had a few happy years, and it is true that Kerstin helped me a great deal during the years on the farm. But she never liked my concentration on work and the firm. She saw another life ahead of her.

I didn't exactly work an eight-hour day, and I was away a lot. Did she want to come with me? No, she mostly preferred to stay at home. Slowly but surely we were drifting apart, and we thought it was because we had no children of our own, although we had tried, been medically examined, and very much wanted to.

We adopted a little Swedish girl in the hopes that that would bring us closer to each other. That gave us a brief respite. When we finally decided to divorce, I took it as a personal failure, and I can't cope with that kind of thing. At work I am allowed to fail, that's all part of it, included in the concept, but not in private. The divorce affected me badly, and I missed our little girl.

When we separated, my wife demanded so much, even her lawyer was surprised. We finally agreed on a reasonable sum, but still there was a bitter aftermath. She was shortly to fall ill, and she died a few years later from the after-effects of a bout with tuberculosis she had suffered when young.

I was not allowed to see my daughter for a long time. I could only yearn for the little one I had known. She and I have now made it up. She has married and lives with her husband, who works for a building firm. We see each other once or twice a year and have a very good relationship, though she is not involved in IKEA.

My first wife and I managed to be reconciled before she passed away. But the whole matter pains me and still hurts. I considered myself a real shit. Had I really done all I could, or were we perhaps too different from the start?

The 1950s, therefore, turned out to be a time, in equal parts, of personal anguish and commercial success, a time marked by the growing pains and intoxication of the business as well as by a personal search for a new harmony. The latter was at last to present itself on a trip with the staff to Italy, when Ingvar met the young teacher Margaretha Stennert. They married in 1963, and in 1964 their first child, Peter, was born.

At this point, Ingvar Kamprad was no longer regarded as a wonder child from Småland. He had turned into a self-assured, polished, and feared competitor, whose methods were sometimes regarded with contempt and ill will. The competition was no longer confined to the mail-order market but had spread to the entire furniture trade, which could feel the threat coming from this cut-price upstart from the Småland forests.

The competition amassed for a counterattack, a herd of elephants against a roaring mouse.

"Dream Home for a Dream Price," it said on the front of the still simple catalog in 1955. A rival put an advertisement in the *Smålands-*

Posten with the heading: "If your dream house at a dream price becomes an overpriced magpie's nest, then come to us next time."

Ingvar can laugh at it today, but not then. At that stage, he was being chased by a conventional trade that wanted to halt his progress at whatever cost. They called for a ban and tried to put an end to his exposure. Various boycotts took place. Suppliers suddenly flatly refused to do business with the young company. Some did ship the furniture, but without a sender's name and in unmarked vehicles so that it could not be seen who had ordered the delivery. Yet others made furniture for IKEA, but only if it was clearly changed in design, for some furniture dealers refused to trade with any firm that sold the same furniture to Kamprad as to them.

At trade fairs, Ikéa (the spelling varied) was banned for the first time in about 1950. Even as a private person, Ingvar was banned from certain trade fairs. As usual when under pressure and with the wind against him, he reacted with a mixture of tears, bumptiousness, and shrewdness. In this period, he started a large number of different firms and companies so that he could act in several roles as both vendor and buyer. Svenska Silco was the first in 1951 (an attempt to export furniture), then in 1953 he started Svenska Royalimporten (largely carpets), and in 1955 he opened Svenska Sencello (famous for foam rubber mattresses), which together with IKEA is the best known and has a popular shop on one of the main shopping streets in Stockholm. Another business was the mail-order firm Hemservice (Home Service), which eventually laid the foundations for Accentensortimentet (the Accenten Range).

Trade fairs in the 1950s were important crossroads for what was new at the time; the most successful one, St. Eriks Fair, was also eventually opened to the general public, but the exhibition management sought to sabotage IKEA's progress. In Göteborg, Ingvar was smuggled into a fair in the back of a Volvo Duett. A good friend and carpet dealer threw a Wilton carpet over him so that he could get through the gate unseen. When he crept out of the car among the exhibits, no one had the courage to throw him out.

Another time he was fined for twenty-five days at twenty kronor per day for having sold carpeting and rugs at a local provincial fair. In

Stockholm he was forced to rent premises of his own close to the leading St. Eriks Fair in order to be there at all. Naturally there was a rush: people like a fighter, especially if his prices are low. A flurry of newspaper correspondence on the matter served only to arouse interest in "the Småland furniture." At the same time, certain suppliers were given a definitive ultimatum via a circular from the National Association of Furniture Dealers: "If you sell to IKEA, we will no longer buy from you."

Some manufacturers gave in. They didn't dare defy the association, and now, afterward, Ingvar Kamprad can understand: their survival was at stake. "Perhaps I would have done the same myself." Other manufacturers did not give in, however, either on principle or because they were powerful enough.

The increase in boycotts gave rise to costly troubles, and the company more and more often faced the ignominy of not being able to deliver what it had advertised in the catalog. In the short term, it could put up with that as long as it had alternative goods. But in the long term, the situation looked as if it might be devastating for the new company, now leaping ahead.

Suppliers who courageously and loyally maintained contact with IKEA used fictitious addresses; Älmhult was sometimes replaced by Killeberg or another place as a delivery address. At some manufacturers, employees didn't dare fetch goods in the daytime. There were strange nighttime drives, as though transporting illegal spirits in the days of Prohibition, only it was sofas being transported. The atmosphere became increasingly rancorous, and Ingvar Kamprad had "many tearful nights" as he lay awake wondering how he could solve the problem. One of his biggest problems was finding a way to fill orders for twenty thousand chairs.

In 1957 the National Price and Cartel Commission and the Council for Free Trade (now the Monopoly Commission) became aware of what was going on, and a special report was published in issue number 5 of the journal *Questions of Price Cartels*. With hindsight, it makes amusing reading: a powerful monopolistic establishment, set up by the Stockholm Chamber of Commerce and a special commission of the St. Eriks Fair, tried to make IKEA's presence at fairs impossible and to prevent the company's popular prices from reaching a price-conscious public.

With limited resources, IKEA had exhibited at fairs since 1949, initially with nothing but brochures, but from 1950 almost entirely with furniture and household goods. Superficially, the battle was about whether fair exhibitions could sell to the visiting public, which IKEA did, or whether only wholesale trading could occur. Less superficially, it was about breaking an upstart.

Anonymous letters and newspaper articles appeared, and in an early letter to the fair, Ingvar Kamprad complained about the tense and painful atmosphere in the stands created by the abuse from rival furniture dealers.

Year after year the same complaints against IKEA were made; by 1952 restrictions had gone so far that exhibitors were not even allowed to take orders, and the young director was summoned to the chamber of commerce for "questioning." A few years later, the National Association of Furniture Dealers succeeded in forcing the fair to ban IKEA from even giving the prices of exhibited goods.

From today's perspective, an almost ridiculous game developed in which petrified conservative sales thinking was up against a new and insolent price pressure. IKEA was banned again and again from doing anything but kept finding new ways of getting around each ban. If the company was not allowed to appear itself, it would send another Kamprad-owned company exhibit, or some reliable supplier.

In a letter from the National Association of Furniture Dealers, IKEA was likened to a monster with seven heads: "If you cut off one, another soon grows."

There was now open warfare against IKEA in the name of free enterprise by directors who otherwise praised the advantages of competition as opposed to a planned economy. The European trade goods insurance company was brought in to "try to restrain these methods of selling," and there was deprecating talk about "rampant retailing." IKEA hit back, more shrewdly each time.

Whatever people did, IKEA was always there, putting in an appearance in every small Swedish town, in every place where fairs were organized. If IKEA itself was not there, it was represented by one of its subsidiary companies or a Småland supplier allowed to exhibit—with all exhibition expenses paid by IKEA and referred back to Älmhult.

St. Eriks Fair, and the powerful pressure of the trade associations behind it, responded by limiting the public's right to visit the fair to only four days of six. The number of visitors fell, and even other exhibitors started objecting to the boycotts. The destructive forces were biting their own tails.

This battle of fair participation was really over only one issue—the low prices of the upstart. It finally abated, not because anyone changed their opinion, nor because the Price and Cartel Commission intervened (Kamprad did not want that), but mostly because IKEA was growing at record speed and acquiring its own exhibition premises in the three most important cities. The Älmhult people could not be bothered with the battle, for they were fully busy with succeeding.

When it came to IKEA's factory purchases of furniture, however, the harassment continued and became cruder. When Kamprad asked whether he might make purchases, small factories said they wouldn't dare sell to him. Others delivered despite the threats, but by truck instead of by rail, which they considered easier to spy on.

In one of the letters in its 1957 report, the National Price and Cartel Commission mentioned a manufacturer's description of the difference between IKEA and other furniture dealers. IKEA paid within ten days, with a deduction for a cash discount of 3 percent. Others did not pay for three or four months and yet made the same deduction. Nursing the supplier is one of Kamprad's hobbyhorse principles—one he still imparts to his staff—but it could be said that he was compelled to adopt the practice.

I have personally suppressed most of the difficulties of the boycott days. I drew one conclusion: that it never pays to work negatively. That was what was wrong with my colleagues. They acted "negatively," trying to put a brake on things and banning instead of competing positively and meeting us with their own constructive ideas. Who knows whether we would have been as successful as we were if they had offered us an honest fight. That, if anything, might have stopped us. The boycott simply reinforced our unity. It was a crisis that became a noncrisis as we kept finding new solutions.

In fact, the pattern was to be repeated for IKEA in the outside world. In several countries—in Germany, for instance—the trade reacted negatively to us, and thanks to that we had the wind behind us there as well.

In IKEA's business philosophy, the whole matter should be inscribed as a golden rule: regard every problem as a possibility. New problems created a dizzying chance. When we were not allowed to buy the same furniture that others were, we were forced to design our own, and that came to provide us with a style of our own, a design of our own. And from the necessity to secure our own deliveries, a chance arose that in its turn opened up a whole new world to us. That chance was to be called Europe or, to be more precise, Poland.

Then Came the First Self-Assemble Furniture

> "Oh God, then let's pull off the legs and put
> them underneath," said Gillis. And, my good-
> ness, what a neat little parcel it was.

To the general public, IKEA is a company that supplies furniture you have to take home and assemble yourself, preferably with a peculiar little key. Musical numbers have been based on this, and thousands of newspaper columns have hilariously described struggles with instructions, missing screws, and keys that don't fit properly.

Today self-assemble furniture has become a matter of course, and IKEA's competitors in this market have become successful as well. Employees who have worked for IKEA for ten years are presented with a silver key to fasten in their lapels—and with a gold key after twenty-five years.

Ingvar Kamprad learned to keep down prices on the factory floor from his great predecessor, Josef Anér, a master at negotiating low prices by making use of manufacturers' low seasons. Ingvar went in the same direction, but he moved one step further, taking self-assemble furniture as his starting point in the actual manufacturing process and changing this here and that there, cutting away a millimeter here, a centimeter there, all with the aim of saving material and keeping the price down.

It could be said that it was chance and casual meetings with talented collaborators as much as the increasingly tough competition that organically led to the much-debated self-assemble furniture, a fully developed knockdown range, and the production-geared company that is the founder's pride.

This is Ingvar Kamprad's own account of how it came about:

When one of the first IKEA catalogs was to be completed, we were short of time and needed someone who could quickly design the originals for the printed ads, so I got in touch with a young draftsman named Gillis Lundgren at an advertising agency in Malmö.

In time he became one of our most faithful collaborators, eventually a close friend of the family, and the designer of innumerable products and many of our bestsellers. Without him, we would never have got going so quickly with self-assemble furniture, which became IKEA's mark, reputation, and basic idea.

We had a meeting at Elfs Möbler, a factory in Älmhult that supplied us, in which there was a large space we used as a primitive studio when we were to photograph goods for the catalog. Gillis traveled up with a newly acquired secondhand Rollieflex (a Japanese camera) and rigged up a few lamps; together, we furnished one or two simple interiors.

He thought we ought to have flowers in a vase, and I rushed out to buy five tulips in town. By the next morning the first tulip had begun to droop, and on the fifth day the last one started to lean over. But Gillis stuck a needle up the stalk to straighten it up, we painted a beer bottle black to use as a vase, and the photograph appeared in the catalog looking perfectly professional.

I wrote the texts myself at night.

Those were the days of simple operations, improvisations, times of joy, and sudden impulses. We were feeling our way along, failing, trying again, and succeeding.

It turned out that Gillis was generally inventive and skillful. We often hit on ideas together, but I've never been able to draw, whereas Gillis was incredibly good at making what I envisioned concrete. Sometimes he changed a piece of furniture so that competitors couldn't maintain that the manufacturer was selling the same furniture to us as to others. The boycott was beginning to be felt in every way, and we and our suppliers were under constant surveillance by our competitors. Gillis would make a sketch and show it to the manufacturer, saying, "Do this instead, then it'll be a new item."

That was the beginning of our designing our own furniture, essentially avoiding the boycott and its problems. But on one occasion when we had photographed a table and were to pack it up again afterward, it was Gillis who muttered something like, "God, what a lot of space it takes up. Let's take the legs off and put them under the tabletop."

Then one fine day—or was it a night?—we had our first flat parcel, and thus we started a revolution. In the 1953 catalog, which was ready in 1952, "Max," the very first self-assemble table, was included. After that followed a whole series of other self-assemble furniture, and by 1956 the concept was more or less systematized.

Perhaps it could be said that reality forced the innovation upon us. We had begun to experience a worrisomely high percentage of damaged furniture in transport—broken table legs and that kind of thing—and the European insurance companies were beginning to grumble. The more "knockdown" we could produce, the less damage occurred during transport and the lower the freight costs were; that was the logic of it.

Gillis began traveling with me to the manufacturers. He saw their products and how they were made, made lightning sketches, and wondered whether they couldn't be made differently. Thus, self-assemble bookcases, chairs, beds, and other pieces successively appeared.

In my "Appeal to People in the Countryside" in 1949, I had written about the costly middlemen and urged people to buy direct from the factory through us. But not until now, in the mid-1950s and the year before our first real store was opened, were we ready to combine design, function, and price. Early on, we traveled around unannounced and checked the quality at the factories, always looking for small savings that made a great difference to the ultimate price.

I had a kind of awakening on the idea level when I went to the Milan Fair and visited a large carpet supplier. Thanks to him, I was able to see ordinary Italian households, the homes of simple clerks and workers. What I saw surprised me: heavy, dark furniture; a single lightbulb above a heavy dining-room table; a chasm between all the elegance at the fair and what could be seen in the homes of ordinary people.

It is hard to say when a philosophy begins to take shape in a person's head. I don't want to exaggerate my farsightedness, but I think Milan gave me a shove in the direction toward what our future marketing manager, Lennart Ekmark, excellently described as "democratic design": that is, a design that was not just good but also from the start adapted to machine production and thus cheap to produce. With a design of that kind, and the innovation of self-assembly, we could save a great deal of money in the factories and on transport, as well as keep down the price to the customer.

I am often asked when the fundamental concept took root in my head, but that is not easily answered. I can't have been more than fifteen when I began to wonder about the enormous differences between factory prices and prices in the shops. I could buy Japanese ballpoints from the wholesaler, Olov Gustafsson, for half an öre each if I ordered by the gross. If I bought them locally in Agunnaryd at Rickard Magnusson's grocery store, they were already, in the 1940s, ten öre each. The difference between the two prices was bewildering to a boy.

I kept asking myself later: Why does a product that is so cheap to produce get so expensive so quickly once past the factory gate? Why are we so sluggish on the last stage to the customer when we're so rational on the production floor? Distribution loomed larger as the major cost problem the further I progressed in my simple investigations of these questions.

As I said in the previous chapter, shoe shops were excellent examples of old-fashioned distribution, with the ladders along the walls and the need to chase shiny cardboard boxes containing tissue paper and varying sizes of brown and black shoes—a huge amount of work for a fairly small return. That couldn't be the most profitable way of selling. I remember thinking along those lines while still at the commercial school in Göteborg. Not that there was any teaching of business economics there; these were my own conclusions.

It was not difficult for me to see the advantages of self-assemble furniture and the superiority of flat parcels. Flat parcels saved enormously on storage and freight, and in the long run they were to be the prerequisites for the next step: customers taking home parcels of large furniture themselves. But we didn't get that far for quite a while.

We were not the first with the basic idea. NK in Stockholm already had a series of what was called knockdown furniture. They just didn't realize what commercial dynamite they were concealing. IKEA was able, thanks to the dialogue I later carried on with innovative designers, to be the first systematically to develop the idea commercially.

The inspirer of this development, apart from Gillis, was Erik Wörts, who worked as a designer at NK's interior decorator workshops in Nyköping. He and Bengt Ruda, who also worked for NK, together became IKEA's greatest established furniture designers; they dared to defy conventional truths and the contempt of colleagues for mass tastes and start working for us.

It must not be forgotten that it had hitherto been impossible for a Swedish architect to do anything for IKEA. Suspicion of us was great, and after all, Gillis was "only" an advertising draftsman who had gone "astray" in Älmhult and knew about putting needles into drooping tulips.

The Man Who Pulled off the Legs

Gillis Lundgren, born in 1929, is an example of the down-to-earth, energetic, and yet imaginative and very creative people Ingvar Kamprad attracted to him. He is the man who one day was able to "pull off the legs" and put them under the tabletop, thus creating history and a distribution revolution with IKEA's first-ever flat parcel.

He and Ingvar met once in Landskrona in 1953, when they were twenty-seven and twenty-three years old, respectively, and the layout was causing difficulties. They spent a whole day and a night talking seriously about life, the entrepreneur from Elmtaryd communicating his visions, and the youth from Lund listening with astonishment, for it was as if he had met his brother and a philosophy to his own taste.

Gillis had a good eye and had learned his skills from a grandfather who was a carpenter, another grandfather who was a blacksmith, and a mother who designed shoes. The simplicity and thrift that characterized his working background (his father was a mechanic) was typical of many of IKEA's pioneers. He had learned to draw at Malmö's technical school, then fiddled about with layouts, photographs, copy, and printed matter at the Gumaelius Advertising Bureau in Malmö.

The meeting with Ingvar in Landskrona in 1953 sealed his fate. Not even he himself knows for certain, but he has designed perhaps four hundred pieces of furniture and other items for IKEA, and no one knows when it will end. His has never been a widely acknowledged name though he is mentioned internationally; his signature, however, is behind best-sellers that have become famous, like the bookcase "Billy" and like "Mila," in its time the bestselling armchair of its kind.

Gillis is actually a master at everything. For over fifteen years he was responsible for the catalog: photographing, setting up interiors, seeing to the printing, occasionally heading information services and advertising. Moreover, for a while he was responsible for the product range, as product manager, and he has always been a constant friend of the IKEA chief, the two "as thick as thieves."

"If things go well for me, then I promise they'll go well for you," Ingvar said when Gillis was appointed with a handshake, and Gillis Lundgren has never had any other contract. "I have been more than rewarded," he has said.

They looked at hundreds of factories. In the small community of Tibro alone there were 125 possible suppliers, most of them garage-sized. Here and there, the two young men were literally thrown out; the price of the boycott was high. Among those who took the chance of listening to IKEA, some were still successful half a century later.

Gillis Lundgren involuntarily came to be the first full-time designer ("designing any packaging or any chair is much the same thing"), but there were other names that were to bring honor to IKEA. In the 1961 catalog, the Swedish architect Bengt Ruda headed a group of four skilled Danish colleagues: Preben Fabricius, Erik Wörts, Arne Wahl Iversen, and T. Herlev. The talented Ruda had shown true professional courage by leaving NK and putting himself at the disposal of IKEA in the Småland forest.

Malicious professional criticism was not slow in coming. The most common charge against IKEA was plagiarism, a charge that is still made today, sometimes with some justification. In 1997 the company put out a game called Labyrinth manufactured in the Far East, but much to the dismay of Ingvar Kamprad, it was largely a copy of the famous game from Brio, the Swedish toymaker.

Gillis Lundgren, who has lived in Switzerland for a dozen years but is still active in IKEA, thinks that "all design learns from other designs" and that the boundaries of what is more or less copied when it comes to furniture are vague. "Sometimes a new form is in the air, and several architects come to the same solution at the same time without having any idea of each other's existence."

Now and again, the accusations of plagiarism led to businesslike controversies, but neither Gillis nor Ingvar can remember a single case ending up in the courts. Gillis recalls that "Dux wanted to sue us for breach of copyright of a 'unique' bedhead designed by Bruno Mathsson that was supposed to have been plagiarized by our designer, Karin Mobring. Our lawyer was extremely worried. Then I found a similar bedhead that I myself had designed a few years earlier, and the case ended with IKEA promising not to sue Dux for breach of copyright."

Poland: "The Other Woman"

> We were with Ingvar, finalizing conditions for over two hundred different items, haggling over every öre, and we had been negotiating until eleven at night without coming to any agreement, so were totally exhausted. Then I said, "Let's break now and go to the students' nightclub." Then we danced into the small hours.
>
> The next day we continued, and the next evening we were in agreement. That's how it went. For us it was a matter of bringing in as much foreign cash as possible; for Ingvar it was a matter of bringing the price down to nothing.
>
> —SYLVIA LUKASIK

If Elmtaryd Agunnaryd baptized the company, Älmhult confirmed it and Germany married it to Europe. Then Poland appeared in the myth-filled history of IKEA as a combination of the "other woman," adventure, and a turning point.

A Communist country hungry for economic contact and human sustenance in the early 1960s, Poland received the Swedish capitalist with open arms and became a savior when the delivery ban was threatening to cut the ground from beneath his company's feet.

Poland was to be more than a drawbridge to the world for the furniture store that fifteen years later conquered the European continent and eventually one or two other parts of the world. The satellite state's furniture industry became a technical-commercial training institute for a firm that had hitherto managed well in Smålandish but now suddenly had to take out its German grammar and find that there was a universe south of Osby offering even better business.

Toward the late 1950s, the ban on supplies to IKEA by the regular furniture trade had begun to make itself felt. A few manufacturers were strong enough to offer support. The Stockaryds chair factory, for instance (at the time the number one seller), was the only one to dare to deliver wooden chairs. But IKEA's requirements had grown drastically, in both quality and quantity. By 1961 it needed forty thousand wooden chairs to fill its orders but could find only half that number. Sweden was not sufficient. IKEA needed more suppliers.

Ingvar and his newly appointed colleague for purchasing furniture, the experienced commercial engineer Ragnar Sterte, looked high and low for new capacity. They went to Denmark first and built up a supply network. But in 1960 Ingvar read in the *Svenska Dagbladet* that the Polish foreign minister, Professor W. Trampczynski, was to visit the Stockholm Chamber of Commerce to seek collaboration with Swedish companies. Ingvar wrote a letter to him, stating his interest. Months later the reply came: "Welcome to Poland."

On January 21, 1961, Ingvar, his father, and Ragnar Sterte landed in Warsaw. Their visit lasted a week and can still be tracked almost step by step in the documents the Polish secret police drew up.

The visitors were received by a delegation from PAGED, the furniture industry's export organization. In the delegation was young Marian Grabinski, a timber technician, architect, designer, and eventually diplomat. Twenty years later, soon after the fall of the Berlin Wall, he was to be appointed by IKEA as senior adviser and troubleshooter in Warsaw. With nostalgic tenderness, he still keeps the copy of the negotiations that show how the regime's secret police knew exactly what the Småland visitors were up to and where they were staying at the Grand, noting their conversations and, against regulations, giving them special permission to leave the capital and visit a furniture factory in the countryside.

With the same enthusiasm, Grabinski produces statistics that show the astonishing consequences of Ingvar's idea of writing a letter: From 1961 to 1998, IKEA's involvement in Poland went from a modest 69,000 kronor ($8,625) order for chairs to an account worth almost two billion kronor in pure exports from that country, along with investments and local business activities ranging in the billions.

Poland was transformed from a last-resort asylum for supplies to a prime example of what Ingvar Kamprad passionately thinks of as "the revolutionary explosive effect of 'the good capitalist.'"

In 1961, in the middle of the cold war, a relationship of reconciliation began that departed from the norm; today it is far from over and, in fact, looks to be intensifying. Thus, Poland was transformed from a mere supply country to a model market in Eastern Europe, with IKEA as importer, retailer, producer, and exporter.

The very first visit resulted in orders: the three musketeers, as Grabinski called Ingvar, Feodor, and Sterte, signed for their first furniture order the day after their arrival, then went by train to Poznan to look at manufacturing. Today IKEA has a large store there, as well as two in Warsaw and one each in Gdansk and Wroclaw. Six or seven primitive manufacturers have been replaced by a sophisticated network of 160 production-managed suppliers plus a considerable buying organization in Janki outside the capital. There IKEA's shopping center is taking root "in the potato fields" (Ingvar's expression) more and more successfully.

When they first went there, however, the question was whether Poland could rescue IKEA from the supplier mess and, metaphorically, allow the company to "sit on two chairs" at the same time. Ingvar recalls today:

> When we saw the first wretched photographs of their products and the prices they offered us at the PAGED office, and when they also implied that we couldn't even leave Warsaw to go and see the manufacturers, I announced our definite lack of interest. We were close to packing our bags and going home.

The crisis was solved, and the delegation went out into the provinces to meet a weary, grubby, industrial people's planned democracy. But not even a centrally controlled Communist bureaucracy had been able to obliterate the Poles' traditional affinity for furniture and timber. And the prices were incredibly low! "I seldom paid more than 50 percent of the corresponding Swedish manufacturing costs," said the retired Ragnar Sterte, taking out his thumbed order book from those days as if he were handling one of the Dead Sea scrolls.

For the Poles, quantity was what had mattered hitherto. The Russians had laid hands on almost everything. Moscow's thirst appeared to be unquenchable despite thousands of trainloads. Quality, Ragnar Sterte's hobbyhorse, was practically an unknown concept, and it took a long time before consumer quality standards (quality assurance) took root in Poland. Ingvar continues:

> At first we did a bit of advance smuggling. Illegally, we took tools such as files, spare parts for machines, and even carbon paper for ancient typewriters; the poor office girls had to write out invoices twelve times because they couldn't make copies.
>
> We bought nose and mouth protectors when we saw the dreadful environment, and we took a whole lot of secondhand machines from a firm in Jönköping and installed them in Poland instead.
>
> Alongside all the bureaucracy, and driven by a mixture of hunger for profit and compassion, we rapidly established sympathy for our Polish friends, working effectively rather like a privatized aid organization. Slowly and with repeated reverses, we helped to build up a modern furniture industry.

The infrastructure provided stiff resistance. A telephone call from Warsaw could take a day to make. There were no ordinary newspapers, but there was plenty of vodka to drink morning, noon, and night. Problems arose with war-damaged timber: bullets in the tree trunks caused catastrophic damage to saws and planes. But there was plenty of oak, which created a sales boom at home in Sweden.

Conditions on the factory floor could be bizarre. In the middle of a semirational assembly line, the process suddenly turned into little old women with wheelbarrows: Poland still lacked the resources to take the step into full modernity. However, in this environment some of IKEA's most beloved favorites were created.

The managing director at the Wielkopskie Fabryki Mebli, Jerzy Pawlak, shows with obvious pride the Orrefors vase he was given by IKEA when the Wronki factory passed the million mark in "Tore" chests of drawers (and that was only half of what had been produced under the Tore name). Two million "Billy" bookcases and three million "Ivar" shelves were also supplied from Poland, plus loads of the "Ingo" table. Records are still kept for the "Klippan" sofa. The list is endless; innumerable Swedish households are in this way furnished by Poland without knowing it.

The "Ögla" chair was made in bent beechwood in Farmeg, the legendary Thonet factory in Radonsko. It was here that the first order was placed, and one million Öglas were manufactured before plastic took over. Today it is still a fascinating, rich, almost preindustrial experience to follow the manufacturing there. In the shabby workshop with its hot furnaces boiling the beechwood, powerful men bend the round staves for arms and backs of chairs in the classic manner.

Nearby are the supermodern plants where five thousand chairs a day are spit out, of which IKEA takes a large part. Just four years after collaboration with Poland began, Ögla became the image of Ikean quality at a low price. The chair was just as good as the one people paid a lot of money for on the "posh street," to borrow an expression Leon Nordin used in a noted series of advertisements.

"There were two or three obvious advantages that differentiated IKEA from other overseas interests," says Sylvia Lukasik, a leader within the now privatized PAGED (and the person who remembered the visit to the nightclub in Poznan).

One concerned the decision making: it was always one man's decision, and you could rely on what had been decided.

The other was the most important in the long term. We were given long-term contracts and were able to plan in peace and quiet; we very rapidly became one of the main suppliers. A few years into the 1960s, Polish goods were to be found on over 50 percent of the pages of the catalog.

Today one-third of the contents of the Polish catalog are of Polish manufacture. "A third advantage was that IKEA introduced new technology. One revolution, for instance, was a way of treating the surface of the wood. They also mastered the ability to recognize cost savings that could trim the price."

Later on, this generous transfer of technology turned out to be risky. In one factory, Mosina, IKEA had invested up to $5.5 million in new machinery for the manufacture of bookcases. After the Berlin Wall fell, the Poles broke the signed agreement, and although the machines were eventually paid for, they went to work for other people. Profoundly disappointed, the Swedes were forced to accept huge price increases.

One condition for long-term contracts was naturally low prices. Certain shortsighted political bureaucrats in PAGED began comparing IKEA with German companies and others in terms of payment, and they decided to strike a hard bargain. A key man at the end of the 1970s became PAGED's senior furniture chief, Jan Nandurski, a man with insufficient industrial marketing sense. The negotiations between him and Ingvar Kamprad curdled completely when the Poles raised their prices sky high. IKEA began to back out and, with its usual mobility, turned to other low-priced East European suppliers. Between 1978 and 1984, relations with Poland became severely strained and the value of orders fell like a stone, from 100 million to 50 million in only a few years; other countries delightedly took over the role of major exporter to IKEA.

The background to this schism was the practice of buyers from Germany and England of trading in small series of so-called spot purchases, then paying a high price for quick delivery. IKEA, on the other hand, made long-standing contracts for large volumes at low prices, sometimes buying large stocks of articles just to keep to the contract.

Actually, IKEA's model perfectly suited the Polish centralized system, which required a long time to switch over and in which new dimensions or raw materials caused headaches. But the conflict—superficially a battle between antiquated planning and a radical marketing economy— almost torpedoed all the patiently built-up activities in which IKEA had invested since 1961. Not until a clever woman, Barbara Wojciechowska, took over the matter at PAGED was the problem solved and passions again cooled.

Total reconciliation was shortly to withstand a test of fire. When the Berlin Wall fell, state-supported industries all over Eastern Europe were threatened with collapse. Overnight the zloty, linked to the ruble, was almost worthless before it was linked with the dollar. Prices in contracts, however, were fixed in the old currency; Polish manufacturers risked losses of at least 40 percent, which often meant bankruptcy.

Sylvia Lukasik, remembering the drama, tells of taking part in a delegation that went to Lausanne to meet Ingvar Kamprad at home with Margaretha in Switzerland to find an emergency way out.

> For Ingvar, the situation was that he never went back on the prices IKEA had once set in the catalog. They applied for a year, part of his business concept to which he is still faithful. For us, it was a matter of finding some way of avoiding total disaster.
>
> I remember that in the middle of the negotiations, Ingvar interrupted the conversation, went out into the kitchen, and fixed a fine dinner for us. We ate first; then he decided.
>
> He backed us. He could see the extent of the disaster approaching. IKEA took on increases in price up to 40 percent but kept their price in the catalog. We went home having saved our firm, our face, and business relations.
>
> It was for that kind of thing we came to love him and IKEA.

The fall of the Wall gave rise to an important change of course for IKEA, and not only in Poland. Since the arrival of the "three musketeers" in Warsaw, the company had skillfully made the most of the low prices in a number of other Eastern European countries. Soon almost one-fifth of IKEA's purchasing needs were fulfilled in the Communist bloc. Buying was carried out centrally; for anyone who had learned how to deal with that process, it did have its advantages.

Now the whole system had collapsed and all was chaos. Old potentates were driven out, and Moscow stopped buying. New bosses no longer felt bound to old agreements but exploited to the full the machines that IKEA had to a great extent been involved in fixing, but now for other clients.

Both Ingvar and his successor, the present group president, Anders Moberg, realized that the company needed a new kind of security that could not simply be bought for a higher price: since the actual apparatus of production could no longer be relied on, the company, in brief, would have to become its own manufacturer.

Never is IKEA to supply IKEA, they had said. That teaching stemmed from the Prinsen television fiasco in the 1960s. By playing with different suppliers, over the years the company had maintained maximum freedom for itself.

The collapse of communism turned that principle upside down.

In 1991 IKEA bought the Småland company Swedwood with branches in Canada and Denmark. "That gave us the necessary knowledge," says Anders Moberg. "Purchasing ability cannot be translated into industrial ability; purchasing and industrial operations are two widely different things. We were excellent at the former and inexperienced at the latter."

With Swedwood, IKEA built up a management capacity to buy into and run companies in other industries. It went into Poland, then to Slovakia, Hungary, Ukraine, and Romania, and it bought up and modernized companies that had been owned collectively or by the state.

As this is being written, Swedwood has invested one billion kronor and turns over two billion, and it will perhaps double that figure within five years. On top of that, the company has been able to send raw materials to Sweden, thus putting pressure on prices domestically. "At first," says Anders Moberg, "it was like getting an alien body in the firm, but now eight years later it feels good. We can make better use of economies of scale, get even closer to our suppliers, see ourselves with their eyes, make demands, and ask questions: Perhaps they can supply directly to the stores? Perhaps be responsible for stockkeeping? Decisions of that kind may lower our prices by up to 20 percent.

Today Poland's importance to IKEA in more than one sense is greater than ever. Since 1990 five stores and more purchasing offices have been opened. But what is really new is IKEA's own production capacity, under the direction of the subsidiary company Swedwood. Five sawmills and a couple of furniture factories have rapidly been equipped with the most modern technology. The aim is to be at the technological cutting edge. One example is the enormous investment in so-called board-on-frame, one of Ingvar Kamprad's own original hobbyhorses, inspired by Gillis Lundgren.

Ten years ago, Ingvar wrote a long letter to the production manager Håkan Eriksson about making board-on-frame into a "giant project." The aim was a model installation that would guarantee IKEA high supply capacity.

In principle, Ingvar has now realized his dream.

Board-on-frame entails replacement of solid wood with chipboard or hard fiber sheets constructed on a frame like a kind of sandwich element. Ingvar calls the phenomenon "thick-wall"; most inner doors in Sweden are made with this technique. The method saves a great deal of wood and weight but provides a solid feeling and even strength and has become a typical IKEA success. Today the wholly owned laquered-table factories Zbaszyb-Babimost in western Poland and Lubava in the northeast produce one and a half million tables in cheerful colors and birchwood veneer with this technique. Manufacturing has expanded twice in less than a year. Sales of board-on-frame products, largely manufactured in Poland, may well amount to 1.5 billion kronor ($187.5 million) to date.

Swedwood has invested over 250 million kronor in its various factories in Poland, and the number of employees has risen to over twenty-five hundred. Ninety-eight percent of the manufacturing goes for export. Part of this industrial venture is integrated backward: from the raw material back to the forest and the care of it.

Poland became not only "the other woman" in IKEA's life but also another home. Here the emigrants again saw on foreign soil the Småland temperament, a kindred spirit that also prized simplicity, thrift, and enterprise. The previous Polish trade minister Andrzej Olechowsky points out that, immediately after liberation from Russia, two million small native businesses appeared as if from nowhere. Ingenuity and obstinacy of the Kamprad kind suited a disposition that under Communist authority had learned to be innovative in order to circumvent a repressive power.

IKEA's simple and open structure of command has become a dream for a people used to inaccessible state hierarchies, and young, well-educated academics have been attracted to private enterprise. In its management structure, IKEA is precisely the opposite of "other almost militarily managed multinational giants," says Olechowsky. "IKEA is an example of a management structure with no barriers." The output of the furniture stores has corresponded to a need in a population that was unable to afford to renew their everyday things for decades, and who also lived in extremely cramped circumstances and so loved IKEA's clever solutions. "Going into Poland is more than right. People are positive; they can look toward a bright future. They have put the darkness behind them," says Marian Grabinski.

Add to this a strategic advantage: wages in Poland are still one-quarter of Swedish wages at most.

Poland also became a breathing space, and many Ikeans were able to "see the world," as the pioneer Ragnar Sterte expressed it. Exciting careers were available there. One example is Håkan Eriksson, the man who built up Polish production and created the success of the bright lack-table, making IKEA a leader in Europe with board-on-frame.

Against this background, it is not strange that Poland came to symbolize both a turning point and an adventure to Ingvar Kamprad. The Poles gave him a price lead that the Swedish domestic furniture producers could never catch up with. Ironically enough, the attempt to sabotage the upstart from Älmhult ended in his becoming even stronger.

Today Poland is the natural bridgehead for the conquest of Russia. In the autumn of 1997, a series of investment decisions was taken by management that will eventually be worth billions: In the long term, IKEA aims once and for all to conquer the Russian market. The large areas of forest with felling rights that IKEA leased in Latvia will fit in well. Advanced experiments are being conducted in the project called "Weeds of the Forest": types of timber are used that the furniture trade has considered impossible to use and are therefore still cheap. Eastern Europe has become the Ikean laboratory.

Without its experiences in Poland, without low prices, without the habit of wrestling with primitive circumstances and working in a country with a different way of thinking, IKEA could not have gone further in Europe with such great sureness of touch.

It went well for other reasons too. Håkan Eriksson, having spent twenty years with IKEA in Poland, explains the company's success:

> Because young people were given responsibility, because employees were permitted to use both imagination and common sense, because the company maintained its humble attitude: "If we don't improve, someone else will, so we must make the effort."
>
> And because from Ingvar Kamprad comes the same perpetually driving question that keeps developments going: How can we make it a little cheaper? What do you think? Of course we can.

So the passion matured into honest love and mutual grateful dependency, a perfect relationship as Eastern Europe prepares itself to become the growth area of the 2000s.

Seen from the other direction, IKEA provided "order and clarity by ordering a long series of orders a year in advance," said Adam Burda, managing director of Polskie Mebli in Poznan. "There were units that over some periods supplied as much as 80 percent of their production to the Swedes." That was an important lesson. A poverty-stricken Communist country's industry was helped along to future prosperity by a "good" capitalist. That's the way things can go.

And the icing on the cake: Ingvar learned to kiss people on the cheek as warmly as Polish beetroot soup is served with a dollop of cream in it.

The Magazine That Made
IKEA Socially Acceptable

> Maybe we were a little childish, but we saw
> ourselves as educators.
>
> —MARIANNE FREDRIKSSON,
> PIONEERING SWEDISH JOURNALIST AND AUTHOR

When test-drivers for the magazine *Teknikens värld* (Technology World), trying out the newly launched Mercedes minicar, turned the car over, a new chapter in the motor car industry was written.

The prestigious manufacturer was shaken. Mercedes had always stood for quality and safety. After various attempts to repair the damage to the company's reputation, sales were stopped, the car was redesigned, and billions were paid out to rescue the company's status and honor.

It is hard to believe that IKEA would allow itself to be afflicted by a similar problem, but the truth is, it has come close. When information was published in Germany in 1993 that IKEA's bookcases contained formaldehyde that leaked dangerous gas into homes, a tremor went through the furniture giant. Measures were quickly taken to resolve the problem, however: the entire stock was withdrawn, customers were fully compensated, and all manufacturing using the dangerous substance was banned. It was all forgotten shortly afterward, and IKEA felt hardly a hiccup in sales.

Time and time again, IKEA has been exposed to similar, more or less serious attacks concerning the quality of its furniture, thefts of its designs, or supposed dangers in its products. However, the management has effectively blunted such onslaughts with rapid, factual, and honest measures. IKEA has always regained customers' confidence. That once again appeared to be the case in the autumn of 1997, when highly publicized television programs on child labor practiced by certain of IKEA's Far Eastern suppliers were broadcast.

The story of IKEA's relations with the media, like all great passions, is full of equal parts happiness and misery, mixed with a large portion of joint exploitation. The media have used IKEA as an example of the ideal company, and Kamprad as an example of the myth of starting with nothing and conquering the world. Equally, IKEA has needed the media. IKEA is certainly not public in the shareholding sense, but few companies have been so regularly in the public eye.

IKEA served for a long time as a favorite subject of reports on the poor boy who built his own Klondike. In the infancy of IKEA, when the furniture trade boycotted the company by blocking supplies, the sympathy of the general public was aroused. The founder's own ability to embody the company motto, his frugal habits, and his notorious inclination to travel standard class even as a billionaire have contributed to an aura of legend and progress, but also of modesty and ordinary humanity.

Two episodes in the history of IKEA provide clear examples of how the media can change history positively or negatively for a company. In the first case, a pioneering journalist on a small home and furniture magazine played the main part. In the second, an attempt by the largest newspaper in Scandinavia to rob Ingvar Kamprad of his honor and reputation failed. Let us look at both of these affairs.

In September 1964, just after 800,000 IKEA catalogs had been mailed to Swedish households, the furniture magazine *Allt i Hemmet* (Everything in the Home) published a sensational furniture comparison. It claimed, for example, that a chair bought at IKEA for 33 kronor ($4) was better than a virtually identical one that could be bought in a pricier furniture store for five times as much, 168 kronor ($21).

The drama behind this sensational sixteen-page report was almost as great as its economic and other consequences.

Allt i Hemmet, owned by the major publisher Bonniers, was at the time edited by Marianne Fredriksson, who later became a widely praised and much loved publicist and novelist. Eight years before, at only twenty-eight, she had become an editor at *Allt i Hemmet,* and from the first she had shown the way toward a new consumer-directed and hypermodern journalism; in a new cheeky but factual language, she drew attention to underlying trends in opinion and trades.

The magazine itself attracted skilled journalists and consciously reinforced its image with a handful of consultants, mostly progressive architects (Swedish interior decorators always have architectural training). Largely for that reason, the magazine had long hesitated to pay attention to, let alone praise, IKEA, which at the time functioned as a large influential mail-order firm (60 million in sales in 1962) with only one large and increasingly famous store in Älmhult.

At the time, it was considered fact that IKEA was the cheapest mail-order firm in the country. However, despite its success, it shared a reputation for doubtful quality that other furniture mail-order firms had. This was just what Kamprad had feared when in 1953 he decided to compete with other mail-order firms in quite a different way. Customers ordering by mail had to rely on the catalog, the distant salesman of an anonymous manufacturer. They could not touch the ordered goods; they could only hope that the goods were as described. All that customers could see was the price, while the trade description could be one empty phrase after another.

As mentioned previously, Ingvar Kamprad was aware of the fact that only decent quality in relation to price would secure his future. But a bad reputation is something that lasts disgracefully long. Although more and more Swedes flocked to Älmhult and often went home in Volvo station wagons very satisfied with the household goods they had bought there, IKEA's furniture was regarded with quiet contempt by the arbiters of taste and the designers of the day. If the company occasionally had a decent piece of furniture, it was deemed to have been copied or derived from a stolen idea.

Marianne Fredriksson, later the innovator of "inner-world journalism" in Sweden, listened to those in the office who doubted IKEA but finally took the matter into her own hands and went to Älmhult. She wanted to see with her own eyes what the company was like. With her she had an experienced designer and architect, as well as a photographer.

Their visit was observed from the office by a nervous Ingvar Kamprad and his cousin, I.-B. Bayley, who was responsible for the product range. Both of them had recognized the editor and feared her. Little did they know she had come to begin an exciting process, a masterpiece of resolute consumer journalism.

Allt i Hemmet was now to settle once and for all whether IKEA stood for quality in all categories: form, function, and price. A group of people, all anonymous, were to buy pieces of furniture (sofas, dining tables, armchairs, bookcases, lamps, curtains, and so on) with similar looks and similar functions, as far as possible, from IKEA and from a number of other furniture stores and manufacturers around the country.

A living room was furnished in a cramped studio in Döbelnsgatan in Stockholm; one part was photographed with IKEA furniture alone, and another with four varieties of furniture from other suppliers. The sizable price difference between IKEA's room (2,777 kronor, or $347) and that of the most expensive competitors (8,645 kronor, or $1,081) was immediately apparent—6,000 kronor ($750).

Nevertheless, the major sensation was the quality test. The furniture was sent to a Swedish design laboratory, still anonymously, and impartial testers, under the direction of two well-known architects, undertook the trials.

The result shocked the industry and the general public. Piece by piece, the IKEA furniture showed better figures than the expensive furniture by well-known companies.

Most astonishing of all were the results for the Ögla, the bentwood chair made in Poland according to the famous Thonet model. It cost 33 kronor, while the price in the "grand shop" was 168 kronor. Moreover, the cheap chair won the test: even after 55,000 tippings in a machine, the Ögla (made in the legendary Thonet factory south of Warsaw) was still intact.

It is possible that other events have had a more direct influence on the progress of IKEA than *Allt i Hemmet*'s intervention in its history, but the importance of this event cannot be underestimated. The resulting publicity, quite simply, made IKEA acceptable in middle-class drawing rooms.

From then on, the absurdity of all contemptuous talk about wretched quality was shown up. The *Allt i Hemmet* episode strengthened IKEA's conviction to continue quality development. Five years later, a young man, Bo Wadling, was appointed to improve the company's test laboratory in Älmhult. He earned a place in IKEA's history by installing testing machines in store entrances—by torturing IKEA's chairs before customers' eyes.

Finally, there was the last redoubt of the opposition, the grouse about indifferent design.

Allt i Hemmet took the viewpoint that customers themselves were probably capable of deciding what looked good and what design was worth what price. On the other hand, the editors did not hesitate to criticize IKEA for the gushing descriptions in its catalog (for a long time written by Kamprad himself). Moreover, the magazine not only pointed out that there were similarities between IKEA's anonymous designs and those of other well-known designers but asked, were they really so sensational? The magazine established that the price tag on the furniture ended up at much the same level whether the piece was handcrafted or industrially manufactured. And although the great furniture designers influenced much of the furniture on the market, that had nothing to do with plagiarism.

The industry reacted with fury to *Allt i Hemmet*'s "trick." A letter went out from the head office of the furniture industry association stating that if the magazine continued with similar test reports, the industry would urge an advertising boycott. The troublesome magazine was to be punished, and Marianne Fredriksson could feel the floor trembling beneath her.

However, she received support from two unexpected quarters. The owner of the magazine, Lukas Bonnier, urged her to stand firm and took the threat of a boycott lightly. Advertising sales would perhaps fall for a while, he thought, but they would then right themselves again, and he was proven right. Several firms and trades that had the courage to stand on the principle of free competition gradually offered to put their goods at the disposal of objective testing by the magazine. They could see the possibilities of the power of the consumer. Anyone who could prove that he was on the side of the customer would thus acquire increased sales.

The deathblow to the trade's attempts to smear both *Allt i Hemmet* and IKEA came when the news program *Aktuellt* interviewed Marianne Fredriksson. She had come across the confidential letter that went out to the magazine's many advertisers urging a boycott. As they had so many times before, sympathies swung over in IKEA's favor.

Marianne Fredriksson and *Allt i Hemmet* survived unscathed. The testing, in fact, became one of the magazine's most important features and increased its sales and reputation. Income from advertisements increased, and overnight IKEA, without having to lift a finger or invest huge sums, was accepted in drawing rooms. It was no longer foolish to shop at IKEA. Consumers could be said to have both good financial sense and excellent taste.

Things like that can happen.

"Per Albin Hansson built the Swedish 'people's home,' Ingvar furnished it . . . but we at *Allt i Hemmet* said where the furniture should stand," Marianne Fredriksson says with a laugh. "The magazine came out in the same postwar boom as the IKEA idea. There were new thoughts about furniture: what was simple was beautiful. Maybe we were a little childish, but we saw ourselves as educators."

In time, Fredriksson also met Ingvar Kamprad. At an annual catalog photo shoot of IKEA furniture, Ingvar Kamprad appeared with a carton of sandwiches and beer for the entire staff. That was his way of saying, "Thanks for your help."

The Miracle Store

> Every person is a cupboard.
>
> —LENA LARSSON, SWEDISH ARCHITECT

The story of IKEA is a businessman's manual. It teaches that few events in the inception and growth of a company can be ignored as unimportant. Both fiascoes and successes build an entrepreneur.

Sometimes even a disaster can turn into a miracle. IKEA's route to progress resembles most of all a process in which every new stage seems to have happened naturally, though perhaps not logically. When the boy in Elmtaryd sold his first box of matches, his innate genius was tested and the driving force of greed was also aroused. When the first piece of mail-order furniture sold better than all of his minor wares, he had the first impulse that turned him in stages from a peddler into a furniture dealer. Yet he still lacked the vision of something greater than money. When falling prices in the competition with other mail-order firms threatened quality and thus undermined the public's confidence in his firm, he gained insight into the relation between price and people's needs. Then he decided to arrange the exhibition in Lagerblad's old joinery, and from that development, everything was recognized as equally important on the march toward furnishing the "people's home."

That is how adversity is sandwiched with progress and opposition creates openings that invite new successes as well as new obstacles.

The flow of customers to Älmhult gave the founder courage and resources to make the decision to build an "impossible" store in the Småland countryside. His success caused the blockade by competitors, who forced IKEA to go outside the borders of the country to seek new manufacturers, thus issuing a world-citizen passport for the company. Production costs dropped, prices dropped, and success in the market was secured.

Without this resolute triumph, the money would not have existed to make it possible to open a store in Kungens kurva outside Stockholm (an investment of 17 million kronor, or $2.1 million), financed by Ingvar Kamprad himself without borrowing a single öre. It was a turning point that provided the foundations from which the modern IKEA would soon conquer the world. As the firm grew into a large company, it would often find inspiration in Kungens kurva.

On May 2, 1964, Hans Ax, a former fire engineer, brick salesman, and son of a worker from south Stockholm, moved into a small office in a derelict building in the very heart of Stockholm. Chosen the previous autumn by Kamprad to be the manager of the new store, he was directly responsible for appointing staff and planning the opening. His own appointment occurred after what appeared to be a confused meeting in the busy restaurant at IKEA in Älmhult. Customers sat down at the same table, then a friend of Kamprad's appeared and wholeheartedly threw himself into the deliberations on the new colleague's salary.

Building the first store in Älmhult, with its 7,000 square meters, cost 600,000 kronor ($75,000); Kungens kurva (45,800 square meters) cost 17 million kronor (just over $2 million). The architectural model, converted by IKEA's own designer, Claes Knutsson, was the multistory, circular Guggenheim Museum in New York. The motive was practical: square buildings, Kamprad had been told, were difficult to make full use of because of their corners. A circular building would provide optimal exposure for the displayed articles.

The budget for this new investment was bold: an annual turnover of 35 million kronor (about $4 million), which was four times greater than that of the store in Älmhult. But *Allt i Hemmet*'s test issue in the autumn of 1964, in which IKEA's furniture had been elevated sky high in both price and quality, made Hans Ax revise the budget to 60 million. Suddenly the company was in the right place at the right time; the magazine had legitimated IKEA as a prestigious brand name, opening up a Stockholm clientele.

On June 18, 1965, the building was opened, and the lines curled like a snake. The store was besieged by eighteen thousand customers in a single day, and the staff in Älmhult had to abandon whatever they were doing and travel to the capital to help their hard-pressed colleagues. Orders that required time to write out, in combination with far too few checkouts, created an uproar. In the rush, some customers couldn't get to the register to pay; some simply took their goods and left. The manager himself caught up with a carpet thief in the parking lot before the police got there.

It was chaos. The government contributed to this shopping madness by deciding to bring in a value-added sales tax from July 1 of that same year; true, it was a mere 3 percent, but for ordinary people it became a sport to make more important purchases before D-day. During the twelve days before the sales tax was instated, the store achieved sales corresponding to an annual turnover of 90 million kronor ($11.25 million), and when the first year's turnover was calculated, it ended up at exactly double the calculations—70 million kronor.

The placing of the store in Kungens kurva was strategic, and the entire arrangement was to be the pattern for decades. The starting point was to purchase a reasonably cheap site at a fair distance from the city center with plenty of parking space and good access roads. Skärholmen, the futuristic suburb, was just about to be built by Kungens kurva, a name that was not yet official but soon would be. The store was, in reality, in the country.

This circumstance partly decided the store hours: 11:00 A.M. to 7:00 P.M. When the morning rush hour into Stockholm was over, it was easy to get to Kungens kurva, and when the evening rush hour was over, the store was still open. This schedule also suited IKEA's large number of part-time employees. Great numbers of homebound wives chose to work there because they could work one full week, then have a week off.

The sign on the roof (which was to catch fire five years later) silently indicated another future choice. Between the dynamic Hans Ax and the "superaccountant" Allan Cronvall, there had been a heated debate over what the store should be called. Cronvall fought for the name Möbel-IKEA (Furniture-IKEA), while Ax wanted simply IKEA, thus showing that the firm stood for much more than just furniture. The conflict ended with the sign to the south saying IKEA, and the one to the north saying Möbel-IKEA.

In quite another story, it was this same object, the sign, that started the fire on September 5, 1970, through an electrical fault. That gave rise to the hitherto largest insurance claim in the history of Sweden. However, the disaster acted as a cleansing ordeal by fire, organizationally, commercially, and ideologically. It gave the restlessly creative Hans Ax new life, enabling him to stay with the firm and convince Ingvar Kamprad to approve of expanding and modernizing the store in the light of the experiences of the past five years. After the fire, when the store was reopened in March 1971, decisions had been made.

Self-service was now IKEA's selling model and has remained so. Self-service, numerous and efficient checkouts in the exit area, and a decrease in order sales provided a formidable boost to profitability and turnover. The customer took over what was perhaps the weightiest element in all furniture sales: delivery and unpacking.

In the after-effects of the opening tumult, Hans Ax soon put into effect a plan to sell smaller, more portable furniture. When Kamprad saw that this meant his old mail-order concept had changed, "he literally wept a tear or two." But a new epoch had blossomed, and later it was Ingvar who promoted the development of self-service.

Some elements at Kungens kurva became style-forming. Not least was the playroom for children by the entrance. The famous colorful sea of plastic balls (which children love to dive into) was discovered by some interior decorators at a fair in England, who developed the idea further. Today the playroom is part of the sacred concept; franchisers wishing to do without it must ask special permission from Inter IKEA Systems in Delft.

Also new was a section called Accenten (the Accent), which was Kamprad's own idea. Articles of a slightly better quality are sold here for gifts. A woman manager, Inga Lisa Lövén, developed the idea and the name.

Another IKEA specialty was also founded at Kungens kurva: home-cooking Småland-style in the restaurant, which also had a license to sell wine. In Oslo, Ingvar Kamprad had found a store offering what it called "Viking Nosh." He at once wanted to try it at Kungens kurva. But what was Viking Nosh?

What had the Vikings eaten anyhow, and could IKEA serve mead? How could it "Smålandify" an idea of that kind?

Hans Ax turned to a radio and television celebrity of the day—the popular ethnographer and folklore researcher Mats Rehnberg. He rejected the whole idea but produced a more intelligent one of his own. Why not offer Småland specialties? The furniture was often from Småland, and IKEA itself was from Småland. . . .

So the classic menu of sausages with potatoes in white sauce, meatballs with lingonberries, and apple cake with vanilla sauce was introduced as typical Ikean dishes. Today meatballs are a global bestseller: Dafgård in Västergötland (also a family business, typically enough) exports hundreds of tons via IKEA plus several tons of lingonberries.

Homely Småland foods are also offered in the overseas stores, but there the idea has been complemented with the Sweden Shop outside the exit checkouts. All over the world now, people can buy Wasa crispbread, Blekinge salmon, Kalle's Bohus caviar, Skåne ginger biscuits, Västerbotten cheese, Jämtland cloudberry preserve, and a pack of Swedish tots of aquavit plus a schnapps glass.

The fire at Kungens kurva was not a blessing, but nonetheless it provided a jump-start to new things. The insurance company paid twenty-three million kronor, which to a decent extent covered the loss of income as well. The "fire" sale a few weeks after the disaster drew a line of eight thousand people—some waited all night, some raised tents. In one Volvo a family had arranged a traditional crayfish party, and the store manager was invited.

The next day the lines on the highway were five kilometers long, and the store was emptied in a hysterical attack on prices that had been reduced, from 50 percent to 90 percent. (On Accenten goods, the clerks simply moved the decimal point one space to the left.)

The rebuilt and renovated Kungens kurva store was opened the following March. Today it is the flagship of the IKEA fleet. From seventy million kronor in turnover and fifty employees it has grown to about one billion in turnover (about $125 million) and four hundred employees. Being the manager of a store there is almost as grand as being commended to service in Älmhult.

Almost.

The Last Supper with the Gang

> I don't trust systems, not in the slightest. I never have.
> I don't trust establishments, groups, associations, nor
> firms. I trust only individuals I happen to believe.
> Sometimes I am thoroughly swindled, sometimes not.
>
> —PEHR G. GYLLENHAMMAR,
> FORMER PRESIDENT OF VOLVO

A business philosopher once stated that no organization should ever contain more than twelve people, including the boss. Look at Jesus and his gang, he said—weren't they thirteen and didn't it turn out that the last one was one too many?

Of the period between 1953 and 1973 in IKEA's history, it could be said that it was the time of the little gang, when the remarkable inner circle of apostles was recruited. In the beginning, they were never more than could be counted on the fingers of two hands.

They were the ones who from the very start had the whole Ikean religion running through their veins, directly from the Master, who was always no more than a bookcase away. They would never forget what they learned from him and in time would literally and spiritually furnish half the world according to the faith.

Never has so absent a person been so present as Ingvar Kamprad during this period. A veteran such as Leif Sjöö—today Älmhult's head of information, who joined the firm in 1958 as customer service manager—does not remember a day without the boss being physically visible or telephoning from wherever he was in the world. How are things? What's selling well? Can I help? How are things with . . . ? His daily calls home to his father were already famous.

The "three musketeers" who went to Poland had certainly opened up a new cosmos; stores were opened at this time in Stockholm, Sundsvall, Malmö, and Göteborg, but throughout those years the hub continued to be Älmhult. His best friend the dentist could still come up and take a morning whisky in Ingvar's office before work, and out in the furniture store Chairman of the Board Feodor strode around inspecting things like a landowner inspecting his son's estate.

The major business was in the making, but the stamp of the small business was still there, deep down. The apostles were not to turn out to be one too many until later.

Torbjörn Ek, the man who made Hemglass into a large firm and built up Hexagon, describes in his book *Dare Grow Win* how, like a stairway, a growing company takes a number of critical steps, each of which has to be taken with care.

Step one is the one-man business level; step two is the firm with up to five employees; at level three between six and fifteen people are involved; and so on up to the sixth step's major-company level with up to two thousand employees. "Seventh heaven" is everything above that number.

In 1973 IKEA had reached one thousand employees, but in practice it was run like a step two or three business. The atmosphere of a family-in-the-country prevailed—reinforced by Feodor's industrious presence (he became a traveling stock controller) and by Ingvar's cousin I.-B. Bayley, who, starting as secretary, became Ingvar's guard dog, big sister, and eventually product range manager.

At the time, we had an office at the top of a red barn. Ingvar sat inside, and I sat outside, with no lamp. I never let anyone in who hadn't come via me.

We began early, sometimes at six. If anyone came later, we used to say, "Oh, so have you read the evening paper?"

"The board"—if it existed—consisted of Ingvar, Allan Cronvall, and me, while Sven Göte Hansson stood outside exerting an influence.

We did the catalog together—Ingvar wrote, Gillis drew, I edited. In the first catalogs, there were few names, but then Ingvar decided to give names to everything—he found numbers difficult. Computer people wanted numbers, but I fought for names, which I usually thought up together with the designer. Suites, sofa and chairs were to have city names, bookcases boy's names, curtains girl's names, and duvets bridge names. An armchair was called "Stabil"—and it certainly was stable. Nothing we had already named was ever changed—"Aveny" and "Sultan" have always been called that—but nothing was allowed to be called "Ingvar."

However, the bookcase called "Billy" has been called all sorts of things, just as what is now called "Ivar" is called both "Bosse" and "Ingo." . . . Small chests are always called "Moppe," and we once had a curtain called "Morot" (Carrot)—it was covered with linnaea flowers. The same names are used all over the world using the Swedish spelling.

Ingvar largely decided everything, had most of the ideas, inspired, scolded, was angry, then patted us on the back. . . .

We had a product council. Ingvar was given the agenda and sent it back with notes: "good," "excellent," "prohibited," and so on.

Apart from I. B., the only woman, the people allied to the company and in a position of confidence had probably been handpicked by Ingvar himself. They might at first be grilled in a great variety of ways before being offered a post. As mentioned earlier, Sven Göte Hansson was interviewed for a day and a half, and Ragnar Sterte was tested at his first meeting with a whole day's exercise at setting furniture prices for the next catalog. Gillis Lundgren, the advertising man and future designer, landed on the payroll more or less by mistake—but the chemistry worked.

Jan Aulin, employed in 1968 as the first of Ingvar's many assistants, tells of how he was practically left on his own for the whole of his first month because the boss was in Poland. He had to find out for himself how this furniture store functioned, snatch Ingvar's mail from the postman, introduce himself to the decision-making groups—everything seemed very free, disorganized, chancy, and full of unwritten laws.

Aulin had to become his own entrepreneur, form his own sphere of influence, and Ingvar approved of that. As immovable as he is in his demands to follow the IKEA concept, he is susceptible to independent mavericks—the combination of lone wolf and herd animal is in fact the sum total of Ingvar's own makeup as an entrepreneur and builder of firms. He knows how to recognize himself.

The truth is that at this time, just before the leap into Europe, the organization was in several respects at step one of Torbjörn Ek's "stairway." In Ingvar's own words: "IKEA began as a one-man enterprise. I was used to making decisions. At home there could be a lot of us discussing things, but I was the person they turned to in the end."

So, de facto, IKEA had gone beyond all Ek's stages but paradoxically enough had at the same time stayed at all levels.

A decisive moment in the growth of a company is when the founder has to hand over the financial function because it hinders his business activities. That happened when Ingvar appointed the economist Allan Cronvall, a bureaucratic talent from Älmhult lacking in Ingvar's common touch, intuition, and business sense. He became so central that Feodor would kid his son when he went out for a walk:

"I suppose you've asked Allan's permission?"

Cronwall willingly became increasingly high-handed in the business press and gave the impression of being IKEA's strong man, with Ingvar as a secondary figure. Sometimes he decided he didn't even have time to speak to the founder, who had an appointment. He was good about enforcing routines and systems but came into conflict with the dynamic go-getters. For instance, he did not want to go outside Scandinavia with IKEA. Finally, he came to betray Ingvar's confidence in a shady property deal, and the two businessmen parted in a highly painful manner. Cronwall was more or less dismissed at a board meeting in front of all the members.

The majority of the old gang became more persevering.

They all lived near each other—at work and outside. As Ingvar expresses it: "I.-B., Sven Göte, Leif, Lisa, Bruno, Gillis, Ragnar, Jan, Håkan—the pioneers—we were all . . . I was about to say . . . in love with each other. . . . I think it was the happiest time of all."

Many years later, Ingvar was visited in Switzerland by a man who was studying at a management school and wished to interview him.

"What is fundamental in leadership?" he asked. I said love, and he turned quite quiet, but that was just what I meant.

That could be vulgarized. You could translate it into "friend-liness costs nothing." In the next step, as a businessman, you say that without winning people's sympathy you can't sell anything to them either.

Then put that emotional edge on my situation as leader of the gang I am to motivate for a contribution. At the time, when we were working as a small family in Älmhult, we were as if in love. Nothing whatsoever to do with eroticism. We just liked each other so damned much.

I find it more difficult when I have to separate what is commercial from my feelings. Take the children's IKEA. Crudely regarded, the intention is to make money, but on the other hand, is there anything more important than looking after children well? If we can offer help for good solutions for stressed parents and at the same time make a bit, what could we have against that?

Deep down is a genuine sense of caring.

Ingvar loved the fellowship of the early days with these men and women. But as he himself says:

However close you think you are to a person, there is always a distance. I used to be, and still am, in the double hell of having both power and money. It is easier for my managing director— he "only" has power, but even that is not easy.

I am sure many of my colleagues in the firm are prepared to

help me in an emergency. That's proven. But daring to be totally open, and directly criticizing me—how the hell can you do that? That's a very long step. With my authority, I have been able to say a whole lot of stupid things without anyone reacting. That's probably the curse of leadership—people look out for themselves. Even when you invite them in to talk it out, a stratification occurs in the actual selection—you choose people of whom you expect something certain. It becomes not entirely honest, not entirely objective.

None of the people from the older cadre interviewed for this book believe they were motivated by the money. On the contrary, salaries were often mediocre, particularly at management levels. Ragnar Sterte, however, remembers a day in the 1960s when Ingvar asked him to come into town with him "if you've nothing else to do." "Suddenly he stopped the car and took out a whole mass of banknotes, 33,300 kronor [$4,000]. 'I've done a good deal quite privately in Norway,' he said, 'tax paid and all that. I want you and Allan and Sven Göte to have a third each.'"

But money was never the main thing. No one was exploited, but "rich we never became." Much later, a younger generation was to express what Anders Moberg feels: "We who wanted to join IKEA did so because the company suits our way of life. To escape thinking about status, grandeur, smart clothes." As Jan Musiolik, the head man in Poland, put it: "I am more in harmony with myself since I joined IKEA."

Kamprad himself likes to talk about "society bearers" in the company. He is thinking of not just the first generation of Ikeans, although they set the tone:

It's all about those people who usually didn't come into the limelight but who did a little more than just their duty—who tested the lock just one more time to make sure the door was locked and the light out, then again on other doors that weren't really their business. . . .

The pillars of society think creatively ahead—"I'll probably be needed tomorrow, although I'm off duty. I'll go there and check if perhaps I can pack up a few parcels."

No society functions without that kind of person, and we had them early, and still do have them at all levels, the non-self-interested who make sure things work. . . . I remember as a model one Mr. Magnusson at the Crisis Commission in Stockholm, to which I went as a young man for an import license. He was the caretaker and knew exactly whether the people in room 25 or room 32 were the best to fix it without any bureaucracy.

So IKEA became "a loyal pillar of the company," a moral corps of porters. "Leisure time and work grew together, and we almost emptied the office on Saturdays to help in the furniture store. The time was unpaid, but it felt like a must," says Leif Sjöö, or in Jan Aulin's words: "There can't be another company in the world where so much company talk goes on around the clock. We sat through nights in semi-shabby hotel rooms thrashing things out, planning, talking, hatching out ideas, sleeping, drinking, and talking IKEA again."

"I lived with IKEA day and night. It was my life, and now I'm paying the price for it in my old age," says I.-B. Bayley. "But it was worth it. Most important was to enjoy it."

The pillars of society passed on the culture to new generations, having adopted the informal *du* form of address, abandoned the tie as its own anti-uniform, and spread thrift and simplicity like a virus in the hierarchies. They sowed the message of democratic design in the suppliers and paid homage to the doctrine of humility to both customers and manufacturers. Not until another time would IKEA people throw their weight about and try to teach old manufacturers what to do.

One evening when Ingvar was recalling this vanished period with nostalgia, he said: "Just think if we could take half of the pioneers and unite them with half of the newcomers—then we would have the best world-class team. Perhaps we do too little to achieve that."

In every one of his Christmas speeches, Kamprad pays homage to his pioneers. They always sit in the same place at a special table. "Through our history, we are building the future on the present. Not that we lock ourselves into what has gone before. Dynamism has to live on, the company has to change all the time, be supplied with new cells or die."

Both the company and its creators find nourishment in the values of the old gang. Kamprad himself likes to be with these original Ikeans to bring himself up-to-date. Sometimes he goes with them on buying trips. One day in 1991 he was on a buying trip in China with Lars Göran Pettersson, managing director for the trading company in Älmhult (which turns over several billion kronor). In Hong Kong they had a brainwave when they saw the clever umbrella sellers making a fortune when it poured with rain. IKEA began to sell umbrellas at sale price when it rained and at twice the price when it was sunny!

Ingvar was with the veteran Lennart Molvin when the idea came to him about the "consumer and discount" club called "Family." He later developed the project with Kenneth Wänman, and Family is now spreading around the empire. Out of this cadre of enthusiasts came the demand that before he left Sweden he was to put into words the articles of faith that were then collected into *A Furniture Dealer's Testament* (see appendix B). At the same time came the paradoxical consequences of this gang fellowship.

It was just this awareness that his closeness to the "old" IKEA and its original workforce was too great and too emotional that strengthened Kamprad in taking his slow, painful, and mature decision to emigrate. The time of physical, loving presence was gone, and the time had come for emotional healing and the beginning of his legendary wanderings.

BUILDING
THE EMPIRE

The Man Who Prepared for His Own Death

You're not to regret emigrating. You must love
America as your young bride and Sweden as
your old mother.

—VILHELM MOBERG, *LAST LETTER TO SWEDEN*

In the early 1970s, Ingvar Kamprad began giving some thought to what would happen after his death. He was concerned not just about the devastating inheritance taxes but also about the fact that there was no place in Sweden where the next generation could inherit a successful family firm.

Another and perhaps weightier problem for Ingvar Kamprad was that his sons were not even teenagers; he had longed for children of his own, but when his sons were born to his second marriage, he was rapidly heading toward fifty.

What would happen if he died before they were adults and educated?

There were other threats—hostile takeovers, for instance. Glossy new brochures kept appearing—dictating how modern capitalism should be run. That frightened the Småland entrepreneur: the tone of the brochures was shortsighted and totally contrary to the policy of building up close production-linked relations.

There was also the recurring question of a future lack of capital. On the executive board that IKEA gradually acquired (during the pioneer days, old Feodor was the chairman of the board), Per Lindblad persisted in trying to convince members of the advantages of going public. He even warned them of what might happen if they didn't. For a long time, Lindblad had the support of Jan Ekman. He questioned whether the expansion of the company could go even faster than it already had—why was IKEA not already in Brazil, for instance? The concept would also be quite suitable there. The necessary capital could easily be raised on the stock exchange.

Ingvar Kamprad resisted such suggestions. He thought the board was keeping only one eye on the core question—partly because IKEA had in principle always been self-financed, and partly because companies, in his eyes, were not just a matter of capital. They were also people, ideas, culture, and history.

> Still today we want to grow at our own pace so that we keep up, not just with what is new but also develop what we already have. IKEA's strategy has long been to take at least half our resources to improve what already exists—the other half to do what is in the future, if at a somewhat slower pace than if we had had access to unlimited money. IKEA cannot—as an eager member of the staff once expressed it—"just drive along *autobahn-anas* finding suitable sites on which to build IKEA stores."

There have been periods when it has felt slightly paradoxical for Kamprad ("After all, I am relatively progressive") to be the one to say, "Stop and think: you don't just plant culture, the soul, and the family spirit *in any old potato patch.*"

The board was eventually convinced—to Kamprad's slight surprise—that the line taken by the owner was sound. Today everyone has been converted to the conviction that going public would do more harm than good to IKEA in the long run. The perils of a quotation on the stock exchange are exposure to the media and demands for constantly increased profit and expansion, regardless of the business cycles of competition and vision. In addition, Ingvar Kamprad likes to point out, the stock exchange is an expensive solution. Public companies like to distribute one-third of their annual profit to their shareholders, money that disappears out of the companies and works against building up reserves, something IKEA needs in order "to take bold decisions." By contrast, the emphasis at IKEA today is on the ability of the owner (the Stichting INGKA Foundation) to adopt another view in the future and act accordingly.

In his drastic way, Ingvar used to say that he "had long prepared for his death." In fact, he began planning "IKEA's second life" in 1973, when the company for the first time went outside Scandinavia with its store in Spreitenbach, Switzerland.

> I asked myself, for several reasons: What do we do now? How can we keep the future IKEA without inheritance taxes bleeding the company to death or family squabbles between the sons ruining it?
>
> How can we avoid greedy interests endangering what we have built up, while keeping a dynamic and creative organization? And how can moves abroad be achieved without personally affecting me and my family in a financially devastating way?
>
> As a result of my ignorance, fumbling, and not understanding that it was necessary to acquire the best possible advisers from the very beginning, it took a long time to find the right solution. I thought you could take an ordinary Swedish lawyer and ask him to help; then everything would be all right. Instead, it came to involve American, Swedish, English, Swiss, French, and Dutch lawyers. It was hideously expensive. In fact, I've never dared find out exactly how much.
>
> It was not only a long life for IKEA I wanted to achieve, but also its independence of any one single country. A stroke of luck amid our misfortune was the restrictive attitude of the National Bank of Sweden. That forced us into a strategy for survival. After a great deal of work, we got out five million kronor ($625,000) to build the first continental store—the one in Spreitenbach near Zürich. But a special clause required us to transfer any profits to Sweden. That seemed tough, as we needed much more money to get started.
>
> The private Nordfinanzbank in Zürich, one-fifth of which at the time was owned by our Swedish bank contact, Handelsbanken, came to our rescue. They lent us what we needed on the basis of our innocence and gave us the assistance of the

banker Jan Ekman, who was later to become a long-serving board member.

But imagine how pleased I was the day I was able to pay back the five million we had from Sweden—it was, after all, the Swedish IKEA's money. At last we were free.

When the family and I moved abroad, we automatically received permission from the National Bank to take with us 100,000 kronor per member of the family. That half-million was enough to start a foundation in Switzerland, where real estate may not be owned by foreigners, and to found a whole series of companies in different countries with different tax regulations—from Switzerland and Holland to Panama, Luxembourg, and the Dutch Antilles. Our many lawyers quite often had completed registration of companies in their back pockets in reserve, so the process was soon completed and not particularly expensive. Many of the companies have never been used.

From the Swedish side, a number of clever lawyers were working on helping us find the optimal solution. I can mention Ola Ellwyn, who for a decade or two was on our various boards. But there were also people such as SE Banken's Nils G. Hornhammar, and Hans Källenius, long employed by us and now the successful head of Malmö Aviation. Like Ingemar Gustafsson, head of our family-owned company IKANO, he has contributed a great deal to providing IKEA with an international organization that can hold its own in the future.

One problem when IKEA went abroad was a complicated private financial situation for Ingvar Kamprad himself:

As early as the 1950s, I was personally insolvent. After the war, wealth tax was considerable. That included then, though not now, the working capital in the company you owned. To pay the high taxes and also part of my own keep, I borrowed money from the firm all the time, which was permitted at the time. I did take out a salary, of course, but not much more than that of my nearest staff.

I used some of this borrowed money for substantial capital insurance for me and my children—the idea was to ease the tax consequences of a future change of generations and secure our old age.

Ingvar Kamprad came to owe the company a great deal of money—18 million kronor in the end. As an individual he was actually bankrupt, while IKEA was thriving—a bizarre situation. There was one way out to balance the wealth tax—you could still sell a company you owned to another company you also owned, and with the profit acquire ready cash. Today that is allowed only if a market price is set.

In this way, Kamprad started from scratch financially and was able to make use of a number of companies he owned in the furniture and interior decoration industry. The profit from this would help regulate his debts.

In the press, a well-known young Swedish capitalist had been seen dancing at the poolside with beautiful girls and a butler serving him drinks while he explained that there was certainly no art in being a capitalist in Sweden: all you had to do was to sell your companies to yourself and make a capital gain.

There were soon whispers about new legislation.

I at once decided to sell off one of my companies for 25 million to be financially free as far as the company was concerned. By the end of the year, my then deputy managing director had obtained 20,000 kronor ($2,500) for stamp duty to close the deal. He did not have time to arrange it all before Christmas, nor the New Year, but as he said, "There won't be any new regulations before January 1, so keep calm. I'll take the risk."

I have often thought about that remark since. When other people say they are taking a risk with other people's money, what do they mean?

Ingvar Kamprad turned out to have good reason to ask that question. A short while later, the Minister of Finance put through new legislation that applied retroactively from New Year's Day. There was Ingvar, still with his debt, stamp duty for 20,000 kronor quite useless and a deputy managing director who had "taken the risk."

"What do you do now?" I said, and he just went red in the face and said that he hadn't believed that of old Sweden.

Later, as I was about to move to Denmark in 1973, my IKEA loan was settled by finally selling one of my own wholly owned companies abroad; at the time, I personally owned IKEAs in Norway and Denmark. Consequently, as a private person I was debt-free and declared a small fortune of my own of 8 million ($1 million)—apart, of course, from IKEA shares, then worth 160 million, but those I reckoned not to be "mine." They belonged to the future.

To the Swedish authorities, Kamprad decided to lay his cards on the table about his plans and reasons for possibly emigrating, with the consequence that he would also have to take capital out of the country. He went to the National Tax Board in Stockholm and, without hiding anything, put his case to the director-general, who listened judiciously. He promised that he would adhere to all the laws and regulations.

He kept that promise. He was not the officious kind. He told me it was the first time anyone in a similar situation had come to him and put his cards on the table.

Later I met his equivalent at Denmark's tax board. I told him what I had come for, and said I was quite willing to pay all personal taxes demanded of me, but that my company's tax problems had to be solved satisfactorily. He gave me some alternatives and said I was welcome to Denmark if I made that decision.

So during the whole of this process of going abroad I preferred to be quite open about my intentions, which were partly to protect the company as far as possible, and also to avoid letting it become a future object of inheritance tax, whether in Denmark or in Sweden. Most of all, I took up the question of succession.

Given these tax conditions, my Danish adviser said I could at best stay for four years in Denmark. After that, one becomes a Danish citizen and subject to tax. During those four years, both I and the company had considerable international freedom to plan for the future. In my first Danish tax declaration, I accounted for which companies I owned in Switzerland, Holland, Luxembourg, and so on, and what income I had, which was sizable. So I was personally taxed very highly, but I did not complain, just as I have never personally complained about taxes back in Sweden. Nor did this concern me—it was the company I wanted to protect.

Thus I became, according to all the regulations, an expatriate Swede. The head office was at first established in a shopping center near Copenhagen and a year or two later in an old inn with a scandalous past in Humlebæk, a stone's throw from the famous Louisiana Modern Art Gallery. I settled down with my family in Vedbaek, just south of it.

We stayed in Denmark for the four years I had been advised I could stay. The children went to school, and we had a good life there. Then a new discussion arose about whether we should stay. Consultants pointed out that from an inheritance point of view it would be better to choose another country, and they suggested England and Switzerland as good alternatives.

That was when a large number of difficult, complicated, and expensive investigations began. Lawyers arranged a two-day conference in Amsterdam—they came from Switzerland, Denmark, Sweden, France, and England, and they all sent sky-high bills afterward. It all ended with a crystal-clear recommendation to form a foundation in Holland. The oldest and most stable legislation on foundations is in Holland. For my part, I wanted it to be a very serious kind of foundation, as my ultimate intention was not just to avoid tax but to protect the growing company from surprise actions in the future from both the family and other directions.

To summarize, the primary driving force behind the decision to leave Sweden was not entirely the hair-raising taxes, but also the inability of the founder to operate in Älmhult—"sooner or later I would risk becoming a nuisance to the company."

Then came the burdensome fiscal aspects, not least Kamprad's personal loan situation. In time, that led to what one of the sons was to remember as "Dad giving the company away," that is, the forming of the Dutch Stichting INGKA Foundation. This foundation took over the ownership following a complex procedure, but Kamprad maintained a seat on the board and thus executive power. A Dutch lawyer conceived this solution, which was implemented during the 1970s. The lawyer was chairman of the board of a well-known Dutch foundation, and he described the long tradition of trading companies and foundations in Holland. He explained that this tradition provided a kind of guarantee against subversive changes in an uncertain future.

On his way out of Sweden, Kamprad had found the time to form a foundation in Switzerland. We shall return to the ownership construction of IKEA later.

There were other reasons Ingvar Kamprad and his family went to live in Switzerland. It would have been simplest to settle in England, like so many other Swedes.

I said no to a certain country, as I had found out that its legislation in these matters was based on fiddling and humbug. A condition for success is that you are dishonest in your declarations—it is considered quite obvious to declare quite different sums from reality. The authorities assume that all those filing tax returns are liars and so assess you with taxes that are perhaps five times your rent or ten times the value of your company car and so on. One never knows where such matters will end.

This made the decision easy for me. I had no desire to live in a country where I would feel like a potential semi-criminal when I was not one.

So after long, drawn-out investigations of the alternatives, the choice fell to French Switzerland—partly so that the children would benefit from learning French (they all speak four languages). Margaretha Kamprad already spoke the language well; Kamprad himself speaks German better than English, perhaps a legacy of his closeness to Grossmutter Franziska. Nowadays he manages to get by in Småland-French.

Moving to Switzerland requires a definite intention to leave your own country, but in our minds we were thinking in terms of a five-year period. Our tax advisers told us that I only had to declare an income corresponding to my living costs, but that did not suit me. I did not want to walk around the streets of Switzerland feeling like a parasite or a tax evader. I wanted to do things properly in my new country.

So I declared the whole of my then annual income of 500,000 Swiss francs, on which I had to pay about 40 percent in tax. Consultants and lawyers thought I was crazy. What was the point of such benevolence?

But that was what I wanted, and that was what happened. In fact, it corresponded to what I had taken as salary in Denmark as head of IKEA. I am still pleased with that decision. I can hold my head higher in the street, and I am more than welcome at the municipal offices. They even arranged a party for me and Margaretha when we moved in. Would anything like that ever happen in a Swedish municipality?

That is how IKEA and Kamprad moved abroad. Ingvar is aware that the move could be described otherwise, and naturally there is a nastier version in some people's minds. It could be described as a rich man's conscious search for an address where he would pay as little tax as possible. The truth is that taxation *and* other circumstances forced the family to leave. They needed to leave Sweden if IKEA was to survive in the form and with the concept the founder had provided for the company.

After the first five years in Switzerland, we all sat cross-legged in the middle of our living room floor and held council, all five of us, Margaretha and I and the boys. Leaving Denmark and all their friends had been tough for the family and the thought of moving yet again was not popular. We now had to choose to move either back to Denmark (which we really liked) or to Sweden, though I personally found it difficult to think of returning to Älmhult.

I think, as I have touched on before, that I would not be strong enough to keep away from the business. I would drive out onto the road to Bölsö and into the office in Älmhult, and as I grew more and more senile, I would become a millstone around the neck of the next generation of management. Perhaps Lund or Helsingborg, but not Småland, for that reason alone. But everyone said, as we sat there on the floor in our house, "We want to stay."

We are all creatures of habit. Margaretha had and still has a circle of involvement and friends in Switzerland and had learned to like it there. The children had friends, already spoke excellent French, and were on their way out into the world of IKEA, which was not just in Sweden any longer. Another move was from every aspect inconvenient and felt wrong.

So we still live in our little village seven hundred meters up—in fine weather we can see Lausanne down in the valley and just glimpse the mountains on the other side of the lake. I have a good study, a copier, a fax, a computer, and a secretary who comes once a week or whenever I need her.

Twenty-five kilometers from Lausanne was IKEA's store in Aubonne. Now IKEA had a Danish head office, a Dutch foundation, a Belgian coordinating group (which we will come to later), and a founder living in Switzerland. Was Kamprad—or IKEA in general—still Swedish?

> I think about the feelings when the Japanese started invading the American continent and took over one after another of the large companies in the United States, owning even the Rockefeller Center. That is what it felt like when foreigners bought our Wasa crispbread, that is what some people felt when Saab became half-owned by General Motors. The question is whether the nationality of an owner matters at all.
>
> Isn't it more the energy in the phenomenon, the organism that drives a business and creates work, that is decisive?
>
> When the construction of ownership and power within the Kamprad sphere is described later, I hope it will show that we built in mechanisms that are positive for the company as a whole, at the same time guarding what is very Swedish, what is Smålandish.
>
> Once upon a time the store in Älmhult was our entire world. Today sales back at home are only half of one percent of the IKEA total turnover, and yet we still manufacture more than ever *in* Sweden, export more than ever *from* Sweden, sell more than ever *in* Sweden. . . . It is Älmhult that decides and guards our culture.
>
> I understand nationalistic atmospheres. I am myself a local patriot abroad, with Swedish moist snuff under my lip and smoked sausage from Liatorp in the freezer. But rationally, it is efficiency that constitutes the success of a company rather than forms of ownership, independent of a foundation or a public company or a family that lives at a certain address.
>
> We were sitting in a product range meeting the other day, all day long. People came in to report, perhaps all in all twenty-five people, but not one single woman. I think that is strange. The majority of our customers are women, interior decoration is a traditionally feminine art, and here were only men.

My boldest dream of all is to one day have women in management. No track would be more wonderful to follow than that. But why has that not come about before?

How the Inaccessible Company Was Created

The truth about the world—does it exist? How can we tell the truth about the whole truth not being in this book?

—INGVAR KAMPRAD

When Ingvar Kamprad decided to go abroad, his ambition was undeniably to give his lifework the best possible chance of "eternal life." Long after he passed away, he wanted the company to be able to develop and flourish. In his own words, "As long as there is human housing on our earth, there will be a need for a strong and efficient IKEA."

But his ambition went further than that.

No one and nothing was to destroy or endanger his business vision, whether a member of the family or market forces or politicians. Barriers were to be constructed against not only hostile assaults but also against the danger that lies in apathy. All the dynamism was to be guaranteed as long as was humanly possible. More than that, IKEA was a concept to be protected in the event of war and subversive political changes. And power—that was ultimately to lead back to the family in the future as well.

Let us take a look at the business structure that Ingvar Kamprad himself, with some understatement, calls "fairly unique in the world." It was thought out in the 1970s and implemented in the early 1980s. It is so legally intricate that no outsider is really able to understand it. The founder is afraid—which may well seem unfathomable to the outsider—of revealing anything in this ingenious structure except what each country's legislation requires. There are great differences between the European openness that often prevails and, for instance, the closedness that is perfectly legitimate in the United States for family firms outside the stock exchange.

It could be said that the modern IKEA is run in a double command structure by "the hand" and by "the spirit." The business has de facto been divided into two spheres—one physical and the other mental, one organization for the actual store and one for the business.

Both command routes are equally important, but in different ways. On the day when Kamprad, who embodies the idea, is no longer around, these routes will be decisive for IKEA's survival. Should any reader maintain that "the spirit" is the more important of the command routes, he or she would not run much risk of being contradicted by this author.

"The hand" grasps the physical ownership, the shares, what could be said to be tangible in the here and now—buildings, factories, goods, things that can be touched, everything that provides the majority of the tens of thousands of employees with their daily routine.

"The spirit" hovers watchfully to ensure adherence to the business philosophy. Put into practice from the store floor up to the sign on the roof, it is carried out 100 percent correctly. The spirit primarily stands for "the concept," a word that has a special, almost sacred, charge in Ikean language.

But let us first look at "the hand."

The owner base in the IKEA companies is the double Dutch foundation, the Stichting INGKA Foundation/Stichting IKEA Foundation, which was made public in 1982. The foundation owns the business as it has grown from the dreams of the seventeen-year-old entrepreneur in Elmtaryd Agunnaryd since 1943. On the board, apart from Ingvar and Margaretha Kamprad, are a Swiss lawyer and at present two Swedish bankers, Per Lindblad and Jan Ekman. Ingvar Kamprad has been the chairman, "but," he says, "never at meetings. They all know that if I am, it all takes so long, no one gets either lunch or dinner in time, and secondly, it would block my thinking. So the chairmanship alternates."

When Kamprad one day retires from the front office, then a maximum of one person with the name Kamprad is to be elected to the board. The jurisprudence around the board's composition is carefully specified and will soon be tested to the full, for Lindblad and Ekman are older gentlemen who will shortly reach the age limit for board members—in Dutch law, seventy-two. Ingvar, born in 1926, came off the board in the spring of 1998 as chairman and has since that day been only a "senior adviser" at IKEA. He snorts slyly at the description.

Stichting IKEA/INGKA is a double foundation on the Dutch pattern: the owner foundation has all the shares in INGKA Holding BV, the group of companies that, to the layperson, consists of IKEA (all the stores and factories and offices). The board of INGKA Holding consists of prominent executives from all parts of the Swedish business community. These are the men who make the weighty decisions about future investments and strategy. In varying degrees, they are Kamprad's greatest confidants outside the family and the close circle of a few handpicked people within the IKEA sphere.

Stichting INGKA also owns 25 percent of the Habitat firm, which holds about one hundred stores. The rest are owned by the IKANO Group, in its turn owned by the Kamprad sons (see chapter 5). According to Dutch custom, INGKA is bound to the charitable foundation, the Stichting IKEA Foundation. The Stichting Foundation is an idealistic fund that receives money from the owner foundation to distribute for specified charitable purposes—to benefit people and advance projects within architecture, design, art and handcrafts, and the environment.

It could be said that the owner foundation and the charitable foundation are Siamese twins with two heads and one body, the physical incarnation of IKEA's ownership. Stichting INGKA Foundation, with the help of the holding company, is the "hand" that manages the IKEA group of companies. And yet this leading hand would be a dead hand if there had not been two executors for the foundation's task, which is to realize the IKEA concept.

The executive function is practiced by IKEA International A/S in Humlebæk, Denmark, which is assigned by INGKA Holding BV to run the store business, including purchasing, product range, distribution, sales, and sometimes manufacturing. International A/S is the incarnation of "the house spirit." In everyday life, by force of the management agreement with INGKA Holding, "International" manages and serves the stores. The propagator of that concept, the genie in the bottle, is called Inter IKEA Systems.

If International is responsible for an executive function, then Inter IKEA Systems is responsible for the caring function. The company, which is an ordinary Dutch BV company, has its address in the picturesque town of Delft on the same property as the company-owned pilot store.

Inter IKEA Systems BV is as weighty as the owner foundation and is part of Inter IKEA, what is called the Red Group, with a coordinating office in Waterloo outside of Brussels. It is headed by Per Ludvigsson. "Systems" owns the "Sacred Concept" with all its brand names, copyrights, regulations, and demands. The company functions as the Vatican does for Catholicism, carefully ensuring that the true faith is practiced in the consumer temples of the market, sometimes, one might think, right down to the rosary level. The "cardinals"—the closest advisers to "Pope" Ingvar Kamprad—include the lawyer Hans Skalin, who is also the architect behind the complicated construction of the business.

Inter IKEA Systems approves the franchise permit to run a store—either for IKEA's own stores or for an outside owner who is allowed to use the IKEA concept under extremely well-specified conditions.

A manager of a store has to write to Systems to ask permission to deviate from the laid-down concept—altering the physical design of a store, for instance, or leaving out a playroom for children, making a much smaller restaurant, or deviating in any other way from the standard range.

If a franchisee breaks the rules, Inter IKEA can order the sign on the roof to be taken down and all supplies stopped. That situation has never arisen, but it is envisaged as a harsh possibility.

In this division between the hand and the spirit can be found what is perhaps the most brilliant part of the construction that Ingvar has had his skilled and expensive lawyers design for his eternal establishment. There are only two people who know the whole intricate formula—Hans Skalin and Per Ludvigsson. The latter is the family's low-profile confidant, the éminence grise, born in 1943. He is regarded by the sons as the "Supreme Court" of the future should they ever disagree on aims and means for IKEA.

With the parent company in Luxembourg, Ludvigsson oversees the Inter IKEA group of companies via four divisions for each: finance administration, franchising, property, and Catella AB. The last runs consultancies in properties in seven different countries, and in Sweden in the fields of finance and the stock market.

As the person also ultimately responsible for finance, Per Ludvigsson has the opportunity to give pecuniary aid should a crisis arise somewhere. Some people describe this internal bank as a kind of "reserve fund," but in the strictly legal sense that is wrong. In practice, Ludvigsson administers some billions of kronor, the majority (about 60 percent) in bonds, and one-third in European long-term stock—a very cautious Kampradish characteristic.

In Catella (which is part of Inter IKEA), famous store images are administered, as well as well-placed properties in London, Amsterdam, Warsaw, Stockholm, and other large cities.

The founding of Inter IKEA is both wise and logical. Now, and even more so in the future—when the founder's all-seeing eye has been extinguished—Inter IKEA will ensure that his concepts remain intact.

When there are franchises owned by both the foundation and outsiders, naturally the head of IKEA International (Anders Moberg today) cannot supervise everything at once.

For the next generation, it would be terribly difficult to stick to the concept if there were no special organization that was a kind of keeper of the seal. Such an organization would guarantee and develop the concept, for without that, even brilliant business ideas die a natural death.

So Inter IKEA Systems was created. The fact that all three Kamprad sons are on the board of the parent company, System Holdings, shows Kamprad's desire for the family to play a large part in the future. Their influence will be instrumental, but Inter IKEA Systems is the superior complex formula for progress, the recipe for the way IKEA is to continue to be what it is.

The role of the founder during his remaining active years is, in his own words, to teach his sons the preservation of the concept, but also to teach them to see its possibilities. Without owning the concept, the sons, according to the foundation rules, are to ensure that the monitor—Inter Systems BV—functions and is kept vigorous.

The construction of Inter IKEA and its related units—the network of financial operations, properties, and concept-givers—reflects to a great extent the sometimes troubled personality of Ingvar Kamprad. In the marrow of his bones is his Småland virtue of not putting all his eggs in one basket, always having a backup plan, and refusing to be backed into a corner. Added to this is his constant striving to find the optimal fiscal solution.

Now that the ownership of IKEA lies in a foundation, and a type of foundation also decides the radius of action for Inter IKEA (the Red Group), the sons have been freed of the burden of wealth. "The Red Group," Kamprad says, "is too burdensome, from a tax point of view, for the children to own in today's world."

As a foundation, Inter IKEA owns and manages the concept regardless of how various countries may come to regard the laws of inheritance and wealth. Through this setup, the Kamprad sons can "control" Inter IKEA (for instance, they can appoint the board of the Inter IKEA Group), but they cannot own it. Their father has ensured that.

The system of colors describing the separate units of IKEA was invented by the lawyer Hans Skalin. The Red Group is Inter IKEA, the Blue Group is the IKEA group of companies, and the Green Group is IKANO—the only group the family still owns.

The foundations were constructed at a time when the Communist threat was considered a reality in Europe and the world was still living with the Iron Curtain. Anything could happen. So Ingvar Kamprad's foundations developed regulations for yet another emergency exit. It has never been used, but it reflects the instinct to have a lair to retreat to.

Historically, these regulations emerged during the war when various well-known companies were brutally annexed—at first by the Germans, then by the Russians. Firms such as Budweiser in Czechoslovakia and Philips in Holland were affected. For important brand names of this kind, including IKEA, a reserve system was created to avoid confiscation. Where an emergency exit would lead—if one, in fact, had to be used—was a question to be settled the day it became relevant.

Behind the construction of the foundation is the founder himself: his survival philosophy has marked IKEA from the start. Thanks to his vision, IKEA may sell furniture that is taken apart and then reassembled, but the company itself can never be dismantled.

C | IKANO GROUP

- 100 Habitat Stores
- Financial Services (credit cards)
- Real Estate Investment
- Insurance
- Banking

SALES: Approximately 7 billion kronor ($800,000)

GROUP PRESIDENT: Ingemar Gustafsson

OWNER: The Kamprad Family

A | THE IKEA GROUP

- 150 Stores in 30 countries (Ikea International)
- Product Design / Research
- Purchasing
- Production
- Distribution
- Retailing

SALES: Approximately 60 billion kronor ($7.5 million)

GROUP PRESIDENT: Anders Dahlvig

OWNER: Dutch Foundation

B | INTER IKEA GROUP
"Owner of the Concept"

Inter IKEA Finance (financial investment)

Inter IKEA Systems Holding B.V. (franchising)

Vastint Holding B.V. (real estate)

Catella Group (real estate / finance / technology)

SALES: 12 billion kronor ($1.5 billion)

GROUP PRESIDENT: Per Ludvigsson

OWNER: Holding Company in Luxembourg

IKANO: The Boys' Own World

> To preserve what has been gained, but to look
> around for new opportunities.
>
> —INGVAR KAMPRAD

In December 1997, the first issue of *IKANO WORLD* came out. It is a simple but proud little newsletter, produced in Amsterdam and aimed at the three thousand people in Europe who work exclusively in the Kamprad-controlled part of the business. As someone expressed it, "IKANO is the boys' own world," meaning that it's what the Kamprad sons have been given by their father to care for in the future, the company they themselves own and run as they like. It is not a toy, but a fast-growing multibillion-kronor business, a future security fund.

To understand the concept of IKANO, it is necessary to go back to the 1950s. That is when Kamprad the entrepreneur began to establish a series of companies owned by himself alongside IKEA—often to adapt to the market, and sometimes to circumvent the threat of the ban on supplies. It was thanks to these companies that the founder was able to build a fortune separate from, if not independent of, IKEA. In this way, IKEA Norway was begun, as was IKEA Denmark and a number of the stores' properties.

As described previously, these companies provided private economic flexibility, which came to mean quite a lot when Kamprad emigrated and freed himself of debt. Emigration in itself brought with it new companies as safeguards before IKEA acquired its final structure, legally and geographically.

Formed early, IKANO was used as an import firm through which the Polish supplies, among others, came to Sweden. Today it is an umbrella name for all Kamprad-owned companies that were not to be "given away" to the INGKA Foundation.

New companies have always amused Kamprad, and this was more and more evident as the furniture business brought in large revenues that could immediately be used for new establishments. Members of the staff describe the period from the mid-1970s to the mid-1980s, when Kamprad still managed the business from Humlebæk, as almost "renaissance-like." Everything was happening at once, and IKEA bulged without limits to its expansion. Ideas and prospective partners poured in, and new investments were constantly being made. IKEA or Ingvar himself invested in various projects both in Sweden and abroad: a private investment in a Swiss airline, a cutlery manufacturer, an interest in an electronics company. Kamprad held all the reins, and he loved to do so. But managing all these concerns took time and energy, and at sixty-three he made up his mind to leave the front line. His successor as group president of IKEA International would have to worry only about IKEA, and nothing else—that was enough.

It had become an increasingly untidy and important task to look after the assorted companies now running wild under the IKEA flag. Per Ludvigsson, Ingvar's confidant, was asked to clean house by suggesting another organization: the green IKANO was set up with its seat in Denmark, Holland, and Sweden. Today, although the group lies outside IKEA, certain ties have been preserved between the two businesses. The head of the group himself is good evidence of that.

Ingemar Gustafsson, born in 1939, was chosen to head IKANO. He is one of those faithful servants from Småland who personify IKEA's leap from the forest into the world outside. Son of a hardworking smallholder family from the same Agunnaryd as the Kamprad family, he is a classic example of the upstart to whom IKEA gave a ticket. He is also the type of leader to take the company over the threshold into the new century.

He began as a twenty-five-year-old financial assistant, a newly hatched graduate of Lund University ("What do we want with an economist?" said Kamprad when he first heard about him), and he eventually became a kind of controller and reporting secretary at IKEA board meetings. He slowly grew to be a trusted leader. As head of Swedish IKEA for ten years, he saw Älmhult grow from seven hundred employees to seventeen hundred; in the middle of the international expansion, Småland took a firm hold of "its" company.

It is easy to see how IKANO fundamentally safeguards the same virtues—simplicity, thrift, and so on—that mark IKEA; with Ingvar Kamprad as chairman, anything else would be impossible. The head office is today in Amsterdam, with a slim staff of nine people and a type of IKEA spirit that is all its own.

The first overhead slide that Ingemar Gustafsson projects when he is describing his organization is of two lions: the caption underneath one says, "Guarding what has been achieved," and under the other is "Looking for new opportunities." So IKANO is a mixture of "safety first" and "controlled progressiveness." Values are to be preserved here, but new things are always emerging.

The group consists of four divisions with a score or so of companies altogether. The finance and bank division is the most profitable, with two banks—the one in Älmhult and the Københavnske Bank, which is far too often a problem child.

Ingvar Kamprad in his time participated with a 10 percent block of shares when this little bank started in 1979, but he let IKANO take over the whole business in 1995. In 1997 the bank was threatened by a failed takeover attempt. The Københavnske Bank now orients itself with renewed energy toward its six thousand selected private customers with assets of about one billion Danish kroner. The entire finance division turns over about four billion Danish kroner.

IKANO has between one billion and two billion kronor ($125 to $250 million) to place on the capital market. Its greatest single involvement is 38 percent in the Swedish brokerage firm Matteus Fondkommission, but IKANO also invests elsewhere in Europe. Neighbor to IKANO's financial sector is the very active insurance division, whose undertakings do not fall below forty billion kronor.

The next largest in the IKANO Group is the retail division, with a turnover of about three billion kronor. Apart from the furniture chain Habitat (about one hundred stores, largely in the United Kingdom and France, with twenty-five hundred employees), there is Micro, the Swedish spare auto parts chain with stores in Poland and Denmark as well. Also in this division is IKANO Private Ltd., a furniture trader in Singapore and Malaysia. Neither Micro nor Habitat have made any meaningful profits, but they are considered to have a bright future.

IKANO's property stock will more than anything else give the Kamprad sons their future economic security. At the core are a number of exclusive old properties in Prague that have been restored to the highest level of quality and beauty. The group invested early in shopping centers near IKEA stores. In the early months of 1998, Ingemar Gustafsson, together with the increasingly common partner SKANSKA, inaugurated a "town" of factory-outlet-quality shops at Barkarby, near Stockholm, a stone's throw from IKEA's store. These factory outlets will occupy a lot of space in IKANO's future strategy.

How strong are the ties between IKEA and IKANO?

The answer is that both definitely emphasize their independence. Ingvar Kamprad's chairmanship—from which he retired in the spring of 1998—had bound the two groups together. The board veterans Per Lindblad and Jan Ekman now reinforce a kind of connection between the two groups. Otherwise, the closeness between IKEA International headquarters and IKANO's headquarters in Denmark is more geographical than instrumental. "We cooperate, but only in strictly businesslike terms," says Ingemar Gustafsson.

That is an outline sketch of the Kamprad family ownership. Whether IKANO becomes the financial insurance for the family that their farsighted father intended depends on the young owners—Peter, Jonas, and Mathias Kamprad.

It's off to a good start.

The Empire Builders

> It was more youthful then. One lived more by
> feel . . . a little more adventurously.
>
> —MARIANNE WIR, IKEA EMPLOYEE

From 1973, when the first store outside Scandinavia was opened in Spreitenbach in German Switzerland, IKEA expanded internationally at a furious pace. In less than six years, twenty new stores were established in Europe, Canada, Australia, and Singapore, not counting the two in Sweden. Germany was in the lead with ten stores.

These were Viking times, a period of great delight and conquest, and IKEA grew in leaps and bounds—in properties, numbers of employees, and millions in turnover.

This was when the company learned the basic technique of opening new markets, a lesson that made it possible to open forty-three new stores during the 1980s, and thus far in the 1990s another sixty-nine new stores, from China to the Czech Republic and Germany.

From the beginning, IKEA liked to try its luck with a small starter store in the city center to feel out the market and taste the local lifestyle and shopping habits. Nowadays the company is more self-assured, consciously mapping out a certain market and buying an attractive site on the outskirts of a large city with a decent reception area and good roads. More and more often, this means setting up a shopping center–like area in which the

IKEA store sits like a great cash cow in the pasture, surrounded by other temptations—banks, small shops, food halls, and modern stores.

New sites are being bought up in the expectation of opening the stores of the 2000s—at the moment Russia is the target for the next leap. Today, in a departure from the strategies of the past, every IKEA organization in each country is responsible for its own new stores. In the beginning, a specially trained team of IKEA people swept like commandos into the new country, landing like parachutists in unknown territory with a bag of money in their belts to build the bridgehead—namely, the store.

The key figure in these times was Jan Aulin. At the end of the 1960s, he became Ingvar Kamprad's first assistant, his right-hand man who, with all the experience of a thirty-four-year-old, was given the responsibility for starting new stores on the European frontier. Around this dynamo assembled a bunch of commercial pioneers who for decades would meet each other in various places and tell tall tales about what had happened when the European frontier was conquered. Aulin became a mentor for them all.

Later a special name was created for this "special force"—Kleine Gruppe. It could be described as a kind of imaginative cell of resistance wishing to drive IKEA into more expansive directions than the founder and the management in Humlebæk really accepted. The ambitious longed to be included; some who came on board later succeeded and today play a large role in the company. After a while, the management of the group grabbed the reins and halted the gallop, but a shimmer still remains around this period of madness.

Otherwise, in practice Europe was by then already conquered: after Switzerland came Germany, then Austria, Holland, and France. In spite of a couple of trying conflicts with Kamprad, the controversial Aulin was time and again taken back into the paternal embrace to carry out great things—not least in Eastern Europe. "There were years," he said,

> when I thought I was living in the middle of a modern history book. In Budapest, where I started our first East European store, I heard liberation poems being read to jubilant crowds when the

Communists were overthrown. I was in Prague the day the Russian tanks crushed a protesting student, arousing the wrath of the world. I arrived two days after the fall of the Berlin Wall, and in Warsaw I found the place where we were to build our first Polish store in the middle of the city.

During the introductory European phase, the pace was particularly fast; as one staff member put it, "We made every mistake in the book, but money nevertheless poured in. We lived frugally, drinking now and again, yes, perhaps too much, but we were on our feet bright and cheery when the doors were opened for the first customers. We always shared rooms on our trips, competing in good Ikean spirit for the cheapest solutions."

The problem of liquidity more than anything else forced the pace. "The stores were seldom ready when we moved in," remembered Jan Aulino. It was hard to get money out of Sweden, so the trick was to make a quick profit and get the cash flow going.

The tricks used were unorthodox and marked with impudence and improvisation. The elk symbol used in the hard marketing wherever IKEA was launched became so popular that German children wrote fan letters addressed to "Mr. Elk." Brand-name specialists of Inter Systems had to discard it—the elk was competing with the brand name!

When stores sold Christmas trees to people with the promise to buy them back after Christmas, customer figures rose. At more than one store opening, Anders Moberg handed out a Swedish clog as a thank-you to customers in the starter shop, then told customers they had to go to the new store to get the other shoe. Lines got longer and longer, and sales skyrocketed.

But these tricks were not the only reason for the success of IKEA and the Swedish style on the Continent. The 1968 student revolt in Europe left some remnants of rebellion in the youth of the 1970s and 1980s. It also reinforced the ordinary rebellion against furnishing habits and attitudes to living: light and simple "matched" the spirit of the time.

For a long time, there was no limit to the expansion of the Swedish company; by the early 1980s, Europe already represented two-thirds of

IKEA's total turnover. Mats Agmén, an ex-merchant navy officer turned store manager who today watches over and develops the IKEA concept with an eagle eye, remembers intoxicating moments in this epoch of growth: sumptuous feasts, opening parties institutionalized as slap-up breakfasts with schnapps and lots of noise, a champagne celebration every Saturday for the week's sales, which yet again had broken all records.

The young pioneers gloried in it all, and so must Aulin have done. Some time would pass before a few of them pulled themselves together and noticed that the substance was not always of the same class as the quickly established shell. The muscles had certain anabolic organizational weaknesses. The pioneers would be accused of being frivolous in their business methods, and gradually IKEA Europe was reorganized in depth. Aulin and Kamprad would clash severely.

At least four times Aulin considered himself fired—in his role as the company's perhaps "necessary" enfant terrible and super-entrepreneur. Fortunately, Ingvar Kamprad has never really had anything against mavericks, however rowdy they are.

After the colonization of Europe, Staffan Jeppsson, yet another of Kamprad's highly appreciated assistants, remembers the conquest of the "West," the United States and Canada. He was involved in setting up the first store in Canada, in Vancouver, twenty-one thousand square meters in area. The move into Canada was marked by sudden bursts of activity involving a troop of engineers, an administrator, an interior decorator, a chief decorator, and a logistician. After a while, the group appointed the future store manager, who in turn had to start appointing staff.

The commando gang set the operation going, and after four to six months' intensive work, day and night, all was ready. The system was charged with enthusiasm and entrepreneurship, but it was misused. Too often the team disappeared to the next scene of action immediately after an opening, leaving the manager of the store on his own. The abandoned store often fell into malaise.

Kamprad remained in the background, at first not restraining these young men bursting with energy. The founder has always had a notorious weakness—some call it talent—for testing the limits of ideas, sometimes "letting the rope run out" on a project in order once and for all to prove what is wrong. As Aulin says, Kamprad preferred them to make mistakes rather than be idle.

The time for afterthoughts soon came, and the company spirit's needs were admitted to be as great as the need for external expansion. Gradually this insight would lead to the phenomenon that goes under the name of the IKEA Way—the global company's "bible study" that takes *A Furniture Dealer's Testament* as its number one textbook. The IKEA Way trains managers to be spiritual ambassadors out in the empire—and one of the first compulsory lecturers was the rebellious Jan Aulin.

A "Kleine Gruppe" would be very unlikely to arise today. IKEA's spiritual and material domains are now more in unison than ever, as will be evident when we take a closer look at the IKEA Way later on. Nevertheless, it could be said that growth within IKEA continues at almost the same occasionally breathless pace. However, the routines are calmer, and more care is taken over what has already been achieved. If it wishes to, each country can organize the start of a store roughly as before, but now it happens with local forces in the commando.

Remote management from Humlebæk has been decentralized, to the advantage of regional managers, and flexibility is better controlled.

Typically enough, discussions take place, to some extent returning to the original concept, the international commando force. Large sums of money are at stake, and the cost of a store can vary. Today the rising cost of land forces innovative solutions. In 1998 outside Stuttgart, for instance, a twenty-thousand-square-meter store was opened on a site of only thirteen thousand meters. At the top of the building are two car parks, below them is the furniture floor, then the satellite department, and at the bottom yet another car park. The price was high—eighty million deutsche marks—and yet this store is number two in Stuttgart.

To be profitable, naturally it is important that a store be in the right situation, but nevertheless it is only one of several determining factors. Most important of all is that the store is able to live up to IKEA's complex, unique business idea, what could be called "the Sacred Concept."

The Sacred Concept

But let your communication be, Yea, yea; Nay, nay:
for whatsoever is more than these cometh of evil.

—MATTHEW 5:37

Nothing in the IKEA business is subject to so much argument and yet so much agreement, so much assembled creative force but also creative unease, as what is called the IKEA concept. Nothing is watched over by the founder with such tender paternal anxiety as the ability of his stores to realize the content of the concept. Nothing is more sensitive to deviations, nor more important to stick to. Yet its application changes in various directions.

"We are a concept company," says Ingvar Kamprad firmly, over and over again, and it sounds like a blessing, an indulgence, an appeal, and an order all rolled into one. "If we stick to the concept, we will never die," he adds when asked the question one late autumn evening in Älmhult, where eager young managers from all over the world have gathered to begin their IKEA Way training.

But what is this magical concept?

To make it difficult, it could be said that the concept (which is not only about how IKEA sells its wares but also about its entire thinking) is the fundamental business idea owned by Inter Systems BV in Holland that is loaned out on a franchise basis to all stores, outside and inside the IKEA business. The concept is like a smart card with which to open Pandora's box.

To make it very much simpler and still convey its substance, it could be said that the concept is stated in *A Furniture Dealer's Testament*, the little bible the staff anxiously asked Ingvar Kamprad to write before he emigrated from Sweden.

Kamprad lists nine "commandments" in his *Testament*. This summary could be said to constitute the spiritual basis of IKEA:

1   **The Product Range Is Our Identity**
    IKEA offers a wide range of well-designed, functional home

furnishing products at prices that are so low that as many
people as possible are able to afford them.

2   **The IKEA Spirit Is a Strong and Living Reality**
    IKEA builds on enthusiasm, a desire for renewal, thrift,
    responsibility, humbleness toward the task, and simplicity.
    "We must look after each other and inspire. Pity the man who
    cannot or does not want to partake."

3   **Profit Gives Us Resources**
    IKEA will achieve profit—"a wonderful word"—through the
    lowest prices, good quality, more economical development of
    products, improved purchasing, and cost savings.

4   **Reaching Good Results with Small Means**
    "Waste is a deadly sin."

5   **Simplicity Is a Virtue**
    Complex regulations paralyze, "exaggerated planning is the
    usual cause of death to companies," and simplicity gives
    strength. IKEA people do not drive flashy cars or stay at
    luxury hotels.

6   **Doing It a Different Way**
    "If from the start we had consulted experts about whether a
    little community like Älmhult could support a company like
    IKEA, they would undoubtedly have advised against it." IKEA
    goes its own way, turning to shirt factories to make cushions
    and window factories to procure good frames for tables, charg-
    ing more for umbrellas when the sun is shining but selling at
    bargain prices when it rains.

7   **Concentration Is Important to Our Success**
    "We can never do everything everywhere, all at the
    same time."

8   **Taking Responsibility Is a Privilege**
     "The fear of making mistakes is the root of bureaucracy, the
     enemy of development. Exercise your privilege, your right, and
     your duty to make decisions."

9   **Most Things Still Remain to Be Done—A Glorious Future**
     A glorious future! "You can do so much in ten minutes."
     "Let us continue to be a group of positive fanatics who
     make the impossible possible."

This is a brief synopsis of the nine commandments. The entire text is
A Furniture Dealer's Testament, which was printed for the first time in
1976. It has been reprinted over and over again and distributed to at
least one hundred thousand employees all over the world. The latest
edition of the *Testament* was published in-house in 1996 and is thirty-six
pages long.

The *Testament* has since been accompanied by its own "shorthand,"
a glossary of frequently used terms at IKEA. These terms have been
collected into *The Little Word Book,* but most of them stem from the
Testament. Sometimes they are entirely Småland dialect terms that can
be complicated, not to say impossible, to translate; some are unknown
even in the parishes beyond Älmhult. So that these terms would not be
misunderstood but, indeed, given new meaning, *The Little Word Book*
came about. A kind of catechism, its explanations are in the spirit of
Martin Luther's teachings to the faithful. Some of the terms it defines are:

- Humbleness and strength of will

- Simplicity and "the many"

- Experience and doing it a different way

- Fear of failure and status

- The IKEA way and bureaucracy

- Cost awareness and the will to give and take responsibility

- Striving to face reality

- Fellowship and enthusiasm

Few think about what Inter IKEA stands for. The truth is that it is the ideological think tank of the empire, watching over the Kamprad business idea as thoroughly as the eunuchs guarded the emeralds in the Seraglio in Istanbul. Each store—each concept purchaser and franchisee—as a rule of thumb pays 3 percent of turnover to Inter IKEA Systems BV.

Today 143 stores work in 29 countries according to the "concept." The IKEA Group owns 125 of these, and 18 are independent. When the stores buy ("franchise") this ownership concept, they have at the same time access to the sum total of what Ingvar Kamprad and his company have learned from IKEA's success during fifty years. They also receive training, seminars, and management advice, as well as manuals that either regulate or strongly recommend what a complete store is to look like to be optimally rational, the way the stream of customers is to be guided through the store, which interiors are to be included, and just where they are to be placed.

The concept is the sum of the master chef's recipe; though it is very secret, everyone can study it for themselves on a visit to a store. Comparison with Coca-Cola is natural—we drink it everywhere, but we don't know the recipe. Or with McDonald's—the same hamburgers, only different addresses.

Ingvar Kamprad remembers exactly how the concept was put into print.

> When I wrote down the concept in 1976, the gang around me at home in Älmhult were all in full agreement that there really was nothing in the world that would be allowed to alter it. Only if we were absolutely convinced that we were utterly wrong, then would we start discussing the details.
>
> But ultimately there is nothing to discuss. People can argue for other solutions, and we listen and try to fit the argument into the framework. The framework is sacrosanct, but within it is freedom, and a wealth of innovation is allowed to explode.

So then I hear an example of what this freedom has led to. In the new store in Frankfurt, they go completely against the concept that says just inside the entrance there should be the living-room settings—instead, they started with bedrooms. In my experience, they are going against all sensible thinking regarding how people set up home—they usually start by planning the living room, and in the living room they begin by deciding on the most important piece of furniture of all, the sofa.

I have actually never experienced any exception to that rule. After the sofa, they usually go for the carpet, the table, then they buy the chair, then a bookcase or shelving, and after that the rest (kitchen, bedroom, and so on). But as people are different, in the first part of the store we always have five living rooms in various styles—one of these interiors is to be a really low-price alternative. Of course, some people come to the store for other purposes—they are intent on finding a single special item for the nursery or whatever—but the average customer, he or she begins with the living room.

If any store now wishes to try something different, they first have to ask permission of the concept provider—perhaps that can be regarded as a value judgment.

Such are the laws of the Sacred Concept, the dynamic code, the business idea that is to be given eternal life.

When for reasons of space the store in Poznan did not want a proper restaurant, it had to request to be an exception. If a store skips the classic playroom in the entrance, it also has to ask special permission. Should any of the franchisees not follow the concept seriously, the management of IKEA Systems BV can ask it to take down the IKEA sign.

Although the concept described here may seem crystal clear, it is nevertheless the cause of a lot of trouble and a great many questions. In fact, many people think it is not clearly written, and few of those in charge are able to say just what in the concept is of the greatest weight.

ABOVE Ingvar Kamprad's childhood home, Elmtaryd, in the old parish of Agunnaryd. From 1943 to 1950, it was also the address of the recently founded mail-order company Ikéa.

RIGHT Ingvar Kamprad and his mother, Berta. She died of cancer at the early age of fifty-one.

LEFT Berta and Feodor Kamprad with their two children, Ingvar and sister, Kerstin, four years his junior.

BELOW Sedonia, Ingvar's paternal grandfather's mother, who traveled from Germany to help with problems following her son's suicide.

RIGHT Achim and Franziska, Ingvar's paternal grandparents.

BELOW Ingvar and his father, Feodor.

ABOVE A churn stand was the first "distribution center."

LEFT Ikéa-nytt was an advertising supplement of the IKEA catalog; today more than 90 million copies of the catalog are distributed.

BOTTOM LEFT Albin Lagerblad's former joinery in Älmhult, where IKEA opened its first furniture display in 1953.

RIGHT The parcel shed outside Elmtaryd, today a spot where company managers at Älmhult are taken for an excursion.

BELOW Önskebo till Önskepris means a dream home at a dream price and furniture from Småland—two initiatives in the early 1950s that prepared the way for the IKEA opening in Stockholm.

BOTTOM The legendary lakeside cabin by the Möckeln, where so many contracts were signed and so many perch were gutted.

Five decades of
interiors from
the IKEA catalog:
1950s (TOP),
1960s (CENTER),
1970s (BOTTOM),
1980s (OPPOSITE,
TOP LEFT), and
1990s (OPPOSITE,
TOP RIGHT).

OPPOSITE BOTTOM
A selection of
catalog covers.
The catalog has
one of the largest
print runs in the
world, nearing
100 million.

The opening of the Philadelphia, Pennsylvania, store in 1985 (TOP LEFT) . . . was followed by the Baltimore, Maryland, store in 1988 (TOP RIGHT), . . . Burbank, California, in 1990 (LEFT), . . . and Chicago, Illinois, in 1998 (BELOW LEFT).

BELOW Leaders past and future: Anders Moberg (left), who in 1986 succeeded Ingvar Kamprad as president of the IKEA Group, is joined by his successor, Anders Dahlvig (second from left), the recently appointed president, Ingvar Kamprad (second from right), and Hans Gydell, vice president of IKEA International.

Much of this controversy has to do with people hearing the same thing but understanding it differently—a whisper at the head of the troop loses its original sense by the time it reaches the tail end.

This has probably also had to do with dynamic store managers. In the past, all army officers were supposed to be able to ride. Within IKEA, every man and woman dreaming of a real career in the empire has to have proved what he or she can do as a store manager. (One thing can be noted on that score—far too few women have been given the chance.)

Within the framework of the concept, the store manager is king, but the temptation to avoid listening to the signals or to tamper with the Sacred Concept is always around. Store managers have actually often found the concept a burden. In the 1980s, some managers tried taking a line of their own in conflict with certain fundamental concepts. The history, the inheritance from the first pioneers, and their experiences were looked down on.

IKEA International, with its headquarters in Humlebæk, which supplies the whole enterprise with management skills and thus controls operations all over the world, has nowadays appointed a man full-time to keep an eye on the ability and responsibility of the franchisees to live up to the concept. He is the link between IKEA International and Inter IKEA, where Mats Agmén is his counterpart. Together they keep watch over the stores all over the world. Together they can carry out tests in Inter IKEA Systems' experimental store in Delft in Holland.

Staffan Jeppsson always saw the same question brought up at the owner's dawn raids. (He would appear unexpectedly at half past five in the morning and start talking with the men delivering goods into the store. What was the security like? What annoyed them most? Were they given morning coffee?) It turned out at his inspections or run-throughs, which might last for up to thirteen hours, that the same 150 to 200 complaints always arose, and the founder was always equally depressed: for God's sake, he had taken that up before—why had nothing been done?

Jeppsson began to note each complaint, requesting that those responsible remedy the matter and also giving them a date by when it should be done. An increasingly more insistent need arose to find an objective evaluation basis for measuring sales efficiency. What does a truly good layout look like for a store? Does the restaurant live up to the previously unwritten basic demands ("to be worth a detour on uncrowded days, to be capable of serving the greatest possible number of hungry people on crowded days").

Jeppsson's trips with Kamprad led to what has now become the systematic "commercial review" he drew up on behalf of IKEA International. For these reviews, nine people are handpicked within an equal number of specialties. They select a number of strategic "victims" and go through the stores according to a flowchart that makes it possible for one "auditor" to cover an area and a store in a day. The auditor ticks off how the concept is being dealt with, then approves or disapproves.

Certain principles are designated as sacred—and it's important that the stores score high in these areas. Among these are the restaurant ("no one does good business on an empty stomach"), child care ("who can do vital shopping with the kids yelling all around their feet?"), the toilets ("a full bladder must not be what decides the customer on buying or not buying something"), and the bistro situated beyond the exit checkout. (Jeppsson calls it the "calming-down department"—when the customer has paid up after a wearying trip around the store and is exhausted, he or she is to be offered something that "makes up for it all," a cup of coffee and an almond cake, for instance, or a hot dog, for next to nothing.)

The audit is based on criteria that are anchored in rules confirmed by the boards of each individual country's organization. Simplicity and clarity are key. The audits are an attempt to codify and judge objectively what Ingvar Kamprad has more intuitively done on his own authority against the background of his long experience. It could be said that they are a sophisticated way for IKEA to guarantee quality, tempo, and profitability after the owner has retired as its first inspector-general.

As a result of the German frenzy, the idea came up of starting IKEA in different places with a small city-center shop, where goods in the catalog could be seen, then ordered and delivered. The method was not unique, but much the same as had been used in the first furniture exhibition in Älmhult in the 1950s.

Jan Aulin, Kamprad's henchman in Germany, Rune Mårtensson, and Lennart Dahlgren, today active in building up a Russian retail organization, searched the map for a fairly large town on the Rhine and found Coblenz. Mårtensson swiftly took on the task of opening a catalog-shop there within a month.

A month later, Aulin wondered how Mårtensson had coped with his assignment and went there—but in Coblenz he was unable to find any shop at all. Coblenz? exclaimed Mårtensson. Didn't we say Constanz? I opened there after three weeks' hard work.

Thus another anecdote was added to the imperialists' increasingly prolific history. To complete the story: there is now a store in Coblenz too.

Better late than never.

Älmhult in the World

I have been to Älmhult lots of times during my seven years with the company, but I've never seen an elk. But last Saturday I saw one on the road. And yesterday I saw Ingvar Kamprad. What a week!

—BRITISH PARTICIPANT
IN THE IKEA WAY PROGRAM

The stairway up to the conference at the inn in Älmhult is crowded. Twenty-two young people, all in executive positions and most in the IKEA uniform of jeans and sweater, have come to take part in the company's important "bible-reading." This is a week's training that is to make them into ambassadors for the spirit of IKEA in the empire.

The atmosphere is rather like a high school assembly, a buzz of expectation, a touch of reverence and selectness. Attendees all have on their chests a green heart with their name on it. Store bosses, chief purchasers, furniture men, environmental specialists, high-level managers, and other executives have all flown in from all over the world and landed at the local airport in Växjö—from Pakistan, Hong Kong, Canada, and the United States, and from all corners of Europe—Swedes too. There are only five women, and the rest are men.

For the next few days, they are trained in various subjects, all with one foot in *A Furniture Dealer's Testament.* Attendees have lessons in history and range ideas, in buying and distribution and store design. In IKEA a good cost-effective leader does not distinguish between weekdays and weekend. Time is "gained" by getting started on Sunday evening. The simple welcoming dinner just over, now they are all introducing themselves. On the wall behind them where they can all read it, like a religious quotation, is IKEA's business motto:

> **We shall offer a wide range of home furnishing items of good design and function at prices so low that the majority of people can afford to buy them.**

Most important on this first evening is that the participants are to meet Ingvar Kamprad himself. They have sent in their many questions to him in advance, and he has sat nearly all day out at a nearby farm, sorting through them and preparing, for that is what he is like (and how he will always be).

Meetings of this kind are never routine. Speaking to groups of people is important to him. He constantly complains about how slow he is with words, and he may well wrestle with a single speech for a whole week. Kamprad, quite simply, suffers from a slight stage fright, particularly when he has to speak in another language.

Regularly every year, he returns to the place of his birth. He calls it a "holiday," but essentially it is the month for balancing the books, attending many long board meetings with IKEA International, Stichting IKEA, INGKA Holding, IKANO, and the other companies before the next financial year. On one occasion, he admits to the local radio station that he has been out fishing only once in four weeks, although he loves fishing above everything next to wild mushrooms.

He and the family often spend Christmas in Bölsö—the farm that became his Swedish address after he and his sister Kerstin shared their inheritance. Bölsö is nowadays an IKANO property that the Kamprads can rent. By the edge of Lake Möckeln are three adjoining houses in a row that the Kamprad sons like to rent every summer. On the farm itself are conference premises with a pool and guest rooms—the top floor alone is reserved for Ingvar and his wife and is furnished exclusively with their own furniture range. However, there is one unusual piece: the Prillan (the wad of snuff under the top lip) table, a present from Polish friends for his seventieth birthday. There is a spring flower arrangement in the middle of the table that constantly pushes up through a pipe small round boxes of wet snuff. The legs are lovely sturdy bottles of Polish vodka.

This evening in late August is compulsory for Kamprad, as sacred as the other IKEA Way week in the spring, and as important as the so-called IK days at the beginning of September when the management of IOS (IKEA of Sweden) presents the entire product range to the founder.

Every year his conviction that a sense of inner mission is the cornerstone in securing company survival has been reinforced: without the concept in the marrow of their bones, they cannot be sure of the future. If these leaders cannot convey the core of the message to their coworkers, things may go badly.

The answers he will give this evening down in the basement's rather provisional museum all point to just that: keep the concept sacred, then things will go well for IKEA.

The fact that the IKEA Way was to take place in Älmhult did not seem at all obvious from the start. As usual, when new things are born in this company, a swarm of eager midwives stands around the delivery table, and the senior consultant Kamprad himself is seldom far away with his anesthesia. When the IKEA Way was invented, the reasons for it were very numerous.

Some would call it the result of second thoughts; in the excitement of growth, a great many had forgotten IKEA's roots. Yet others would maintain that the start of the IKEA Way program was necessary to rescue the company's future interests.

Mats Agmén, today the guardian of the concept within Inter IKEA, was responsible for realizing the idea in 1980. He at first wanted to isolate the participants from everyday life, force the "students" together, and keep them away from the bustle and noise of the outside world. Therefore, they met in a remote conference center in Älmhult, since that was where the concept was born.

It is not just nostalgia that makes Älmhult our Mecca. Rational reasons also speak for it to be so. Take one perspective: we have a special message with our Swedish design—bright, light, and functional. I usually repeat that we are not teaching Belgians to buy Belgian chests of drawers; they can do that better themselves. What we can contribute is what is Scandinavian, and that is part of our living concept.

But supposing we were to abandon Älmhult and do this in Munich. After a number of years, more and more German architects would be involved, more and more non-Swedish product developers. It would be easier to go off the rails from our Swedish line. Add to that that in Småland we are fairly well known—not to say notorious—for being thrifty and hardworking; there is a special spirit that has nothing to do with inbreeding, but with historical and worldly circumstances. Älmhult is to be a prototype. Every company needs its roots—it is from the past that we are building our future.

The IKEA spirit emanates from what we learned during the pioneer years in this district. Both as a Smålander and a rational thinker, I therefore defend the idea that Älmhult is our heart, our spiritual home.

So IKEA becomes something of a nationalistic project in which whatever is Smålandish is just the necessary starting point. In the restaurants, the meatballs and smoked sausages are from towns in Sweden. The furniture is still mostly named in Swedish, and there is no talk of removing the circle above the å or the dots above the ö. What is Swedish is exotic, tempting to buy, and in principle Älmhult decides on the appearance of every product. The Sweden Shop outside the exit checkouts is becoming an even better business with its mixture of Hällevik salmon and Västerbotten cheese. Recently it was said that IKEA dominates Swedish exports of food to France, and a television feature showed a Frenchman who went on a pilgrimage to the store in Paris to eat meatballs. That's what can happen when Sweden is spread over the world.

But this is just the framework of IKEA. Much more important is learning the main components of the concept at the executive level: buying policies, production management, the furniture range, breathtaking prices, democratic design, satisfying many people's dreams on the home level, simplicity, shrewdness.

All this spills over into other parts of the giant. It is not a matter of chance that Anders Moberg, appointed first head of IKEA International after Ingvar Kamprad retired from line operations in 1985, is a farmer's boy from just outside Älmhult, or that Ingemar Gustafsson, head of the IKANO Group, comes from a town a few miles away. Occasionally Kamprad can be heard dreaming aloud about the new head of the 2000s being a woman from the district.

So Älmhult reinforces on more than one level its grip on the empire the more global it becomes. That is how management became spirit, and the moraine became a philosophy, Älmhult, Älmhult über alles. . . .

LEADERSHIP IN TIMES OF CHANGE

The Noble Art of "Hugging" Management

Oh, I must have hugged several thousand.
—INGVAR KAMPRAD

Ingvar has a physical way of being with people he likes, and he likes a great many people. When he meets me, I am given a great bear hug, then when we part, an even bigger one. Sometimes he kisses me on the cheek like a real Russian. At breakfast, caring for my health, he puts a ginseng tablet on my plate. "You can get them for half the price in Denmark," he tells me, in the spirit of consumer information. He takes one himself just to be sure—together with an aspirin against the risk of a heart attack.

When he meets his associates, he moves close to them and usually takes hold of them, gazing straight at them as he speaks, into their eyes. I often see him getting closer and closer as he discusses things with associates, as if this were a matter of confidences between intimate friends. Afterward there is always the obligatory hug—always that hug.

The stories from the pioneer years are legion, and Ingvar loves the memory. He and some of his coworkers are staying in a simple hotel in Eastern Europe, sharing a room and talking into the small hours about shelving and life. Were there only one bed, he would surely lay head to foot, just as he loved doing as a boy with his friend Kalle in Elmtaryd. Thanks to these sleeping arrangements, the hotel bill will indeed be halved. More important, personal bonds will be strengthened.

In the early days, when he and Ragnar Sterte went to Poland, Ingvar would wake up long before his colleague and, while waiting, spend the time cleaning out his fellow traveler's pipe, so that he could have the first necessary puff before breakfast as soon as he woke.

People should lie head to foot more often, so to speak, to understand how they need each other. That is the moral. Kamprad has passed it on to his sons—lying at dawn in their room and discussing the UK range.

Naturally some people wonder what kind of man he is with this need for physical contact. After a long exciting night discussing ideas with a future manager, he takes his colleague in his arms and, full of gratitude and inspiration, kisses him on both cheeks.

Two Polish directors say they love him because he is European in his way of showing his emotions. After the opening of the first store in Budapest, one of them remembers sitting with several colleagues on the floor of Kamprad's room at a small inn out in the country. They sang folksongs, made speeches, and held hands, and everything was wonderful. Ingvar and Margaretha were there with them all night.

When Ingvar is with his sons, the image of the loving father takes over.

The conversation may be about chairs, shelving, or difficulties with plywood, but it is carried on with quiet patriarchal friendliness. The father constantly preaches to his adult sons, giving them lengthy examples of business settlements and visits to distant parts of his furniture empire. He remembers prices, names, everything. Occasionally the sons interrupt, a question or two is given a long answer, but usually it seems to be the tender-hearted indulgence of a father who knows best. His sons are absorbing his experiences while he is alive, while he is testing the limits of their knowledge, involvement, and attention.

Are they maturing well enough? When will one of them be allowed to take over? Which one, in that case? Are any of them going to?

When it is time to say goodnight, Ingvar strokes the boys' cheeks. The next day, when it's time to leave, his hand stops at his eldest son's neat beard, and he strokes the chin several times with a kind of absent-minded tenderness. He kisses his sons, not once but several times in farewell, and they accept these many signs of affection from their father. They adore him, but fatigue is in their eyes (alongside forgiving and admiring smiles)—Dad, you're impossible!

When he speaks of IKEA, the phrases *together, family, belong to each other,* and *fellowship* arise again and again. They are never missing. IKEA is first and foremost a family with an increasing number of relatives all over the world.

The head-to-foot company IKEA.

They should sell a head-to-foot sofa called "Ingvar."

During the 1960s, the tycoon traveled around Europe, not with a secretary, but with his elderly (and still alert) father, Feodor, at his side as the chairman of the board.

So in the beginning was not just the moraine but also the family. The pattern is repeated within the company in various dimensions: as management techniques, as forms of organization, as commercial equipment. If you like each other, you work well together; if you hug each other and show you like each other. . . . What's more, hugging is both free and cost-effective.

If work and leisure ran together organically in the young mail-order firm, if the rule of "one for all and all for one" applied and the company was a part of the family and the family part of the firm (who can keep track of which is the egg and which the chicken?), then it was to take a long time for the founder to understand that not everyone thinks and acts like a member of a family. Indeed, he never *demanded* that everyone work on Saturdays and Sundays in the store. They were only to do so out of sheer family feeling.

When the unions came into the picture, as mentioned before, he took it almost as a personal failure.

He will always retain the memory of the sweetness of the early years' wonderful head-to-foot feeling. That is what he loves most about his creation, the people he's worked with, "the family." To the very end, he will persuade himself that this spirit can survive in a global company wanting to conquer the world in the twenty-first century.

That IKEA won't survive is probably his greatest anxiety. New members of the family, and particularly those who are to occupy important positions, must therefore have the right chemistry or—why not—faith. Because of this, Kamprad carries on long conversations with both the young and the old and broods for weeks, months, and years about who would be best to take over from whom and when. Have they the family feeling? Are they thrifty and humble? Do they understand deep down what is meant by doing something for many? As one of his old coworkers said:

Sometimes Ingvar gets worried. We had appointed a new production manager, and everyone was excited about him, so Ingvar took him out to the farm and made fish soup and talked to him, then lay awake all night. In the morning, he came to me and said he was miserable about the kind of people we were appointing nowadays. [The new employee] didn't recognize basic values. I felt sorry for him. After all, we have whole staffs there to think about appointing the right kind of person.

His other anxiety was also born in those early years in the Småland forest. It is the habitual belief that he knows best, that he decides. For the first ten years, IKEA was, after all, a one-man company, though with some family members. But before his colleagues did anything on their own, they always asked: "What will Ingvar say?," "Do you think Ingvar would . . . ?," or, "Ingvar said that. . . ."

During the first years of IKEA, all ideas appeared to have come from Ingvar's youth. From age seventeen to over seventy, the same expectation was harbored toward him: that he in particular would find the right solution, that he was the one with ideas. Others express it like this:

"It's still the same . . . much is related to him, justified or not. It is easy to hide behind 'Ingvar has said. . . .' A random word suddenly becomes law. One evening Ingvar had driven up from Denmark. It was six o'clock, and he couldn't get in through the door at Älmhult. Frustrated, he said that things were really damned awful when he couldn't even get into his own company. After that, for a long time we stayed open until eight in the evenings, always, for no one wanted to risk Ingvar not being able to get in again. The fact that he would then slip in at six in the morning, no one even gave a thought to, and how he got in, God only knows."

That is what closeness, the "noble art of hugging management," is like—revitalizing, heartwarming, and sometimes detrimental to business. Ingvar's approval can move mountains, and his disapproval can cast a shadow over the best of intentions. Therefore, every single person in this global company asks the fateful question: what will really happen when Ingvar is no longer around?

The person who ponders that most is Ingvar himself.

A Youth and His Errors

Remember not the sins of my youth.

—PSALMS 25:7

The story of Ingvar Kamprad's Nazi and fascist past is an example of how every human being's story consists of several chapters: the collective texts of life overlap and, by digging, new layers are constantly found. Today's era illuminates the aberrations of our youth, unveiling a past of complicated emotions, complex loyalties, and sheer love.

The media also have a story, conveyed with dizzying speed and carrying news of a faded patch of shame all over the world as if it were new. In the long run, self-esteem is shaken, credibility is undermined, friends distance themselves, and sympathizers and patrons flee, for not even legends are invulnerable.

Ultimately, this is the story of the way "news" is received in a company and the way it makes the organization quake, testing the very framework and those responsible for it. It is a story of survival—and of profound sentiments with roots in a personal culture carefully nursed over the years. It is a story that re-creates the image of both the man and the company.

This is the story of Ingvar Kamprad's "youthful sins." It says much about IKEA, its idea, and its founder.

Twice in the 1990s, bitterly, Ingvar Kamprad was made to learn that in our day no human being, least of all a public person, can escape his past. For forty-six days in the autumn of 1994, from October 21 to December 9, the revelation of his contacts with the Nazi Neo-Swedish movement (when he was between sixteen and twenty-five) was top of the agenda in the global company of IKEA. Thirty-seven thousand employees, millions of customers, and other interested parties demanded explanations after publication of a much-publicized series of articles in *Expressen,* at the time the largest Swedish paper.

In the spring of 1998, the aftershock of the same earthquake struck, and things that had not previously come out were brought to the surface.

When the worldwide media campaign was at its height in 1994, it occupied a score of people in IKEA, from the main character himself to information officers and lower-level employees.

Everything began on the morning of October 21, 1994, with a fairly angry conversation between Pelle Tagesson, a journalist on *Expressen,* and Staffan Jeppsson at the head office in Humlebæk. For four years, Jeppsson had been joint assistant to IKEA International's managing director, Anders Moberg, and Ingvar Kamprad himself, an arrangement that Kamprad and Moberg had made so that both would know what the other was doing and they would not get in each other's hair. Over the years, Jeppsson had very often traveled with Kamprad and gained his confidence with a calm and systematic professionalism and an active interest in the environment.

In a heated discussion, Tagesson requested that Jeppsson grant him an interview with Kamprad; he had no intention of revealing why and would indicate only that it was important. "If I don't know what it's about, I can't arrange anything," said Jeppsson, and hung up. A second later, Tagesson called back to tell him what it was about.

"If I say Engdahl, perhaps that's enough," he said, and Jeppsson knew at once.

In the National Archives of Sweden were a number of documents that in 1994 had just been made public. They showed that Kamprad had moved in the circle of Per Engdahl, head of the Neo-Swedish movement, which was driven by an ideology close to fascism. A recently published book, *The Quisling Centre,* on Nazism in Skåne, was based on these papers—in which Kamprad's name appeared.

With that, the opening shot of IKEA's most upsetting media affair had been fired, and Staffan Jeppsson, as Kamprad's assistant, had to put aside most of his work for the next six weeks.

He was, as mentioned before, not entirely unprepared.

Afterward he remembered that late one evening in the autumn of 1990, after a tour around Germany, he, Ingvar, and another colleague, Lennart Ekmark, had landed in Solingen and gone out for a drink. After a hard day's work, they had sat over a beer and talked of the much-admired Vilhelm Moberg and his antifascist book *Ride Tonight.*

Then Ingvar spontaneously compared Ekmark's past as an icono-clastic Maoist in the 1960s with the great confusion of his own youth in the 1940s: his interest in the Nazi-tinged Neo-Swedish movement and his dealings with the charismatic Per Engdahl.

Who was this Engdahl, who had recently died at the age of eighty-five? Judgment depends on who is making it. Everyone is agreed that he was a highly gifted, ideologically flawed, but clever literary academic. He produced a considerable volume of work—numerous statements, a score of books, an edited edition of Hitler's speeches, and also a great deal of poetry.

Engdahl, in his time, had been involved in forming a local branch of the Swedish fascist organization and for a brief while belonged to the pro-German movement that called itself Swedish Opposition, with its base in south Sweden. His own "party"—the Neo-Swedish movement—was based on a mixture of corporative ideas and the dream of a united, racially pure Europe led by the Germanic peoples. In the program of Swedish Opposition, for instance, members openly discussed collecting all Jews into a special organization in the expectation of a "common European solution." Engdahl was a loyal fascist up to the end of the war.

This was the man who in 1942 turned the head of the young Kamprad.

So Staffan Jeppsson was not entirely caught napping when Pelle Tagesson phoned; he had already, so to speak, had the story from the horse's mouth. He knew that this revelation could be dynamite. Kamprad himself had probably feared that as memories of the turbu-lence of the Second World War were stirred as more and more archives were opened, he would also, as a well-known head of a firm, risk having his dealings with Engdahl examined. Close friends had warned him against speaking about these matters—it could raise hell. Perhaps he aired his anxiety that evening in Solingen to his two sympathetic assis-tants to be able to unburden his guilt over an uncomfortable example of his youth's "sickness," as he was increasingly to call it later.

We now know that Kamprad could have gone much further back in time in his story, further than the time that *Expressen*'s revelations touched on, a time that Ingvar himself, in 1994, was incapable of recalling. It all goes back to his childhood on the farm in Elmtaryd at the feet of his beloved grandmother, and also to the influence of his father Feodor, a "squire" given to going around in breeches and boots, and who was clearly anti-Semitic. Ingvar still remembers his father talking about how it was Jews who ran the exchange offices in Germany after the First World War, helping to wreck the economy for ordinary people. It went back to Feodor's conviction that a Jewish lawyer sold the family property for much too low a price and thus partly embezzled the hereditary estate.

Feodor and Berta Kamprad, Ingvar's schoolmaster, Rudolf Malmqvist, and his wife Ellen, often played bridge together at home on the farm, the men always talking about Germany (Feodor for, Rudolf against). Ingvar sat alongside, watching the game and listening "as long as he kept quiet."

It so happened too that Ingvar's grandmother showed him the lavishly illustrated magazine *Signal*, published by Goebbels's Ministry of Propaganda. Its reports on German youth impressed the boy, who thought it great that "Uncle Hitler" was doing so much for Grandmother's relatives.

The farm mailbox was full of similar advertisements from the many pro-German groups of the day, and Ingvar eagerly joined in. He says:

I wrote off for more. On the whole, my eyes were open to everything that was free. In the weekly published by the Swedish Farmers' Association, which was as important in the countryside as *Pravda* was for the Kremlin in its day, I found advertisements with coupons so that you could send off for catalogs and all kinds of free offers. So I received back a whole mass of mail and in that way got to know about the so-called Lindholmers, the most extreme Nazi group in Sweden, and their newspaper, the *Swedish National Socialist*. I don't remember—but it is possible—that after a while I was recruited into Lindholm's Nordic Youth, a Swedish Hitler Jugend. I certainly admired both Hitler and Lindholm.

The fact that in my memory this period seemed very short and unimportant has to do with thinking I later converted to something much better, the Engdahl movement. Lindholm was a genuine Nazi, Sweden's crude führer with his "Heil Hitler" salutes, shoulder straps, and all that. If you liked him, you were a Nazi. Later on, I was ashamed of admitting that I had been a Nazi.

Then, in 1994, when everything was to be dragged into the daylight, Engdahl in my memory came to stand for most of the confusion of my youth. But Lindholm was my first idol on my hopeless ideological journey. Neither my cousin, my sister, nor any school friends I talked to—nor I myself—can remember that I ever appeared in uniform or behaved like a Nazi. Like other young men in the country at the time, I belonged to the shooting club and after national service did voluntary officer's training in uniform, but that had nothing at all to do with the Lindholm setup. Sometimes I was able to borrow my father's breeches when I went fishing—they were useful to wear with rubber boots. Father's high leather boots hung in an attic at home in Elmtaryd, but they were his, not mine.

But one day a roll of posters came in the mail, a large picture of Sven Olov Lindholm on them. I biked up to the village and put some up. I may have tried to recruit a member or two, but if I did, then I have suppressed it. I obviously read a lot about this Lindholm, the leader of the National Socialist labor party, just as I read other German propaganda. The ideas in the brochures were very like what my grandmother thought.

Eventually I went to a rally for Lindholm, though without personally speaking to him. I was really only a child. However much I try, I can find no more than a few concrete memories. I once cycled to Moheda—I must have been about eleven or twelve, and it took several hours. That was in the years before the outbreak of war, because I do remember the film of the Berlin Olympic Games (dimly, because I was never interested in sport). In Moheda, I saw young people in uniform, a man urged us to join, and there were drums and flags.

Another time, probably around 1941, I went to a Lindholm camp for Nordic Youth, despite my mother's and father's disapproval. There were more uniforms there, and in the evening a bonfire was lit and we sang a lot. For me, essentially a lone wolf with no other real friends of my own age, this was a new kind of fellowship that I really liked and deep down yearned for.

I assume I also joined the party then on some occasion, but I have no papers to show for it. On the other hand, as a more mature teenager, I took part in another political weekend meeting in the district of Kalmar, a kind of seminar organized by the Engdahl circle I had got to know in Osby.

In 1942, at age fifteen, I had gone to the Combined Middle School there, which had also been my mother's boarding school. Her parents had put aside money so that I and my sister Kerstin, who was four years younger than me, could attend. I had found ordinary school difficult and was partly dyslexic. I remember lying in bed all night trying to learn foreign words, but failing.

I took my Lindholm propaganda with me to Osby, and at the kiosk I bought the *Swedish National Socialist.* Once three of us boys went up to the school attic to form a secret political party. We each had a little yellow notebook with us, and on the inside we drew a swastika. We also tried cutting each other's arms and mixing our blood to become blood brothers.

There wasn't much more to it, but the headmaster, Bernhard J:sson Ernestam, and another teacher, both strict anti-Nazis, had observed what I was up to. I had gone to certain meetings and even drawn swastikas in textbooks or on desks. I was called to the headmaster's room and told to "stop all that nonsense." It was against the school rules.

However, I went on cultivating my political interests and was careful to hide them. I found a newspaper called *Vägen Framåt* (The Way Ahead). I took it home and read it, then wrote to the editor that I was "interested in genuine Swedish literature and also their newspaper . . . therefore please send me some sample issues of the same, free of charge."

Vägen Framåt was clearly pro-German. This was in the middle of the war and so was not unusual, for Hitler was still very successful. For the first time, I now came into contact with

Per Engdahl, leader of Swedish Opposition, what later became the Neo-Swedish movement.

I thought his newspaper was well done. In one number, it said that Engdahl was to give a lecture at the hotel in Osby, and there were also letters and notices about it. This was in November 1942, and the local book printer had organized it all. I went to the lecture and was greatly enthused. Engdahl was a real seducer. I recognize that today. I probably said then that he was an incredibly clever speaker. But I still think the man was a genius, apart from, of course, his views.

There must have been about fifty people there, and I had the good "luck" during coffee afterward to be seated at the same table as he was. He greeted me in a friendly way and asked me who I was, so I felt noticed and proud, sixteen as I was.

After that evening, I went on reading Engdahl and *Vägen Framåt* even more intently—incidentally, you could buy it in any kiosk. Contradictorily enough, I also bought quite a different paper at the same time—called *Trots allt* (In Spite of Everything) and published by Ture Nerman, socialist, rabid radical, and anti-Nazi. *Trots allt* was also fantastic in its way, I thought, but my heart beat faster for Engdahl.

Nerman was also a clever writer. But Engdahl was a brilliant speaker. I can't get away from the fact that I have never met anyone like him in my life, and I went to hear him speak on several occasions. I admired him and quite often in the following years went to his meetings, where I came across the Neo-Swedish movement's organizer, a man named Palmqvist, and their youth leader, Bengt Olof Ljungberg.

This gang was active both politically and practically apart from Lindholm and other notorious Swedish Nazis. There was hardly a single jackboot in Engdahl's movement—I have a dim memory of Ljungberg being the only exception—no battle songs, no brown shirts. They were themselves, and I found many of them sympathetic. I liked the Neo-Swedish thinking on what was corporative, and I fell for the idea of a greater Europe. This was long before I drew the right conclusion that Engdahl's recipe was not the right way to freedom and dignity for human beings.

When he left Osby, Kamprad went to Göteborg and attended the senior school of commerce for two years. He had left the Lindholm lot and instead quite often went to the Neo-Swedes' premises, where he met "mostly older men, very few young." At one place there was a Swedish flag and a Neo-Swede with the Royal Vasa Sheaf in the middle hung up at the back, some nice old ladies making the coffee, and a smell of freshly made buns. The local leader was Mr. Bergkvist, the biology teacher, "awfully nice and considerate." On one or two occasions, Ingvar was given the task of going down to the station to meet Per Engdahl, who was to give a lecture.

I piloted him to the meeting place. He was almost blind, with terribly thick glasses. He couldn't cross the road on his own. On the way, we were also to have coffee at Bräutigam's famous café. There the visually handicapped national chairman wanted me to read aloud to him from an anti-Nazi paper, first of all the daily column by a man named Torgny Segerstedt. Engdahl maintained that he had great respect for this opponent of Hitler and called him "a simple and fine man."

I have always found it easy, sometimes too easy, to admire and trust gifted people with qualities I myself lack. There was in me a kind of feeling of pity for Per Engdahl because of his blindness, but also respect for his capacity and intelligence. When I had finished reading a column aloud, Engdahl would immediately repeat it by heart, yes, word for word. That impressed me.

I also had the impression that he was putting his cards on the table—that he was what he made himself out to be, no one else. To my direct question, he assured me he was neither a Nazi, fascist, nor racist, but there were extreme phalanxes in his movement.

As I see it now, and against the background of what I later learned, he was, of course, racist, but not, as far as I could see, particularly anti-Semitic. He liked to say that the mixing of races always produced bad results. For instance, he talked about the Malays—a people of half Indian and Chinese descent. He talked about the American Indians in the same way, and I was stupid enough to be taken in. He made me believe it was wrong for the races to mix.

On the other hand, I never heard him pronounce hatred of either gypsies or Jews, or any others. But he was racist. I certainly understood what was in the Neo-Swedish manifesto, but I never read it; I was stupid enough to think that what Engdahl said was so good it had to be enough. The fact that he is later said to have changed his mind makes no difference in this context.

When the war was over in 1945, I left Göteborg to start working for the Forest Owners' Association in Växjö, a job my father had fixed up for me. In town I took part in several meetings of the phalanx of Neo-Swedes that had survived after the war. I still didn't realize that I was a victim of a great flaw in my thinking. Fortunately, I had a good friend in Ivar Peterson, a man who later joined *Expressen* and died young of cancer. I greatly admired him.

I confided in him early on about my "sickness"—my connection with Engdahl—and he told me how far I had strayed and patiently told me why. We became close friends, and he listened in a brotherly way to me, although I was slow to change my mind. I remember a remark he made when, in my normal way of doing business with people, I sold him a clock and later also wanted to sell him a wristwatch. He said:

"My dear Ingvar, I pass the church clock on my way home, and when I am at home, I have the clock you've sold me. What do I need a wristwatch for?"

Ivar Peterson, then a man of forty, gave me, an uncertain and fairly isolated twenty-year-old, a number of fresh ideas that were to help me gradually see through "those gentlemen," as he called Engdahl and company. He was a wonderful person who did everything to bring me back to my senses, just as later on IKEA's faithful lawyer, Ola Ellwyn, did.

But now life was turning nasty, and other things were

making it complicated. In time I had become very close to Engdahl and looked up to him. In 1948 we made an agreement that I would publish one of his books. It was called *Political Education*, with subheadings like "Who Was It . . . What Happened . . . How Did It Happen . . . in Politics?"

It was mostly a collection of political essays with no actual ideological overtones but more of a historical description of Sweden and the world outside from 1809 to modern times. The point was that Engdahl's name was not to figure in it, perhaps because it contained twelve lines on "the party-less Neo-Swedes"; his pseudonym was Sten Jonsson. Our agreement included that as proceeds from the book came in I would pay him his remuneration.

The book had good reviews in a number of provincial newspapers but was a financial flop; I paid off my royalty debt to Engdahl over a long period—one hundred kronor now and again. I like to think, and hope, I finally did right by him.

I found it difficult to break with my idol, and his illness restrained me from doing anything that would sadden him. In stages, I had stopped believing his teachings and was on my way to being converted in the right direction; moreover, business rather than politics had begun to dominate my life. I ought to have left, but I still lacked the courage to say I didn't want to have anything more to do with him. So a long time went by without any break occurring. He sent me his big book, *The Renewal of the West*, with a slightly bitter dedication that spoke of "the silent, oh so silent forests of Småland," meaning I had not been in contact with him and he was hurt. I read bits and pieces of the closely written eight hundred to nine hundred pages of the book. (The books I have actually read to the end can on the whole be counted on the fingers of one hand.)

Engdahl was not interested in me for my money. IKEA was still a modest business and was producing scarcely more than a decent amount of pocket money. Not that his movement wasn't in constant need of capital—few people have asked me to contribute so often, and few have I refused so many times. If he was fond of me, it was probably for other reasons, not financial. Long afterward he expressed his approval of the way I ran IKEA and said that as a businessman I realized Neo-Swedish ideas on classlessness, and so on.

Before I married for the first time, Kerstin, my wife-to-be, and I discussed whether Engdahl should be invited to our wedding. Before we had even decided, he sent us a wedding present—some fine upholstery material from Kinnasands textile mill, where his brother was manager.

There was no turning back—he had also written a special wedding poem in our honor. (Per had already published several collections of poems, and he perhaps met a better fate as a poet than as a politician.) We had invited a few close friends to our wedding in Solna church.

We sent him an invitation, and I also wrote a letter asking him to make an encouraging speech that would cheer my wife up—she had a tendency to pessimism. "My future wife finds it rather difficult because she can in no way find any meaning in life, but thinks everything worthless."

Engdahl came and made a beautiful speech at our wedding dinner at Hasselbacken in Stockholm. The letter with the invitation was published in *Expressen* in the autumn of 1994 as evidence of my alleged connection with the Nazis. That was to be turned into the affair that for several terrible days in November of that year profoundly shook both me and IKEA.

Then it appeared again on a similarly miserable occasion in the spring of 1998. Again it was *Expressen* devoting its columns to me. Now the paper had discovered my early contacts with the Lindholmers and was making a great scandal of my not having said anything about it in 1994. I have now tried to explain why.

I thought I had changed in my opinions—from crude Nazism to Engdahl's more "decent" fascism. Perhaps inside me this became an entirely sufficient conversion from evil: I was so terribly ashamed of the time with the Lindholmers that I never even told my wife Margaretha about it, which in itself was a bad idea.

Engdahl was enough, I thought.

In addition, whatever people say, I was largely a child when all that started to happen. The events that I now, as thoroughly as I am able, have accounted for occurred over sixty years ago. As I have lain awake at nights pondering this dismal affair, I have asked myself: when is an old man to be forgiven for the sins of his youth? Can anyone fail to see my regrets, my sorrow over my error? Is it a crime that I was brought up by a German grandmother and a German father? As I said: when is an old man to be forgiven for the aberration of his youth?

The Affair That Became a PR Case

> . . . the whole truth and nothing withheld,
> added, or changed . . .
>
> —FROM THE SWEDISH OATH
> ADMINISTERED TO A WITNESS

> A friend in need is a friend indeed.
>
> —ENGLISH PROVERB

The story of Ingvar Kamprad's interest in Nazism and fascism when young provides a picture not only of a human being's tortuous route to and away from certain convictions but also of what happens in a large company when a unique event intrudes on everyday business and threatens to undermine the credibility of the business concept and jeopardize sales.

It is hardly surprising that management gurus have thoroughly studied the Engdahl affair, not as a piquant biographical deviation in the life of a businessman, but as a case study on a company management level. This book also includes a view of the matter from that angle.

It would not be an exaggeration to say that *Expressen*'s proposal on October 21, 1994, when the journalist Tagesson was looking for Ingvar

Kamprad, landed like a bomb on IKEA and the life of Kamprad himself.

He was given a period of grace for reflection.

According to their plan, he and his assistant, Staffan Jeppsson, were due to fly to Seattle the following day. Tagesson knew that Kamprad was on his way and flew down to Geneva in the belief that his victim was to take the plane from there.

But Kamprad and Jeppsson were flying from Copenhagen. Nevertheless, four days later, Ingvar met Tagesson with a photographer at IKEA's store in Aubonne outside Lausanne, Jeppsson also present as a witness.

Before Tagesson produced all the incriminating documents, Kamprad had decided to talk about everything and to tell more than he was asked about. Everything went quite smoothly until *Expressen*'s envoy showed him two sheets of paper considered to prove that Kamprad had taken part in a European fascist meeting in Malmö as late as 1958.

Suddenly, this was no longer about youthful sins but about the lack of political judgment in a mature major businessman. It was in 1958 that the very first store was established in Älmhult. IKEA had been growing explosively, and Ingvar had by then abandoned all political interests. He had certainly not taken part in any such meeting. Moreover, he couldn't have—he was up to his ears in work for the company.

Kamprad was horribly upset. Jeppsson had never before seen him like this—his face scarlet as he crashed his fist down on the table. This was a lie, and he would prove it.

Tagesson and his victim, to say the least, parted in discomfort. At IKEA they knew what charge would shortly detonate in the media. At that time, certain decisions were made that came to be guiding principles for how the company and Kamprad himself were to act in the near future.

Everything was to be put on the table, he said. If, by chance, he had been mistaken on any point, if he had suppressed or forgotten unpleasant facts, well, then that was that, they were to be brought into the light of day. No attempts were to be made in any way to conceal the truth. That was the order of the day—and it had only one snag.

Ingvar himself had forgotten the extent of his earliest interest in Nazism, which had led to the next step of contact with Engdahl.

But now, in November 1994, the entire management of IKEA was activated by this order of the day. A kind of crisis group was formed, consisting of Jeppsson, Elisabet Jonsson (head of information in Humlebæk), and Anders Moberg, safely in the background. They occupied the room that Ingvar himself used when visiting IKEA International. On Sunday, November 6, Ingvar went to Älmhult, where Leif Sjöö, the Swedish head of information, was his combined backup and sounding board.

That day a large number of store managers had flown in to Älmhult for training in the IKEA Way program. In the evening the founder was to meet them and give them the first lesson in *A Furniture Dealer's Testament,* the entirely necessary sermon on the culture of the IKEA family, the spirit of Småland, everything that had been born there in the magical 1950s.

A special war headquarters was set up in Älmhult on that Sunday, as it was wrongly believed that *Expressen* was going to publish its revelation that day. Leif Sjöö took on considerable responsibility—as soon as they knew what *Expressen* had written, he was prepared to go straight to the National Archives and comb through the special archive that Per Engdahl, for posterity, had donated.

All these preparations were made at the same time in order to gear the staff up on separate levels. Kamprad found himself in one of his recurring annual dry periods, when he touched no alcohol at all. He drank some coffee that someone had left behind after the Friday afternoon office meeting, and he found two stale buns—that was all he ate during two days' work.

All the papers had now been produced, and the strategy for meeting the gunfire from the media was in place. When everything was summarized by Sunday evening, a kind of relief spread through them and someone cried out:

"Now, let's all have a drink. We've earned it."

"Not on your life!" said Kamprad, as disciplined as ever. "I'm on the wagon this month."

That evening, when he met enthusiastic store managers from all over the world—for several of them this was the high point in their career—he was outwardly calm and collected in spite of the pressure. In the middle of the session, Sjöö slipped in with a box of all the documents that were to be shown to the press and employees, the documents that would either reject or put into perspective *Expressen*'s still unknown accusations.

That evening Kamprad drove down to Humlebæk, where the next day he made himself available to the media.

The first article in *Expressen* came out on Monday, November 7, with placards, large headlines, and four pages of reports, the gist of which was: Ingvar Kamprad was an active Nazi. On the same day, the entire staff was informed via in-house newsletters and meetings. In Humlebæk, as expected, television, radio, and print journalists besieged all headquarters north of Louisiana; on the screen appeared a hunted Kamprad, angry, despairing, tired, and miserable, all at the same time. "I who have so much to carry out for the future—do I have to spend time talking about what I thought and felt as a young stripling?"

With that, he provided an image of his determination to resist, to overcome. Actually, this was a specialty of his. Only those who are asleep make no mistakes, he repeats like an invocation. Problems make possibilities, he could have added, faithful to his preaching habit. The truth, nothing but the truth—he might have quoted from the oath for witnesses.

Reverberations in the media all over the world were not slow in coming.

Two days later, all the media on every continent had the news—Italian, Dutch, French, American, German, and so on. With varying degrees of forced wit alluding to the furniture company, the matter was presented with headlines such as "Nazi Skeleton in IKEA Cupboard."

Before the reports were published, however, Ingvar Kamprad had given out a long handwritten letter to all his employees (he still writes all his letters by hand), aiming particularly at the people at home in Älmhult, the core troop, the famous close "family." The letter was published in the *Älmhult Bladet* (Älmhult Tribune), which is to IKEA what a government organ is to a political party. It was rapidly translated into all the languages in the world of IKEA.

In the letter, which he wrote in several drafts (one is headed "Ten days—hitherto—I will not soon forget"), the regretful father speaks to his family and indeed starts with the words, "Dear IKEA family," under the heading, in capitals, "MY GREATEST FIASCO."

With that, Kamprad set the internal tone of the affair. He clothed himself in sackcloth and ashes and confessed everything. Many think he asks for forgiveness rather too often, but that is his style even in personal conflicts. He compared his youthful sins with what were, in his opinion, well-documented fiascos—for instance, his loss of millions on a television factory in Helsingborg in the 1950s. Briefly and precisely, he told of his tearful Sudeten-German grandmother who liked Hitler—revealing the details of the background to his pro-German sympathies and his contact with the Neo-Swedish movement. "This is a part of my life I regret," he wrote before confessing his work as the unhappy publisher for Per Engdahl—a book that turned out to be another fiasco (serves me right, he seemed to be saying).

Kamprad's letter was a brilliant personal document, even if collectively addressed. He wrote as if to friends, revealing an internal journey that did in fact test the spirit of IKEA:

You have been young yourself, and perhaps you find something in your youth you now, so long afterward, think was ridiculous and stupid. In that case, you will understand me better. Add to that that all this is forty to fifty years ago. In hindsight, I know that early on I should have already included this in my fiascos, but that is now spilled milk.

He ended his letter with a reminder of what IKEA now had to deal with—the launch in China. He rounded it off with his classic magic formula: "Most things remain to be done—a glorious future!"

Perhaps the most hurtful article in the press on Kamprad was produced two days later in the Swedish tabloid *Idag/Kvällsposten*. It contained the "revelation" that "Nazi money had financed the start of IKEA," a piece of information that came to be repeated in the spring of 1998 and was then verified by Per Engdahl's son.

If sorrow and dismay had marked Ingvar's reaction hitherto, he was now furious. For a person who all his life had made it a point of honor to preserve his freedom by never being in debt to anyone, an accusation of having borrowed money was a stab straight to the heart. Whether the lender were fascist or not, it was the charge of not having stood on his own feet that hurt.

"They could have accused me of murder, but not of borrowing money!" he exclaimed, for he does not lack a talent for absurd gallows humor.

"When I read that story, my courage really did begin to waver." A few minutes later, he literally burst into tears—but for another reason. A fax had come from Älmhult, and above hundreds of signatures of his employees was the following simple text:

INGVAR,
>   WE ARE HERE WHENEVER YOU NEED US.
>   THE IKEA FAMILY IOS [IKEA of Sweden]

Then the father of the family broke down and wept like a child.

Later that day, after he had collected himself, he sent a two-page handwritten fax to the Älmhult newsletter headed: "COULD NOT STOP THE TEARS."

In it he gave a letter-hug to all the IKEA employees for their action. Once again, he spoke of how ashamed he was for collaborating, and he categorically denied that he had ever borrowed a cent to build up IKEA; at the time when IKEA allegedly borrowed funds, the company was actually turning over about one million kronor and would have had no reason to borrow money.

While all this was happening and hundreds of merciless articles from the world's press were floating in to IKEA by fax, Leif Sjöö finished digging in the National Archives collection of Per Engdahl's voluminous correspondence and speeches. Sjöö's assignment, given him directly by Kamprad, was to seek out all documents that might have any connection with him and the neo-Nazis and, regardless of their content, to show them to the press promptly, but to send him a copy. The truth and nothing but the truth was to be the word.

Sjöö, in Älmhult since 1958 and brought up the hard way, found a number of documents that spoke of collaboration. In an early letter (as stated previously), the always thrifty Ingvar asked to be sent a few copies of the paper *Vägen Framåt* and signed the letter "with a Nordic greeting."

In another, undated letter, there was talk of the Neo-Swedes wanting help from Kamprad to bring in money from a society in Göteborg, and another was about a vanished hundred-kronor note that Per Engdahl was asking about. This letter is even more interesting because it reveals that the young Kamprad was worried about the National Association of Furniture Dealers, which had just forced the St. Eriks Fair to prevent IKEA from taking part. (Kamprad said in the letter to Engdahl that he hoped the leading social democratic newspaper in Stockholm would support his case.)

In a third letter, Ingvar Kamprad ordered two volumes of an Engdahl book (*The Renewal of the West*) for one hundred kronor (twelve dollars), delivered a favorable opinion on *Vägen Framåt*, and hoped that Engdahl would come and see him if he happened to be passing by Älmhult.

Finally, Leif Sjöö also found the document that the press had given as evidence that Kamprad had taken part in the Fascist European Congress in Malmö in 1958. In fact, it was a list of donors to the chairman, Engdahl, who was to turn fifty at the New Year—according to the list, Kamprad donated nothing. But most important of all, it turned out that he had not been politically active as late as *Expressen* maintained.

With Kamprad's personal letters to his staff and his obvious regret over the actions of his youth ("I'm ashamed," "I regret . . . ," "I was stupid enough," and, "I didn't dare say no"), the potential scandal died for the time being.

There was nothing more for the journalists to get hold of—though the whole matter had not subsided abroad.

The Jewish world movement in the person of Rabbi Abraham Cooper of the Simon Wiesenthal Center in Los Angeles wrote to request a detailed account—they were considering the possibility of boycotting the IKEA stores in the United States but first wished to find out the truth about why IKEA did not have a store in Israel but did in the Arab countries.

IKEA immediately intervened on this front as well, partly via a letter from Anders Moberg, and partly by sending IKEA's U.S. head, Göran Carstedt, and the future Seattle store manager, Bjorn Bayley, to Los Angeles for a personal meeting with Cooper. Their arguments and Moberg's letter convinced the rabbi that the company had never discriminated against Israel, and that, on the contrary, it had long purchased from and supplied goods to Israeli customers and positive investigations into the possibility of setting up a store in Israel were already under way.

The center in Los Angeles was satisfied with this. Kamprad's "bitter regrets" over his involvement when young and the fact that he had assured them he had never supported any Nazi, whether an individual or an organization, were accepted. The potential boycott was called off.

With that, the "Nazi affair" was over—for the moment. The crisis group could be wound down. IKEA had ridden out its worst media crisis ever, and there are those who think the company emerged stronger than when it all began. What settled the matter was certainly the main character's resolute determination to take the initiative immediately, his very personal message to all his staff, his accessibility to the media when the matter came out into the open, his clear words stating that absolutely nothing from the archives was to be concealed—even if later it unfortunately turned out that not everything had been revealed.

At this stage, everything was working positively toward silencing the media. On December 7, 1994, Staffan Jeppsson noted for the first time in his war diary that, since October 21, no questions at all from the media on the matter had come either to him or to Elisabet Jonsson. The next day they were at last able to start working as usual on "current matters." But Jeppsson is still coping with "harmful" books and documents from this youthful sin of Kamprad's—including the unread *The Renewal of the West*.

So far, this account of the Engdahl affair is an almost perfect case for any mass media seminar at management level: practice total openness toward the public, put everything on the table, make no attempts to feed snooping newspaper reporters with fake sweeteners but give them only the actual raw material—the truth. And also get the truth straight from the horse's mouth.

There couldn't have been a better PR textbook.

In the spring of 1998, however, before there had been time to publish this book, with all the relevant replies to the questions about Kamprad's life, revelations were made about the part of his relations with Nazi movements that he had only implied or previously suppressed. The farm boy's visit to the meeting in Moheda/Alvesta, when Sven Olof Lindholm spoke for Swedish Nazis, now produced gigantic headlines; yet again, and not without reason, the same barrel organ as in 1994 started grinding. But this time the suspicion was also cast on Ingvar that he had, after all, tried to keep secret parts of the truth about himself.

In the previous chapter, he himself tried to describe the psychological fog that stopped him from seeing himself clearly—a sheltered, fairly isolated youth, brought up by a bitter Sudeten-German grandmother and an openly anti-Semitic, pro-Nazi father.

Ingvar Kamprad was undeniably shaken again, and many of his friends did wonder. He had made innumerable telephone calls to people involved at the time in order to be able to check up on what had really happened. I myself have asked him numerous questions to try to revive his sluggish memory, and he has been close to despair when time and time again he has been mistaken about years and events.

As the head of a large company, Ingvar Kamprad must be unique in that he has never kept a diary or journal that can be referred to later. He is almost allergic to collecting photographs and letters and seems almost maniacally oriented toward the future, toward the next day. His memory is excellent but hugely selective: he remembers the name of a Pole with whom he did a large furniture deal but is constantly wrong about years and names that are of no direct importance to his business.

After the death of his parents and a change of home, he made a drastic suggestion to his sister: "Wouldn't it be best to throw everything out?" His sister, Kerstin, did the opposite: she kept things, and thanks to her, important parts of this story are well sourced and documented. When I asked whether Hitler's *Mein Kampf* was among the books on the farm, Ingvar did not know, but his sister quickly told me: "It's still in Father's old bookcase, a German edition in Gothic type, almost untouched." And then Ingvar remembered that as a boy he had leafed through it but never read it. It was his father's. On the back of the cover it says in pencil that the book cost 7.20 deutsche marks—presumably a gift from the family near Leipzig.

Finally, a documentary account in a "memoir" of this kind reaches a critical boundary. Ingvar has been through painful interrogations not only by me but by his kin in this matter. He has tried to answer but has not really succeeded. In the end, the search in a case of this kind must—if the subject is worthy of it—be handed over to the experts, the professional historians. Ingvar himself ponders on whether he has said everything that is reasonable and relevant about the "sickness" of his youth—he thinks so, but does not know.

Not for sure.

The "Ten Hot Dogs" Strategy

> I say to the economists, "What the hell is 'percentage' anyhow?"
>
> —INGVAR KAMPRAD

In 1995 the IKEA furniture store started selling hot dogs at five kronor each, as opposed to the usual price of ten to fifteen kronor. This investment was at once successful, and today it contributes to the growing restaurant and food sector by turning over 1.6 billion kronor in 1997, and alone answering for exports from Sweden amounting to 700 million kronor ($87 million). That makes IKEA Sweden's leading food exporter.

But behind this success is a special story. The "ten hot dogs strategy" says a great deal about the way the company regards price, competition, and the needs and desires of the customer.

One of IKEA's basic principles is that of "the substantial price difference." This is engraved in the first commandment in *A Furniture Dealer's Testament.*

The reasoning is very simple. Since IKEA turns to the many people who as a rule have small resources, the company must be not just cheap, nor just cheaper—but very much cheaper. In short, the stores must sell things that, in the eyes of the public, are astonishingly cheap to buy.

So the goods must be such that ordinary people can easily and quickly identify the lowness of the price. That was how Ingvar Kamprad—for it was he—gave birth to the idea of selling hot dogs for five kronor.

He thought IKEA needed a new kind of item at what he calls a breathtaking price. It was to be sold in the little bistro, which in a complete store is always just where customers emerge from the exit checkouts.

> Everyone, including myself, who likes sausages knows what a hot dog costs at a stand. At present it is between ten and fifteen kronor. I suggested to the directors that we sell them at five kronor. They looked at me with dismay and surprise. Perhaps they thought the idea foolish, or perhaps I didn't explain it very clearly. Talking about selling hot dogs in a multibillion furniture store was not really on the agenda.

To realize the idea, the originator had to participate himself. The target he set was that two people at the counter would be able to sell three hundred hot dogs an hour. A number of trials were carried out, and the best working position as well as the most functional fittings were tested.

It all took time, but it soon became a reality. It was an almost immediate success—today hot dogs are sold all over the world on the five-kronor principle. Each country has its exact price level (preferably so that only a single coin is necessary), so in Switzerland a hot dog costs one Swiss franc, in Germany one and a half deutsche mark, in the United States fifty cents, in Austria ten schillings, and so on.

> The next objection arose from my staff, who are always concerned with what they call the gross profit margin. We're selling hot dogs for almost the same amount it costs to make them. Shouldn't we raise the price and take six or seven kronor in profit?
>
> In that case, the project ought to be abandoned, I replied, as the whole idea is based on the substantial price difference, the easily understood price. The hot dog went on costing five kronor regardless of the cost of raw materials. We don't lose on

the deal, nor do we make much profit, but at least we make a little on each hot dog.

In the end, that is what matters.

It is common knowledge within the company that IKEA usually has a breathtakingly priced product in its range—a "hot dog." That has now acquired its own in-house meaning, and Ingvar Kamprad has added yet another eagerly guarded task to his many others.

A little while ago, we advertised a mug costing ten kronor. Come to IKEA and buy the mug, it said. I was upset—the price was much too high. It should have cost five kronor at the most, although it did look pretty nice and was of good quality. It was the price that was wrong.

So it came about that I wrote down my philosophy about the ten (twenty nowadays) hot dogs. We have ten different products that live up to "hot dog" pricing. A rule of thumb is 3 + 1 + 1—three kronor to the producer, one krona to the Ministry of Finance (tax authorities), and one krona to ourselves. Each time we are unable to follow that equation, we should think twice.

Take the mug from the above example, called "Bang."

In Switzerland it costs exactly one franc at IKEA. I haven't found one on the ordinary market for less than three francs, and even in that case our mug was much better in both design and quality. Before, we sold at the most seven hundred thousand mugs per year, and now the "hot-dog mug" sells twelve and a half million.

But Ingvar Kamprad is still in search of new hot dogs.

One day I found a wonderful English beer glass for eighteen kronor at our Swedish co-op competitor—I always go and look at what my competitors are doing. It was the kind of English glass with a level measure on it, forty centiliters, heavy and really good to hold. I thought it would be a good "hot dog."

I went straight to our most superb buyer and said: "Björn, can you get that glass out at one krona? You can order two million." He replied: "Nix—I can't, but maybe in an edition of five million." The whole thing had the support of the product head, whom, as usual, I had bypassed. The last time I met Björn, he had a supplier who would do the glass at 1.08 kronor.

It'll work out. So in a short time we've put twenty or so "hot dogs" up for sale—the whole organization is up and going.

The reader is right to ask himself or herself why, as the retired head of the firm, I go on with this kind of thing. There are three answers: one is that I find it difficult not to; it also says in my contract that I have a veto in matters of the range; and people in the company often say, "If you're on to something, let me know."

So I let them know.

I'm going on with my search for new "hot dogs"—lots of associates are involved. I recently saw a multi-plug we sell for under twenty kronor, while competitors take about fifty. My belief is that this "hot dog" will sell millions.

Our pricing policy is fundamental.

The stumbling block is when we price ourselves out of the market. Our economists constantly go on that we must keep our "total gross profit margin" to a certain percentage. I say to the economists, "What the hell is 'percentage' anyhow?"

Percentage is something mysterious. The only thing that interests us at IKEA is what is left in our pocket when the season is over.

They talk about "cash flow," and I say that I don't know what cash flow is, but I know what I have in my pocket.

If we had taken ten kronor for that mug, and not five, then we would, of course, have "earned" more on each mug— perhaps one and a half kronor—and had a better "gross profit margin." But we would have sold only half a million of them instead of almost twelve million, on which we now earn one krona each.

These learning experiences are easy to suppress or ignore. But after having been the subject of endless bickering for over a decade, in this respect we are beginning to wake up with a vengeance.

That pleases me enormously.

The Dream of the Good Capitalist

What . . . keeps me going is the feeling that
in a wider sense I am participating in a
gigantic project of democratization, though
quite a different one from what is normally
talked about.

So I am dismayed when we make a
mistake, faulty products. . . . It seems to be
my fault, and I must get in there and do something, though there are so many of us now.

—INGVAR KAMPRAD

Can capitalism be good?

In what way can I as an entrepreneur be of the most use?

How is an empathetic businessman to orient himself between a centrally governed society with in-built economic and social support for its citizens and a market economy that only too easily bolts at top speed at the expense of individuals?

I admit that I have thought a great deal about these matters.

I have always disliked the harshness of American capital-ism, and I admit that I do have some socialist sympathies. But I recently reacted when I heard a woman in a television discus-sion condemn the market economy; she wanted to put a stop to it, and she said the good of the people was now to come first.

I ask myself how. And what is "the good" of the people?

In China I see how those in power allow a few to earn huge sums of money, the idea behind it being that the people will eventually benefit. Communism today is clearly allowed to take on any appearance. The question is whether, as an entrepreneur, I can combine the good in a profit-making business with a lasting human social vision.

I like to think it must be possible.

I don't mean to say that capitalism can avoid fiascos. I myself have been the cause of several. To fail is part of all evolution. But every day, IKEA strives to develop and achieve a better future for the people, our customers.

A company goal of that kind influences those working toward it.

Studies show that people who work for IKEA believe that they really are working for a better society and that they therefore like working for IKEA. They believe that in their daily lives they are contributing to a better world.

Expressed a trifle solemnly, our business philosophy contributes to the democratizing process. It makes good, handsome, and cheap everyday articles available to a great many people at a price they can afford. That seems to me to have something to do with down-to-earth democracy.

My closest colleagues and I began using the expression "the majority of people" very early on. As has been touched on before, it was on a visit to a fair in Italy in the mid-1950s that, without being aware of it, I was the first to put the concept into words. In the daytime, I saw the most modern and luxurious furniture exhibited at the fair, costing vast sums. In the evenings, I had the good fortune to go home with some Italians and saw with my own eyes the difference between the exhibited luxury and the furnishings that ordinary people could afford in their homes.

I asked myself, why do poor people have to put up with such ugly things?

Was it necessary that what was beautiful could be bought only by an elite for large sums?

I went back home with those questions ringing in my head. They were to go on demanding an answer from me all my life.

Democracy as an instrument for evolution can lead to remarkable inertia. If everything in a company is to be questioned, nothing gets decided. In an increasingly technological world, democracy can get almost out of hand. How can I knowledgeably vote on nuclear energy? Can I, in all my ignorance, judge safety and investments on that level?

And yet democracy has one over-shadowing advantage—all the alternatives are so much worse.

Even the most enlightened dictatorship ends badly. The great greed that is unbridled jungle capitalism leads to the destruction of humanity. In my confusion when young, I played around a lot with corporative ideas, and as I have implied, I reckon that to be one of my mental fiascos.

Today I grieve over the difficulty, perhaps impossibility, of inventing regulations that, without damaging the basic system, would be able to ward off the worst drawbacks of free enterprise.

On IKEA's part, I am proud to aim at the majority of people and their living conditions. It defines our range and informs our demands for the lowest prices. It is imprinted on our search for effectiveness and beauty in design, and it motivates us in environmental matters. The mass of people can achieve a high material standard of living only through the efforts of entrepreneurs obsessed by the idea of satisfying a market.

Antipathy easily turns on successful people, who use their success to misuse their money and live in luxury. It is so easy to forget that most businessmen are like most people. They live a normal everyday life in relative simplicity. They invest most of their wealth in developing their firms further, and they very much want the next generation to continue doing so. I am one of them.

To those who constantly criticize the business establishment, I put the question: What is the alternative? Planned economy, centralization, socialism?

If that is the answer, the signs are frightening, and now after the fall of the Wall, most people know the truth.

When IKEA began to do business for the first time with a

Communist country—it was Poland—we received fierce criticism, most of all from the middle classes. It was wrong to fraternize with a loathsome system.

Such thinking is understandable, but let he who is without sin cast the first stone. We were driven to Poland because in free-enterprise Sweden there was a furniture trade that started a boycott against us because of our low prices. Capitalism, said to favor competition, could not tolerate an upstart with a new view of the production and selling of furnishings to a wide public.

I had many a tearful night when I sensed that the very existence of the firm was threatened. That also gave birth to a greater determination to fight and find ways out. Thus came about a paradox—that we in the abused name of the market had to go to a Communist country to safeguard our supply of goods to sell in a free country.

This, and nothing else, governed us when for the first time we laboriously established business contacts with the Polish furniture export organization, PAGED, in 1961. At the time, it was purely and simply a matter of surviving or dying. We lacked chairs to sell, we lacked shelving, tables.

After a while, slowly, alongside the need for profit, grew a more mature view of our new business partner: perhaps we could be of some help to this isolated country?

We met people in Poland who were thirsty for contact with the world outside. Later on, they came to us in Älmhult, and they hardly wanted to leave the place. They loved Småland. It struck me that only athletes, merchants, and perhaps artists could open a peephole for the people imprisoned in communism. When they were able to see our Swedish model, live our lives, shop in our stores, and visit our homes, they began to question their own system. I like to think this might have helped people throw off the yoke.

That first time in Poland we visited factories with environments that were downright unhealthy and might have come from a Dickens novel.

We saw others that were semimodernized, but there, in the middle of the conveyer belt, were several old women with wheelbarrows shifting the half-finished products.

Everywhere we went, we felt the need to intervene and yes, to help. Slowly, we had an influence on the Polish furniture industry as it modernized. It was a matter of give and take—we undeniably bought cheaply from them, just as now, thirty-five years later, we are accused of doing in Romania. The Poles, in turn, learned new techniques from us and made long-term contracts with a buyer they could trust, in contrast to other foreign buyers who came, bought, and then simply disappeared.

Today we have results: Poland exports to IKEA alone more than one and a half billion kronor; our first offer, as far as I remember, was less than seventy thousand kronor. Poland today is one of the leading producers in the European furniture industry.

That's what can happen if capitalists intervene.

That is how I see "the good capitalist" in his prime role. In discussions, I usually use a fictional example. You are Yeltsin. There is a knock on the door, and in comes your secretary with a check for $20 billion. Here you are, Mr. President, do what you like with this money to develop your country, the World Bank will write off everything in twenty years.

What does the wretched Yeltsin do? How does he get the wheels to start turning?

Where should he begin? How is he to know which industries ought to do what and how? How is he to find out whether they can do what he wants? And how much money will vanish in the process?

Compare this with a few thousand Swedish entrepreneurs going to Russia and each starting up a business of his own. Results would appear very quickly. One starts a toothpaste factory, another makes ultra-modern furniture, and a third manufactures paper clips. Capitalists are enormously inventive when they get wind of a need on which they can make a profit.

Poland is proof that trade is better than aid, that good capitalism can work. We went in at all levels—not just ordering, but gradually as retailers and trend-setters on the market. Today few Polish homes or offices have nothing from IKEA in them, or something inspired by IKEA. We have renewed the home furnishing concept and helped modernize the distribution of goods.

I admit that complications can arise.

Take Thailand, for instance. As this is being written, the country has been shaken by a currency crisis and anxiety on the stock exchange. The people are discontented. We have bought quite a lot there. Far out in the jungle, we have chanced on a small manufacturer in a ramshackle property who would very much like to make the "Justus" hat-rack for us.

It's easy to realize that this factory would never have been approved by the authorities in Sweden or any environmental organizations. Reporters would be able to write articles on the scandal of this factory. Television would do a hard-hitting exposé. The shack in the jungle is a threat to nature. The question is then, shall we beat a retreat, be off as quickly as possible and evade the problem? Much better to go and find a more modern factory that, indeed, is 5 percent more costly for us but operates on an environmentally sound basis.

Or?

Or do we sit down with the owner/factory manager and start talking about whether, despite everything, we can work together and help modernize and improve his factory?

My reply is that it would be wrong to always flee the field in a case of this kind. Naturally we cannot have suppliers only on this level, but we would very much like to have some of them working all the time and growing with us. In these semi-derelict factory buildings, sometimes with no access to roads and with a battered aluminum kettle puttering away on an open fire, small miracles can be achieved.

I remember a factory that made bicycle baskets. They had old machines held together with steel wire and antique, extremely dangerous welding apparatus in cubbyholes with no ventilation.

Nonetheless, we stayed there and made friends for life. Today they have modern machines and have expanded (not just with our help). We have given them a little technical advice and backed purchases of modern equipment. Things are beginning to straighten out.

It is simple for people to sit at home making judgments about using suppliers that don't correspond to Western technology. But think about it! How can we best contribute to turning the development in a more positive direction? Are we to go out into the jungle and tell that Thai man, "Now listen, do something about the air in your building first, and get yourself slightly better machinery, and stop letting barrels of poison stand leaking there in the corner, and we'll come back and order goods from you"?

Or shall we try to be of some help, step by step?

I had to answer the same questions again, of myself and our employees, when television did a program condemning the use of child labor in India in factories that were our suppliers.

In our contracts, we say that the use of child labor is unacceptable and suppliers have to live up to UN regulations on these matters.

We keep tight controls to ensure that our suppliers do as they have promised us, but naturally we are sometimes kept in the dark. According to our written policy, we must then break the contract, and that is where I have a guilty conscience. Is it really right simply to break it off immediately?

Yes, we have done that sometimes, and I have only some idea what happened in the districts concerned. On the farm back in Småland, we children helped as best we could. In all cultures, children have very early on been incorporated into the sense of solidarity in work. This was for different reasons, but one weighed heavily—the family needed the children's hands. On the other hand, we are against any form of abuse of children as a labor force, like any other form of slavery.

Our decision to break a contract after the revelation of the use of child labor brings about tragedy—for the children. What is their alternative? Is it the street? There are often no schools. Where are the children to go? How is the family to manage? It surprised me to receive so many letters from the Far East after the television program, letters from ordinary people who said to us at IKEA: "Please don't abandon the Filipinos. Don't abandon the Indians and Vietnamese. They need you for their growth on their way to greater prosperity and a better standard of living." I admit those letters influenced me considerably. IKEA did not wish to let anyone down. We wanted to be part of development.

Reality does not always match up with our ideologies, our dream image of what life should be like. Business life can't make itself out to be better than it is, but "the good capitalist" can play an important part. Admittedly the capitalist is always out to do good business, but the results of his contribution can lift both workers and customers.

I detest capitalists who go to underdeveloped factories and buy up everything they have—ten thousand bicycle baskets straight off—and then just leave. Our way is to return, build up a relationship, contribute with our knowledge, draw up long-term contracts, emphasize the importance of delivery on time, quality, and the environment. That is what we did in Poland, in Yugoslavia, in Hungary, in the Czech Republic, and that is what we are doing in Taiwan, Thailand, Vietnam, and China.

Where, for instance, would IKEA have been if we had not gone outside the borders of Sweden and learned to trade with Communist Poland or other developing nations of the day?

The truth is that in the long run no Swedish production capacity was sufficient for our needs. Nor would we have been able to keep prices as low as we did had we not been challenging Swedish producers to become better and more efficient. In the long run, we would not have achieved our international expansion, which today brings billions in income to Sweden and low prices for our Swedish customers.

Some time ago, I had a letter from the chairman of the local council back at home in Älmhult, asking IKEA to set up more businesses in the area. But we are already extremely strong in the district that saw the birth of the firm and that undeniably helped us grow. We could increase our influence in that beloved area, of course, but in the long run it might be harmful and create an imbalance. We need suppliers from all over the world to secure activities back at home in Sweden. We need Sweden to reinforce our profile in the world.

All business is local, they say. Without our heart in Älmhult, IKEA becomes less of a good company. Feelings and business do not exclude one another—we learned to love Poland as our second home, first as a lifesaver when we couldn't find enough chairs and tables for our Swedish customers, then later because of the people, their good hearts, and their skills. They came to mean a great deal to us, and we to them.

As I often say: the best deal is when neither buyer nor seller loses, but both gain.

A Christmas Party in the Warehouse

A big hug to you all.

—INGVAR KAMPRAD

It is the day before Christmas Eve 1997 in Älmhult. An uncertain covering of snow is dissolving into a misty nothing, but there is still the illusion of Yuletide peace over the neighborhood as the stream of cars makes its way across to the huge parking lot in front of one of the warehouses called DC Nord, the so-called Cementan, to celebrate Christmas.

Since 1953 Ingvar Kamprad has invited his workforce at Älmhult to a simple Christmas party during the days before Christmas Eve. The very first time, they totaled thirty pioneers, who listened to his gospel and received a fine Christmas present not yet considered by the tax authorities to be indirect earnings. This time, 44 years later, with 37,500 more people in the workforce in a company that is fifty billion kronor ($6.3 billion) larger than when it started, about 1,000 of the 1,600 Älmhult employees have come.

Twenty-four hours have gone into preparing Cementan for the party: the stock has been cleared, and fifty long tables are laid out, flanked by thirty or so illuminated Christmas trees. Cartons of sacks of this year's Christmas presents stand behind a counter outside the party area—today within the framework of what is fiscally legal.

Close to the speaker's platform is the table for the pensioners; a few gray veterans are already there an hour before the party, and they know that the boss will do today what he has done for forty-four years. He'll turn to them in particular, the much-discussed generation that laid the foundation stone of the IKEA empire.

People start pouring in through the huge doorway and fill the premises, dressed in scarves and hoods and padded jackets, some with heated cushions to sit on. In the background, the loudspeakers are playing Christmas music.

At two o'clock sharp, an amazing ceremony takes place—trucks are driven slowly along between the tables, laden with brightly colored bowls of Christmas rice. Ikeans dressed in red speedily unload their burdens as if feeding the starving masses, and in the shortest possible time everyone has drunk a toast, consumed the rice, milk, and open ham sandwich, followed by coffee and ginger biscuits.

What is being experienced is the greatest event in IKEA Älmhult, a participatory high mass, a kind of holy service, and the parson, no, read high priest, is in his place.

Someone leads with a prayer—as it should be at all services. He is Mikael Olsson, the managing director of IKEA of Sweden; his prelude speaks resoundingly of exciting delivery and production statistics. As if following a productivity rosary of its own, in compact figures he shows that IKEA has grown by 20 percent since the last Christmas party. Referring to A Furniture Dealer's Testament, he lauds the efforts that everyone has made to create better living for the many and notes that this is ongoing work between IKEA and the customers, each doing half.

Since the previous year, the United Kingdom has become number two statistically and Spain has been incorporated into the empire, just as China soon will be. In Groningen, Nottingham, Hanau, Bologna, Zürich, and Sindelfingen, new stores have been opened. Next year there will be just as many new ones in Shanghai, Genoa, Brno, Krakow, Gdansk, Stuttgart, and Saarbrucken.

Olsson, a natural Ikean, speaks quietly and at tremendous speed, as if hastening to clear the way for the main speaker (and everyone knows who that is). He touches quickly on statistics—over one million lacquered tables and ten million five-kronor "Bang" mugs sold. In passing, he points out that IKEA buys two-thirds of all its goods in industrial countries and has never bought more in Sweden than it does today, but the aim is to double purchases in Eastern Europe and Asia within five years.

As he is speaking, a solemn hush falls over the crowd, for success is a drug that silences people. What everyone is partaking in is a kind of house prayer for growth, in which the figures for the wine are mixed with the redeeming self-criticism of the broken bread, pious wishes (trim the stock and the range), deeply felt prayers ("trade is better than aid"), and finally, a blessing on Älmhult, "our cultural center."

Then the time has come for "Our Father"—for Ingvar Kamprad. Indeed, out by the Christmas present counter is the *Älmhult Newsletter*— IKEA's own *Pravda,* obligatory reading for anyone wishing to research Ikean Kremlinology—with the whole speech already printed in it. This year, however, the founder has decided to rearrange his statement, and so it is wise to listen carefully to what he says as well as between the lines.

He is in great form. He is a Billy Graham, a preacher who has become a household god, a revivalist speaker and moralizing pastor. He makes jokes, tells stories, and literally sheds a tear when afterward the staff leave eighty thousand kronor ($10,000) to the cancer fund named after his mother. He is as formal and tearful as he is humble and visionary. He speaks of his wife Margaretha in the same breath as he takes employees "all into his great embrace."

The day before, television has broadcast a documentary about the use of child labor in the Philippines and Vietnam, but the founder makes no reference to unpleasant investigative reporters. On the contrary, he thanks the producer for the media pressure on the company because "we must have journalists both for the sake of our good deeds and our sins."

Everyone laughs. They all understand.

It is a brilliant speech by a pastor who has no need to worry about positive vibrations in his congregation. Some people would call it populist, but whatever it is, it is altogether a repetition of forty-three previous Christmas speeches. The theme is the same: IKEA's philosophy, cost awareness, the majority of people, the dream of the good capitalist, hard work raised to the highest morality, regrets and penitence when faced with past sins of omission, a mission to seek profit and glory. It is the restrained self-praise that gives everyone a lift and the eternal reminder that they are right at the beginning and that most has still yet to be done.

Then the applause breaks out and the father of them all goes and stands by the exit as the good capitalist, between the pallets of "Billy" the bookcase and "Emma" the sofa. He shakes everyone by the hand, and one thousand hands are shaken. Each person is given a kind of inner laying-on of hands, as if they were at once promised that their sins will be forgiven and given top marks for order and behavior at the end of a school term assembly. They depart with a fine Christmas present in their arms—three green towels with face cloths. They can go home to their dear "people's home" in the best of IKEA's furnished worlds.

THE
GREAT LEAP

Most things still remain to be done!

—INGVAR KAMPRAD

To Inherit but Not to Destroy

I shall never forget one late autumn evening at home in 1974 when Margaretha had let all our sons stay up to await my usual late arrival. I had been working for fifteen hours and was tired, hungry, and worn out. Peter was ten, Jonas eight, and Mathias five. They were in their pajamas, sitting on our yellow sofa. Peter acted as spokesman and said: "Daddy, we've discussed the matter, all three of us. We are sorry that you have so much to do. So when we grow up, we've decided to help you."

When Ingvar Kamprad had a child of his own for the first time, he was almost thirty-eight. He had been longing for this moment—not least because of the pain associated with being cut off from any contact with Annika, his adopted daughter from his first marriage.

He took an intense part in the arrival of his firstborn, which for his wife was as difficult a delivery as the two following turned out to be easy. But all went well, and the proud father staggered exhilarated out of the maternity unit, phoned his best friend, the dentist in Älmhult, and said "Brother, you must now join in on something that has never happened in my home and won't happen again. When we've drunk a toast and finished our drink, we'll do what the Russians do—throw the glass over our shoulders against the wall."

Ingvar Kamprad was happy.

Peter, the first heir, had been born.

The other two sons appeared at two-year intervals, and the primary school teacher became a full-time housewife in Älmhult, while Ingvar was absorbed in the constant building of his empire.

Afterward he would say that the price was far too high, and that he has never really been able to forgive himself for not being around more as a father, for having become largely a business father and letting their good mother create a home, listening to the boys and giving them an ethical base.

In one respect, he has tried to compensate. From the moment he took his family and IKEA abroad, Ingvar kept on thinking about his ambition not only to protect his children from becoming involved in bitter inheritance battles but also, if necessary, to teach them so that one day they would be able to step into the company. Inherit but do not destroy it—that was his motto.

So he constructed an ingenious system that protected his creation, IKEA, from every conceivable horror and guaranteed the company the possibility of "eternal life," if there is such a thing.

Looking into his feelings about these matters is a delicate matter. Who can dissect other people's motives, dreams, and anxieties in matters concerning their descendants? Who dares have an opinion on a powerful capitalist's visions of the lifework he wishes to leave in safe hands?

The founder's fears about one point were nevertheless unmistakable—he wouldn't have time to finish his work before the boys were mature enough to take on the responsibility, should they want to. Over recent years, blood ties had come to play a more important role for the aging Kamprad, perhaps greater than he had once thought.

Today Ingvar Kamprad truly hopes and desires that his sons will be involved in running his empire in the twenty-first century. Not at any price, and not that he has ever promised them anything, but he has increasingly and purposefully attempted to make sure they are brought up to their vocation.

The sons have been pleased to be part of the plan. In ruling families, the kingdom is always the central daily subject of conversation—indoctrination begins at the breakfast table and continues into the darkness of the night. The Kamprad boys are used to the stream of foreign visitors, to deals being made at the worn old table in the fishing hut, to life being all about IKEA. All three of them—Peter, Jonas, and Mathias—have for many years now tried out various activities within the business, each adapting those activities to his talents and temperament but in principle following Ingvar's desire, as he puts it, "for all three to have an overall view."

They have worked in different parts of the world—in the Far East, Poland, and Canada. They have shadowed their father over a year's intensive training, not least in the art of judging stores. As this is being written, Peter is a manager, Jonas has established himself as a designer (with several products of his own for IKEA) and purchaser, and Mathias is extremely interested in the range of goods; his next dream is to manage a store.

They are serious young men who think before answering, careful to keep a low profile. They avoid political questions, but "their hearts are probably mostly to the right," while at the same time all of them distance themselves from "wild capitalism." Two of them have children; one is a bachelor, one is married, and one lives with a woman from—well, guess—Älmhult. They have previously agreed not to be interviewed or to be photographed together. There has been talk that the risk of being kidnapped (they would be recognized) is a reason, but their aversion to publicity stems more from a desire to nurse their modest image.

Showing humility is all part of the durable platform for a Kamprad upbringing. The Smålandishness is genuine, just as their inherited thrift is. Their personal simplicity of manner is a copy of the genuine lack of affectation in both their parents. Their varying brilliance in many languages (Danish, French, English, and German) was a result of leaving Sweden. However, they complain of not knowing any language properly and ask for help when they do not grasp certain words. What they have mastered perfectly, however, is "Ikeanish"—the words and currencies used within the company, IKEA's own dialect.

Living as billionaires, if only on paper, and being multinational heirs, they do not reveal any extravagant habits. On the contrary, like any ordinary citizens, I hear them talking about "saving up" for various things. Indeed, the motor boat they keep in Älmhult was purchased secondhand and after much searching around south Sweden. The art of haggling and arguing over the price they have learned from above.

One of Peter's hobbies, riding his Suzuki Savage (he also parachutes), looked like it might end in disaster a few years ago when he broke his leg so badly that he had to go through a series of difficult operations. This shook his family in more ways than one. He stubbornly went on working at half-speed, and on crutches.

Jonas is an enthusiastic musician who used to play drums in a band in Älmhult and Lausanne and likes to practice on his electric drums in his small city apartment. Mathias, the youngest—like his father, snuff under his lip—studies a great deal (ethics and morality at the moment) and likes fishing. They are much like any young men, with the difference that they were born into a life of potential responsibility that they have not chosen but would probably exchange for anything else only with considerable anguish.

Peter, thirty-four, is an economist, and Jonas, thirty-two, a designer. Mathias, twenty-nine, has defied all attempts at formal schooling but has worked the longest in the business, lately in Habitat.

So few IKEA staff have had such a multifaceted internal training as these young men have, from the sweaty warehouse up to the chilly management level. In INGKA Holding, Jan I. Carlsson (a member of the board and a head of personnel) has been given a special mandate to keep an eye on the management training of the boys, alongside their father. The man the boys themselves rely most on is Per Ludvigsson, the Red Group eminence in Brussels.

I have had one or two very long and very frank conversations with the Kamprad brothers, in Småland and in Humlebæk. They have emphasized their desire to remain discreet. So the edited version of several hours' conversation in the next section is to a certain extent anonymous, the various answers not linked to any particular brother. There are other reasons as well to be oblique: their internal power as the company's most exposed trainees is not detailed to any great extent but is nevertheless a capricious factor for in-house interpreters looking for signs. For the time being, they should be judged as ordinary, though slightly special, employees among what will soon be thirty-eight thousand others.

Yet their opinions in these summarized conversations provide a picture of the personalities that, in the spirit of their father, may come to manage IKEA for decades ahead. They are heirs to one of the largest furniture companies in the world, run in foundation form, but they are also the very rich young owners of the large home furnishing company

Habitat. Each of the brothers naturally also manages his own fortune, but their involvement is modest.

Everything else in their lives touches IKEA—and IKANO. Ingvar Kamprad regards his sons with a mixture of uneasy tenderness and professional distance, as only a father with ultimate responsibility for global business groupings can. Although he points out that he has also made an agreement with his adopted daughter that places her outside his business interests, he admits unconditionally that he is ambivalent concerning his expectations of his sons.

This has several roots: in time, in the brothers' characters and knowledge and wills, and in Ingvar's own ambivalence.

> I would hardly wish for the next generation to be as tied to their work as I am. I don't want them to relinquish the pleasures of life, such as leisure time, golf, a quiet family life, and so on. Not one of my sons wishes to tie himself down in that way. And if he does, then presumably his wife does not. At the same time, my sons are noticeably keen to acquire a thorough training before they themselves feel they can take operative responsibility. But before they have gone through the necessary phases, I will have grown old.
>
> Take Peter—he, for instance, needs to learn the weaknesses of our product range. He must spend some time in Älmhult to know the company and be able to do something well. Mathias must learn the job of the store manager thoroughly before his training is complete. Only Jonas is ready, in the sense that he has a training he himself stands for, one that can be of direct use to the company.
>
> Several models of my sons' participation in the management have been discussed, all of them with pluses and minuses. In one instance, there could be room for a Kamprad on the second level as deputy managing director, and the brothers could be considered to relieve one another at certain intervals. In another model, since we have three different branches (the

Red, the Blue, and the Green Groups), the sons could be responsible for one each but meet at the crossroads on the management level in the other two branches.

My hope is to see the boys placed in positions they feel they
are capable of managing. All of them have potential on different
levels—Jonas with his sterling experience of production conditions, Peter with his aptitude for structure and organization,
and Mathias with his feeling for marketing and totality.

I don't want my sons to compete for glory. So I have to
pinpoint someone, sooner or later. If none of them regards the
matter as I do, then I shall have to recruit someone internally.

However, it is not really up to me to dictate the oath my
sons will eventually have to take. The operative leaders of the
organization will have to do that. If they say no, you wouldn't
be able to manage that job, then the son in question will have to
find something else.

The company's number one problem is the lack of prospective leaders with experience in the entire IKEA field: production
(where everything begins), design/purchasing/range, marketing.
Staying on top of all of these divisions is a complicated process
that IKEA's future leaders, as I see it, must master. To manage
all of it you have to know the details—that is my philosophy.

I myself have now left the chairmanship for seniority
reasons, both in Stichting and in IKANO, and am reduced to
"adviser," for such are the laws of Holland. Perhaps I can
remain somewhere else in the organization—as chairman in
another country, as a practitioner somewhere else. Outsiders
may say that our organization seems odious when so active a
person as I am rushes around erecting trip-wires for the director
of IKEA. But all that is based on a rational decision between
him and me the moment I left the daily operation of management. As long as I have the energy and am capable, I shall take
part in matters concerning our product range and continue with
my work on the buying side, where I feel particularly at home.

Can I keep myself from interfering?

I think so. When something is wrong, I find it difficult not to react, but when things go well, no one is happier than I am not to have to react.

Conversations with the Heirs

I remember the moment very well. I must have been twelve, and he came home late one evening and told us he had given IKEA away. Then he explained how he had managed to keep the power in his hands and so could make the key decisions, but that we no longer had any money.

At that age I understood only the word *money*. It stood for Saturday sweets and pocket money. I was appalled. What has Dad done? Haven't we any money left?

Who are the Kamprad sons?

All three of us have been brought up as typical Kamprads. We've learned a tremendous lot from Ingvar, his way of thinking, his thrift, stubbornness, his closeness to the ground. From Mother we've learned to care, and the ability to see through people—can you trust them or not?

We were trained to handle money very early on. Dad asked us, "Are you really sure that's what you want to buy? Have you thought carefully about what you want and if it's worth it? If you buy that, you'll have nothing left." That's how he went on.

What did your father say about the future?

We would like him to have been clearer, but on the other hand, we don't always know what we want ourselves, and so it's difficult for him to be clear. Peter once said to Dad, "Be impatient if you want to be, but then you must do something about it—say what you expect of us." Father's perhaps rather too headstrong, while we tend to sit on the fence. That makes him seem unclear.

We like listening, we're polite, and it's awfully difficult to assert yourself when he's around. Even if you think one of his ideas is not so good, you wait until after the meeting to say, "Now, listen, don't you think we should do this instead?" If you're in a meeting with five or six people and Ingvar, then everyone waits to hear what he has to say, and it doesn't make any difference what you yourself were thinking of saying.

But today are you prepared to take over the responsibility?

First of all, we have an important inheritance to manage. We could go off to the moon instead, or do something quite different, but that would be a pity. There are so many opportunities. So our task is to refine our inheritance, to improve it.

We don't really know how we are going to tackle this. We'll be in the firm somehow or other, but just how, we don't know. If Dad had been ten years younger, then we would have had time for internal training and he would have been able to place us wherever he thought appropriate.

But every day Ingvar increases the pressure on us—"Now you must take over." That started a few years ago. He has always wanted to prove to himself that he is just as strong as ever, but he knows that at some time he has to slow down. Things often happen in people's lives when they are between seventy and eighty.

When one of us wanted to work in America, Dad protested—that was too far away to keep close contact. We all work in different directions and seldom meet. So we rarely talk about it, but we have to be prepared should anything happen to Ingvar.

What do you think will happen if "anything happens"?

There is a precise plan that is to be set in motion "in the worst case"—set up for the next hundred years—that dictates exactly who is to do what. Ingvar would be replaced by three or four people wherever we or our representative could step in and manage on different levels. Let's call it a kind of senior family council. Then there's sure to be an awakening. We would have to decide, all three of us, where we could be most useful. None of us hankers after Anders Moberg's job.

Only one thing is quite clear—we'll be close to management. We have confidence in most of the top people. If Ingvar got on well with them, then, so will we. Choosing what we are to do later is complicated. We can't just bluff our way through. We need clever advisers to put us on the right track, and we have them.

How long have you been prepared?

Ingvar has talked about preparing for his death since 1976. I remember the moment very well. I must have been twelve, and he came home late one evening and told us he had given IKEA away. Then he explained how he had managed to keep the power in his hands and so could make the key decisions, but that we no longer had any money.

At that age, I understood only the word *money*. It stood for Saturday sweets and pocket money. I was appalled. What has Dad done? Haven't we any money left?

Only when you're older and earn money of your own do you realize you can't just go on consuming. Then you know that money is about being able to buy a house, a car, a boat, and being able to afford to have a family and a dog for the children. Then when you've done all that, there's nothing left but what is unnecessary. When you've realized you can have control and influence but escape the trouble of dealing with a gigantic bank account, then you've matured and understood that money is nothing—it is power that is important.

Ingvar was probably like us when he was young. I bet when he was thirty and had bought his Porsche, then he was damned pleased and perhaps wanted to buy an even grander car next time. He simply wanted more and more things. Then when things went so well that he had everything he needed, he seemed to shut himself up inside himself. He became like a closed circle that wasn't going to let money run out of the company. He wanted the company to live much longer than himself. IKEA became an entity with a life of its own.

Today, as adults, we know how to appreciate the solution Ingvar came to for the company structure. It's built for our safety, although the company is not entirely protected from us. No high position can keep us from making the wrong decisions and thus risking what has been built up. But it feels good not to have to be burdened with a whole lot of ownership.

Can IKEA go on infinitely growing?

The possibilities are great if we look after the concept. Size in itself doesn't have to be an aim, but it is clear that it gives us a chance to be stronger, make better purchases on a large scale, and so on. To say that IKEA is now big enough would be wrong. It would take away motivation and internal strength. IKEA requires energy, confidence, and strength to grow. On the other hand, we can call a halt for a few years to gather strength. A great risk is that it is more fun to occupy yourself with new projects than it is to go on the weekly round of a store.

Can you already influence IKEA today?

Yes, but then, so can our warehouse staff. That's what's good about our system—that every sensible employee willing to produce ideas says what he or she thinks. Every one of them has a productive mind, and together we can develop an immense capacity. Management is otherwise the forum in which we brothers can express ourselves and be heard. But in everyday life too, at coffee breaks, you can be an influence. Everyone who wants to can. Today we're on the board of Habitat, IKANO, and Inter IKEA Systems. We also sit in and listen in on the other heavyweight boards in order to learn.

So is it on the boards that you'll be most active?

The board is good for an overall view, but just sitting on it and not having any concrete knowledge of the floor is not so easy. I noticed that in IKANO, for instance, when some insurance matters cropped up, I was totally useless.

What are you hoping to do for IKEA in the future?

It would be ideal to open twenty-five new stores in a year. That'd be amazing, because it would mean we had done our jobs well. I don't know whether we can do that in a year, but it would be a wonderful yardstick.

My *highly personal* aim is to take over a store as manager, which I would do for three years. I like being in stores and have written several memos on possible improvements.

My favorite stores are the small ones. The products are closer to you, the passages more narrow. Cinesello Balsamo in Milan, which is horribly cramped, is really quite wrong from the point of view of the concept. But you can find your way around it and enjoy the experience, thanks to a whole lot of intelligent solutions made by the salespeople and the interior decorators.

Is franchising to outsiders the future?

Probably, and that entails new major responsibilities and an awareness of what we can do and what we want. Can we support this project? Can we acquire goods for everyone? If we manage things badly centrally, then someone else will have to pay out of his own pocket.

So far, IKEA International has had first pick. In the future, a store may even be run by anyone—as long as it is someone judged to be strong and competent.

What does it feel like to be so rich?

You don't really think of yourself as rich, a fact that people find hard to understand. There are people who wear elegant jackets and have large cars and a need to show they are someone. But if you really are someone, you have no need to show it.

We don't live a life of rich men, any of us, and none of us wears a tie. I just happened to have bought some new shoes, but I dress less well than the average man on the underground. I like that.

Who are your friends? Can a billionaire have any real friends?

I have close friends I can talk to and even cry with, friends from home in Lausanne, quite outside my work. Whether you can rely on friendship when you are rich depends on how you cultivate that friendship. If you are yourself, honest, and can imagine giving someone a helping hand. . . .

Friendship can't be based on getting something back. But I know several people who would stand up for me in a difficult situation, and several I would do the same for.

How do you want IKEA to be?

Nowadays I like it when Ingvar says we should try to make daily life better for most people. During my early training, I thought that was some damned marketing trick; a company has to earn money, full stop, that was nothing to hide. To survive, a company is to hand out as much as it can to its shareholders, that's what it's about. But we also have to ask ourselves what values, what morality guides us. We must know what culture we stand for. We must be decent and honest. It's important to make it clear in our culture how we are to act in other countries.

It's to contribute to development in the field of housing that we give reasonable opportunities for people to grow wherever we have partnerships and business relations. It's about developing our competence, checking that things look good wherever we produce. We don't just look at how cheap and reliable supply goods can be for the right quality, but at whether we can influence a producer so that the canteen in which the workers eat is pleasant, so that the workers have a quality of life. We make the environment a top priority because we have to respect the quality of life of future generations within the commercial limitations reality has given us.

Things such as child labor come into play here. The problem is more a matter of development for the country in question than for us. The debate has been slightly twisted. But we nevertheless have some responsibility, not least by telling people how things are in those countries and how we regard our business contacts. We do not want child labor, but why does it exist at all? It's not enough to say just that we don't want it. We must also ask the question of what happens to the children if we abandon an order. Are they to go back to selling themselves on the streets instead?

All three of you live abroad. How are you going to maintain what is "Smålandish"?

IKEA of Sweden (IOS) is still in Älmhult and decides the product range, so that means a great deal. We have often talked about it being too expensive, and it can be difficult to get qualified people to move there. Designers from Italy are perhaps unwilling to live in little Älmhult. But it's important that Älmhult is a model and decides the pace, so that it doesn't turn into a sheltered workshop. We've met people who think that in Sweden everyone is always taking a coffee break and that we

Swedes are a bad example for everyone who comes on a visit.

Yet there's nothing better than Älmhult. Despite certain problems, I can't imagine anywhere better. It's true that the work pace in Asia is faster. We take a break, yes, but while working. And Älmhult, like nowhere else, has furniture know-how. Nowhere else in the world is there such a tremendous fund of knowledge contributing to IKEA's future.

It *is* true that decisions take a longer time in Sweden. It takes up to two years to get a product out in IOS and only one in Habitat. The difference is that Älmhult demands that everything is perfect down to the smallest detail. What you lose in speed, you gain in superior quality. IKEA puts more energy into quality today than it did ten years ago, as it does on the linking of design to production.

What have you learned from Ingvar's management style?

He's good at "speaking to the masses," at getting people with him. He hasn't really ever let us in on the conversation. We've had to find our own ways. He's put us under unnecessary pressure, because we're his sons, but on the board we are met with the same respect as others are.

Ingvar has changed over recent years. Before, he used to discuss an idea until everyone was in agreement. He can listen and change his opinion if he hears a good argument, but he himself finds the umpteenth argument for whatever it is he wants just right. I've never heard him say, "Now, do it like this even if you don't want to." His strength earlier on was that he was always careful to market his ideas in-house.

In recent years, Ingvar has grown more impatient because things haven't turned out the way he wanted them. He is disappointed when nothing happens in the case of something we've all agreed on. He is angry because he knows he can't always be there checking up on things. There isn't enough time, which is why he is so impatient. It's a matter of getting a lot done. Now.

He probably treads on lots of people's toes. While the founder of the company is still alive and active, a manager capable of being decisive has to be a strong person. Ingvar likes to interfere; he sees something that doesn't fit the basic concept, and then, of course, there is a terrible fuss when he objects. That is not always easy to take, but it really is part of a kind of learning process when the new generation is to take over from the founder.

Sometimes Dad goes too far in his criticism of others. I've asked several times, "Was it really reasonable to send such a brutal fax? Don't you antagonize people?" "You're probably right," Ingvar would say, then work all night canceling the fax before the recipient has time to read it, then sending another friendly one instead. He is also aware that on some occasions he is bad-tempered, so he makes an effort to be more diplomatic.

Who will produce the visions in the future?

We can't see that person at the moment. The creepy thing is that many of our new projects have been initiated by Ingvar himself. That's a bad omen. We brothers will have an extremely important part to play over and above the operative management, and we will have to find new ideas, put them down in print, and send them out to the entire organization. It is expected that there will be Kamprads in the IKEA management, otherwise IKEA's soul will not survive.

We will be instrumental, that's our task—to find and, between the four of us, set up strategies. I think that will work.

We are much more cautious than Ingvar and will have to find another management style. He doesn't see it himself, but when he says something, it becomes law. As a result, problems have arisen that he didn't anticipate. We will be forced to have our own feelers out, forced to find different ways from Ingvar's, to learn to listen.

We are trying to learn to be creative. To do what Ingvar has done—convince people and let others do the rest. Sow the seed, water it a little before it starts growing.

What if you don't agree among yourselves?

Within the organization is a man in whom we have the greatest confidence. That's Per Ludvigsson, head of the Red Group in Brussels and a key player when Ingvar one day leaves the stage. He will never be visible from the outside. He's the gray eminence in whom we very much believe. Sooner or later we three brothers are bound to think differently, so then we rely on him to modify and find good solutions.

What to you is "typical IKEA"?

I think it's the driver's seat we found at a tractor manufacturer's in the Czech Republic. We sell it as a chair now—one of those small bottom–shaped pressed metal chairs with holes in them . . . quite cheeky. It is probably manufactured in a tremendously simple way. Bing-bang, a kilo of metal, and it's finished. The fact that it became a chair is "typically IKEA." The same thing was repeated with bicycle saddles that became three-legged chairs.

A designer once showed me an idea that I didn't really understand. I said it was a really good bench and table. "Bench and table?" said the designer. "Can't you see they're storage boxes?" But a bench and table came out of it. I saw something quite different from what he was showing me. There are hundreds of examples of products in which we began at one end and ended up with something quite different.

That's typically IKEA.

A Quiet Moment on the Board

Some people have a need for their smallness
in order to feel. Others demand their great-
ness. Yet others need you for their disguise.

—HENRI MICHAUX

It was October 1986, the place was the headquarters in Humlebæk, and it was time for the annual accounts to be presented at Ingvar Kamprad's last appearance as company director. The turnover had, appropriately, just passed ten billion kronor ($1.25 billion), and Ingvar's young successor, Anders Moberg (thirty-six at the time), had recently taken over.

But Hans Gydell, the equally recently appointed financial director, remembers the day for another reason: it was the first time INGKA Holding BV was able to report profits of over one billion.

Should it be champagne and pâté de foie gras?

Applause as the curtain is raised?

Should the board be showered with flowers and bouquets?

They all waited for the company director's comment. He finally spoke and said, approximately, "Gentlemen, may I suggest a minute's silence—so we can feel our satisfaction."

That is what happened. Ingvar Kamprad is always the same. Never boast, always show humility, take nothing for granted, always think about and prepare for bad times ahead, never let anything go to your head—deep down in the marrow of his bones is the conviction that success is the worst enemy of success. Many years later, after yet another brilliant balance sheet, he would give the deputy managing director some homework for the next board meeting—to present a horrific scenario of a profound cash flow crisis.

But as Hans Gydell was later to say apropos of 1986: "If the same principle were applied in future to mark good profit years, there would be total silence at board meetings."

At another INGKA Holdings annual accounts meeting of the board in Helsingborg in November 1997, Ingvar broke the long silence that should have arisen (if we put it that way) and started applauding. He had very good reason to do so, and his delight seemed to come straight from the heart. He was both proud and happy. With something like a tiger's leap, the entire company had hurtled forward. Compared with the previous year, the turnover had increased by over 20 percent to almost 46 billion kronor, the net financial result (before tax) to 15.5 percent, or over 7 billion.

The result after tax was 5.4 billion kronor—an 11.8 percent rise in turnover.

Over the year, the labor force had increased together with the turnover, from 33,400 to 37,500 employees, while at the same time costs had shown a relatively downward trend.

How is an outsider to regard these results? Are they typical of IKEA? Are they unique? What do they really reveal?

In the children's pages of weekly magazines there is sometimes a "connect the dots" puzzle—an image with several scattered numbers. Children draw a line from one number to the next and eventually a profile emerges of perhaps a bear or a horse, a wolf or a castle. Reading the annual financial statement for INGKA Holdings, it is as if the numbers draw the contour of a personality—Ingvar Kamprad himself.

Or as he prefers, the picture is an outline of a very special company spirit.

The profile of the annual accounts on August 31 for the financial year 1996–97 was in itself a demonstration of strength and energy. This does not mean that INGKA Holding—in everyday language, the IKEA Group—had shown mediocre results previously. As an average for the last five to ten years, the results before tax and net financial items had been over 12 percent—a bit below 8 percent after tax. But when Anders Moberg solemnly presented the figures for what was the company's best year ever, in a typical IKEA manner he and Gydell swiftly pointed out the "extraordinary" circumstances that had contributed to this success.

Most obvious of all had been a positive currency and rate-of-exchange effect that could be calculated to about 650 million ($81 million) and an unusual restraint in investments in new markets. But no strokes of fortune in the world could hide that a series of factual strengths also constituted the basis for this great leap:

- In 1996–97 investments in Eastern Europe at last began to produce a return after years of hard work.

- At the same time, the United States turned from large deficits to positive figures—also after a great deal of blood, sweat, and tears in the 1980s.

- The trends of rising costs were broken; awareness of simplicity and thrift, the basic IKEA virtues, was returning.

But perhaps it is the sum total of many years' activities that was the major factor. By drawing lines, as children do, from year to year, Hans Gydell (Anders Moberg's running-mate as deputy managing director at IKEA's office in Humlebæk) sees the shadow of the founder and his economic company morality.

With a liquidity of 20 percent and a solvency of 50 percent, both IKEA and Ingvar Kamprad reveal themselves. The accounts simply reflect the message in *A Furniture Dealer's Testament*. For thus have the laws been since the birth of IKEA:

- A good cash reserve must always be ensured.

- All property must be owned.

- All expansion is to be largely self-financed.

- There shall be no boasting.

Look at those basic nuts and bolts. They have held up the wagon on a journey lasting half a century and are not the slightest bit rusty. Ingvar Kamprad bought his first "store" for thirteen thousand kronor in cash when he opened his furniture exhibition in an old joinery in Älmhult in 1953. In the same way, twelve years later, he found the seventeen million required to build Kungens kurva, the flagship that set the course for the future. Just when other companies might go into crisis or demand a new share issue or go to the bank to borrow, that is when IKEA has always had access to its own capital. Only currency restrictions and an intractable national bank prevented the first continental store (Spreitenbach) from being paid for in cash—a temporary loan of five million kronor ($625,000) from Nordfinanz Bank untied the knot at the time, until the Swiss profits could repay the debt.

Independence is a sacred economic principle for the founder.

Very occasionally, for legal reasons, IKEA has had partners (as, for instance, in Brussels and Tokyo), and it has always been uncomfortable. On the other hand, stores are financed up to 70 percent during construction, but IKEA never uses stock as security.

IKEA today owns 139 stores all over the world. Calculate for yourself: a large modern store costs between 150 and up to 300 million kronor (and some are approaching half a billion). They are written off at 4 percent per annum and are included on the balance sheet as a successively increasing hidden reserve.

Naturally the company would easily be able to capitalize on all of these huge possessions by, for instance, going public on the stock exchange with the properties. Nothing could be more alien to Ingvar Kamprad. Owning the properties perhaps slows the pace of growth but provides security: "No landlord can come in ten years' time and raise the rent by 20 percent."

This emphasis on ensuring liquidity and solvency demonstrates how Ingvar the farmer's heir has wed Ingvar the businessman's heir, a strong dose of both moralities producing optimal freedom. The farmer knows from bitter experience that an unfree base is his enemy, and the merchant knows that as long as you have money in your pocket you can take the golden opportunity by the forelock.

"It is this policy," says Anders Moberg, "that means we can afford to take risks, wait out difficulties, and await progress in a country like Poland or the United States. It is the long term that matters. As long as we look after the base—that is, the concept, the actual trade—we are safe and at the same time have a margin to take a business chance. So I can go to a store and hear that the sites next door are being bought up. "Why don't we at once go in and ensure room for expansion?" I say. "We'll need that land in a few years, after we've continued to grow, so let's strike now. We've got the money."

At IKEA, swift decisions that in other companies would make accountants pale are made by turning to ample reserves for unexpected expenditures. Nowhere in the accounts is there any sign of recklessness—here a reserve is being put aside, and here a fortune is being built.

"There's quite a lot of Småland in the accounting," say Moberg and Gydell, describing it all with controlled understatement. "IKEA is like the farmer who has just done his sowing: the year's harvest is behind him, and the seed corn already in the ground."

This is the result of decades of the simple life now resting safely in the coffers that the various groups in the business administer, today amounting in total to twenty billion kronor in funds. There are thoughts of coordinating these considerable fortunes more effectively.

What are these reserves for?

Early on, I learned the old rule that 1 percent in reduced sales produces 10 percent in reduced profit. We are making good money today, but supposing we hit a head wind for a few years? With a 15 percent drop in sales, over half our entire profit would be wiped out. That's why volume means so much to IKEA. I have been appalled when we've played our war games in Humlebæk and soon realized a positive development can turn into the opposite.

That is why we push cost awareness at all levels with almost manic frenzy. Every krona that can be saved is to be saved. That also marks our view of taxes.

Once at a conference I saw the term "noncreative costs" and wondered what it meant. The answer I was given was taxation, of course. And whatever attitude you take, tax is and remains a cost. In Sweden corporate tax is 28 percent—the IKEA group last year paid 23.5 percent on the annual profit, no dramatic difference even if small percentages also produce large returns on our level.

The income of the Inter group is based on license fees (3 percent on sales, minus costs). The money does not belong to any special country, and so we do everything to minimize the tax. That occurs via one company in the Dutch Antilles (where Habitat also is), which taxes dividends lightly. This is even more important as the Inter group in time has administered its assets skillfully through fortunate stock investments.

Holland has advantageous conditions for holding companies, and the link between Holland and the Antilles is normal for both small and large international companies. When I bought my many companies in connection with leaving Sweden, some companies were already registered in the Antilles—it seemed to be standard—and both Inter and IKANO also have this link. We are in good company.

The IKEA business view of taxation is simple and straightforward. We follow all the laws and regulations, but if the laws give certain reliefs, we exploit those opportunities. We are often offered tax relief in connection with establishing ourselves in a country or a province—we don't refuse that. Swedish investment funds really provide the best opportunities, allowing us to deposit part of our profits free of tax. These foundations have helped us build most of the stores in Sweden.

It is worth pointing out that tax legislation varies a good deal from country to country. Many countries now take 0 percent in capital tax, while both Germany and Sweden take 30 percent. The tendency is that differences are leveled out step by step.

Building up reserves is a fine old tradition in IKEA, connected with our need for independence and freedom of movement. The Inter group, with its accumulated assets, by no means serves as a savings bank for the family, but as a safe and growing reserve should things at any time go badly for the IKEA business. From that perspective, it is our duty to reduce all kinds of costs—even if the cost is called tax, not least taxation that touches our international capital.

Like a mantra, Ingvar repeats that money is no aim in itself, only a means. Against the background of his philosophy, it can be seen how IKEA is taking the step across the threshold into a new century. The old founder will retire for age reasons, and a new generation will be at the head. What chance have the young leaders of making the great leap? The answer is that, whatever else, they have a financially strong company with a unique business concept to use as a catapult.

"The man lacks any ability to be satisfied," the IKEA veteran Hans Ax once said about Kamprad. And in exactly the same way, he himself never admits that he is satisfied. But what he nevertheless did perhaps grant on that drizzling November day in Helsingborg in 1997 was a reflection of his pleasure at having welded together the management team that is leading the company into the twenty-first century. Things don't look at all bad.

At only thirty-five, Anders Moberg was asked in a bar in Amsterdam whether he wanted to be Ingvar's successor, and he was then given a month to think it over. Moberg, despite his youth, had something of a veteran's status in IKEA without being one of the original gang from Älmhult. Not least, he had the right Småland blood and so had been brought up in the same morality as Ingvar Kamprad. In a typical Ikean manner, he had no higher qualifications in economics than ordinary high school competence, but he had a reputation for being a good handball player. Unbeknownst to him, he was one of the first young people to be picked for IKEA's management training launched in the early 1970s.

At only twenty-four, he was placed out in Europe, given the responsibility for an establishment in Cologne two years later, and became one of the irrepressible, day-and-night working gang of young men headed by the mythical and dynamic Jan Aulin.

Anders Moberg, depending on how one counts, has between ten and fifteen stores "on his conscience," in the sense that he set them up and got them going. With rare courage, he also refused the offer of the command of the flagship in Kungens kurva—he simply couldn't tear himself away from entrepreneurial activities in Europe.

After some considerable thought, he realized that he would find it difficult to look in the mirror if he refused the offer, and he said to Kamprad: "It'll be a greater misfortune for you than for me if it all falls apart."

All went well instead. Even as IKEA has become increasingly complex, the basic business idea appears to be more indestructible than ever. In the necessary successive process of transformation that has to continue all the time, Moberg is a leader with a low profile, consciously avoiding competition with the Kamprad legend. On the contrary, he realizes that IKEA needs its founder as long as he exists, and that to neglect his unique qualities would be almost dereliction of duty.

Between the restless Kamprad and the apparently unruffled Moberg, a division of labor has existed from the very start. The former's veto on the subject of the range is infamous; in this company, truly "the founder knows best." They also share an assistant, a post filled by a variety of young talents. This creates the advantage that both know what the other is up to. The one who has freedom of movement in all fields of the business is, of course, Ingvar Kamprad. Like a squirrel, he can leap from shelf to shelf in IKEA's vast warehouses of problems and possibilities, traditions and visions. Moberg has to see to it that the shelves are in place and that they remain intact.

The concept was born in a period when the originator's ideas, opinions, and decisions were expressed in a circle that had it all straight from the horse's mouth. Today the distance is great between the center and the periphery, and the demands for clarity in manuals, direction instructions, and decisions are proportionately even greater. It is up to Moberg to keep all this organizationally together. At the same time, as long as he is alive, the founder's task and responsibility is to distribute his favors of inextinguishable knowledge, charisma, inventiveness, and energy.

"It mustn't happen that in the growing new IKEA we get people who just do what's written in the manuals," says Anders Moberg. "We must have space for what has been IKEA's and Ingvar Kamprad's historic strength: enterprise, mavericks, new ideas." "No store is to be like any other," Ingvar once said, then added, "only with a certain uniformity and gathering of strength in behavior shall we achieve a breakthrough for our business idea."

So the younger generation is faced with the double task of defending and deepening the original recipe in the spirit of Ingvar Kamprad, and at the same time being wide open to integrating what is new and unexpected, which may grow locally in various directions in the world, or as a result of technical and political development.

Anders Moberg consciously avoids grandiose scenarios. He keeps his feet firmly on the ground and distinguishes matter-of-factly between visions that are to be realized beyond the turn of the century. "At the moment," he says,

> we're changing things in practically all of the twenty-five major stores. We don't have enough checkouts, the warehouses are too small, the restaurants are inadequate, and so on.
>
> Twenty of these major stores, all situated in capital cities, make up over 35 percent of IKEA's sales, and account for over 60 percent of profit; developing them is the actual basis for being able to realize other projects. These stores, some selling over one billion kronor, must have more parking space, more toilets, more bank machines, and a greater capacity for everything that makes shopping more tolerable for customers and keeps the wear and tear in check.

In city after city, building continues rapidly; in Chicago a mega-store is going up. Forceful consolidation is in progress. Next in importance, according to Moberg, is to penetrate every market more deeply so that competitors are kept at bay. IKEA began everywhere as a niche company, but today it has to fight with the giants for important segments. When it comes to market share, Sweden is "best" with a stake of between 20 and 25 percent. In other markets, the company usually falls below 10 percent in market share.

"But we can become stronger everywhere—we *have to* be."

The potential is limitless in a group that is expanding and developing further already conquered bastions. There is Australia, where nothing much has happened, but which is now to be upgraded (just as happened in Canada after IKEA bought back the franchise rights in the late 1970s). A new model is being discussed in which franchisees will be partners in existing stores. That could not only provide a new career route for skilled businesspeople in the company but also give a lift for entrepreneurship, without which even the best of global small companies can risk lockjaw. With a warm hand, Moberg and Gydell are handing

Africa and South America over to the next generation ("They have to have something to sink their teeth into").

> In the United States (where things are going better and better), an expensive marketing strategy demands a higher marketing cover. But elsewhere as well, the rule is, the deeper the penetration, the better the cost structure, the more IKEA can invest in the volume that is its trump card in competition.
>
> Today and in the foreseeable future, Europe weighs heaviest, with about 85 percent of IKEA's turnover. The United States and Canada have to grow at their own pace. I have great respect for the United States, their ferocious competition, their sophistication in methods and attitudes. . . . People ask us why we don't expand faster, why is it taking so long? But I reply that I think it's very good that we take our time.*

America and the Reluctant Immigrant

> Give me enough Swedes and I will build a railway right through hell.
>
> —JAMES J. HILL, LEGENDARY RAILROAD
> BUILDER IN THE NORTH AMERICAN WEST

The gentleman meeting me at Seattle International Airport on a mild January day represents, you might say, the sum of the original IKEA spirit and the new direction in which that spirit is headed, whether Ingvar Kamprad likes it or not.

In this case, he happens to like it.

Björn Bayley, a quiet, gracious fifty-two-year-old with young children and a healthy physique hinting at a passion for life, doesn't quite look the part he plays. He is really a hard-selling old-timer, who in his

---

* Anders Moberg was in springtime succeeded by Anders Dahlvig as president of IKEA Internationl.

exuberant youth was part of the renegade team that propelled IKEA's successful expansion in Europe during the 1970s. Heaven knows that he learned IKEA and its notorious *Testament* almost intravenously. Not only did he spend his summer holidays in Älmhult toiling in the stockroom and customer service. He also happened to be the son of I.-B. Bayley—the company matron who coined the names of thousands of products and served as Ingvar Kamprad's feared right hand during IKEA's first record years.

Ingvar Kamprad, perhaps because he had no grown-up sons of his own at the time, kept a close eye on his young relative. In one instance, Ingvar anxiously intervened in his life. Bayley, having barely reached legal age, country-bred in Småland and with an accent flavored by its moraine, was on his way to marry a young English girl. Kamprad warned him of such an early commitment and wondered whether a career in IKEA might not be a satisfactory alternative to consider first.

Kamprad got his way; this would not be the last time someone married IKEA.

His wedding plans scrapped, Bayley, with less than a high school education, started his exciting journey into the furniture kingdom. It would take him through both highs and lows, including pioneering work and (originally troublesome) projects in Canada and the United States and an infamous departure from the business after the inauguration of today's top-performing store in Elizabeth, New Jersey. Later, after a period of pain and sadness, Bayley's career would be marked by a remarkable comeback: in partnership with his best friend, he would become IKEA's first independent internal franchisee.

Bayley and his partner, Anders Berglund, are majority owners of the IKEA Seattle store, which, since 1994, has proved to be a huge success in terms of sales, profit, and culture. It has also made Bayley and his partner potentially very wealthy men. Already this experiment is being repeated in a Swedish store and will soon be followed by yet another partly franchised store in San Diego. This might only be the beginning of a quiet mini-revolution. As Ingvar Kamprad himself has put it: "The Seattle alternative represents the future IKEA"—in other words, a new career choice for veteran Ikeans who otherwise seem to have reached the ceiling in the company. It is a form of enterprise that will nurture the spirit in a maturing IKEA where the twenty largest stores (the mega-stores) tend to steal all the thunder and where the smaller stores need to be defended. Their staunchest supporter happens to be the founder himself.

That IKEA North America is spearheading this new era might have to do with Kamprad's complex relations to the world's largest and most sophisticated retail market. To better understand, let us look at the history.

In 1961 Ingvar Kamprad, accompanied by his old father Feodor as always, made two trips abroad—both with decisive consequences. The first journey, as we recall, was to Communist Poland, which in many respects created the immediate platform for internationalization, propelled the conquest of Europe, and became a model for using underdeveloped countries as suppliers.

The second journey in October was to the United States, the magic selling machine of the world, the dreamland for every entrepreneur. Ingvar Kamprad described himself in a letter home to I.-B. Bayley as "almost dizzy" from everything he saw of shopping centers and gigantic outlets. He and his father felt like "confused chickens" when invited to a swanky country club outside New York. In Las Vegas, Ingvar did the otherwise unthinkable—he took to the gambling tables. True to his character, however, he followed the golden rule: "Never gamble, but if you gamble, only win, and if you win, stop at once."

He bet twenty dollars and won twice that much, doubled the winnings—and quit.

Ingvar brought back to Småland two crucial impressions of the United States: first, the unforgettable impression of the Guggenheim Museum in New York. Four years later, he built the flagship store of his growing empire, Kungens kurva, outside of Stockholm, in a similar design of a homemade variety.

Second, he took back with him the feeling that the United States might not be for him or his company. As he still maintains: "The Americans have everything, an abundance of products and services. What can we add to all that?" The Old World was a whole different matter, still being rebuilt from the ashes of the war. And the developing nations later on—they all needed the Ikean concept; there the "good capitalist" could still flourish and be of benefit to the "joy and comfort of the masses." America didn't need IKEA, or so he thought.

Kamprad used to say, "The next generation will have to take care of North America," and his successor as president, Anders Moberg, did not hesitate in picking up the thrown gauntlet. But the founder's original message still influences the whole organization even today like an echo of an ancient proviso. For an associate, a trip to the United States is not as obvious as a trip to the Far East.

This feeling of alienation might have played a subconscious role when Kamprad, in the late 1970s, sold the franchising rights in Canada to some local interests, while at the same time leaving the question open regarding IKEA's future policy toward the United States. But as had happened so many times before, circumstances were playing their own game with IKEA.

The Canadian franchise holders started quite boldly, building six stores during three short years, but then they gradually and fatally slid away from the concept. They mismanaged both the company name and its customers and were close to tumbling into financial ruin before IKEA back in Europe woke up.

In 1979 the thirty-one-year-old Björn Bayley was sent to Canada, leaving a position as store manager in Kamen Dortmund in Germany. He insisted on bringing with him the controller Anders Berglund ("He is even more stingy than I am") to save what could be saved before the market, today valued at U.S.$250 million, got out of hand. The franchisees were almost too benevolently bought off ("Maybe they should have been made to pay"), the collapsed distribution of products was resumed, and one store was closed while the others were brought into the right doctrine. From that moment on, the well-grounded pair of Bayley and Berglund have been recognized as maybe the most loyal standard bearers and near-orthodox followers of the Ikean doctrine outside Sweden. As Bayley himself repeats even today: "The concept is so strong that you almost don't need to do anything but follow it."

And slowly but surely, the double-B team got Canada on the right track, just like that.

For Ingvar Kamprad, the young men's success in Canada felt like a confirmation of everything he continues to preach. His concern for what will happen to the Ikea culture is deep and permanent when stores increase in number, distant markets are penetrated, and independent bosses feel a risky yearning to try methods other than those described in *A Furniture Dealer's Testament,* Inter IKEA System's manuals, and Anders Moberg's motivating "musts" for how a store is to function (arrows marked on the floors, price tags in focus, "childish" thinking, and so on).

No wonder that Kamprad, one day in 1984, called from a telephone booth at the railway station in Hannover and asked Bayley to start up IKEA USA, leaving Berglund to manage Canada. First a store would be built in historic Philadelphia (1985), near Delaware, where Swedish immigrants first set foot in the New World. After that, as early as 1986, another store would go up near the American capital itself.

The United States has been called the graveyard of European retail. A host of well-established but naive European companies have dared the leap across the Atlantic only to have their dreams of profit dashed. IKEA, accustomed to being greeted almost exclusively by applause in the markets it had already conquered, now had to learn the bitter lesson that even a strong concept might need a little humility. It would in reality take twenty-two years—from the start-up in Vancouver in 1976 to the opening of the Chicago mega-store in 1998—before IKEA North America, now under the leadership of the former president of IKEA Sweden, Jan Kjellman, could report that all the region's twenty stores were in the black. And not until 1999 did IKEA North America pass the magic benchmark of U.S.$1 billion in sales.

One might think that this was an indefensibly long apprenticeship for a world consortium. During the starting period, stimulated by an economic boom, deceptive signals had been reported promising "instant success." Americans appreciate new ideas, and curiosity about "the impossible furniture store," which painted its buildings in the blue and yellow of the Swedish flag, seemed insatiable, especially when nurtured by the many Scandinavian descendants. Sales were exploding at the same speed as new store construction, until the situation suddenly turned really tough. Even as late as 1993, fourteen of the twenty stores were running at a deficit, and in 1996 only half of the stores were showing profit.

There will always be differing internal accounts regarding what really happened in the transition stage between Bayley and his successor, Göran Carstedt. The sometimes quietly philosophical Bayley today looks at his forced departure as "one of the best things that ever happened to me." It gave him fresh energy for a new start in life; he later invested the compensatory money he received in the Seattle store. At heart, maybe the problems were less about a personal dimension and more about time. As Bob Kay, the Elizabeth store manager, laments: "It takes time to build a name in the United States. Time must be allocated to break through the enormous amount of already existing and forever new messages." Today nine out of ten Americans are familiar with the name IKEA, but only three people out of ten connect it to furniture and home furnishings.

It's easy to compare the U.S. market to the much smaller (but for IKEA much more dynamic) one in Great Britain. IKEA first arrived in the United Kingdom in 1987 by way of a store opening in Warrington. But it took less than ten years before the British market, with its current eight stores, became the second-largest IKEA market following Germany. An unexpected kinship seems to be present between the British and the Swedish character.

While the British gobbled up IKEA with abandon, the start-up problems in the United States were many. It was difficult to compensate for the subtle differences between European and American buying habits and the corresponding differences in lifestyle. Generally the object was to grab only a small piece of the enormously large North American pie (a furniture retail market worth a minimum of U.S.$45 billion, of which IKEA today has fully $1 billion), but these "pie crumbs," time after time, appeared to be more unattainable than any outsider could imagine.

The furniture business in both the United States and Canada is split into a number of regional or local companies, while large department store chains also sell considerable quantities of furniture and home furnishings. IKEA's concept of serving the customer with "everything under one roof" by using the same suppliers for deliveries all over the world was and is (even today) such an odd and unique thought that it couldn't easily be sold to the American public. However, it was IKEA's basic range and concept that generated success in the United States, enabling it to gain popularity through innovative products and sensationally low prices. (As a customer in Chicago said during the grand opening in November 1998, "When do you raise your prices to full? This must be only introductory.")

When Anders Moberg chose the former Volvo head in France and Sweden, Göran Carstedt, as the new chief for North America, the decision not only hurt Ingvar Kamprad (blood is thicker than water and Bayley is his cousin's son), but it carried a taste of cultural transference. Carstedt came from quite a different management sphere—the somewhat sophisticated Volvo (today owned by Ford). He used a visionary language that, to many old Smålander Ikeans, sounded as foreign as Chinese to the American. This son of a retailer turned scholar was sometimes regarded as "an egghead among the peddlers," to quote an associate.

With his primary loyalty to Anders Moberg, Carstedt never became close to Ingvar Kamprad. Still, his five years of leadership (1990–95) left distinct marks on the North American organization. Not that he had enough time to color the year-end balance sheets with any triumphs; the prognoses were overoptimistic, and the market turned generally down, hitting especially hard on the important California business (damaged by earthquakes and riots in the ghettos). And not that Carstedt's organizational model was adopted (it was cut down effectively by Jan Kjellman, who reduced personnel, centralized the sales offices, and closed a few stores). However, Carstedt's feeling for the American buying culture had a decisive impact through all of IKEA. This applied from Älmhult to the boardrooms. "It was a question of translating *A Furniture Dealer's Testament* into American," remembers Göran Carstedt, "to get three thousand coworkers inspired and devoted." As his former staff member and today's marketing and sales director for North America, Kent Nordin, comments, "No stock exchange company would ever have accepted the weak development we reported in the beginning. But since long-range timing and patience is an IKEA credo, we had time to rethink and build a partly new base for survival."

Nordin, in charge of the U.S. market's product range, methodically studied one product group after another in order to determine American needs. He will never forget an occasion in the new Houston store when he suddenly got one bright idea. A woman had stopped in front of a double bed with a look of admiration and puzzlement when Nordin offered his help. Yes, the lady was crazy about the bed, but what in the world did "160 cm" mean? Nordin remembers delving into a complicated lecture on buying facts and the metric system, explaining that this was an accepted measurement of a double bed in Sweden. The woman looked at him quizzically and said: "Young man, I have no clue what you are talking about! You really have no king-size or queen-size beds?"

And she walked off.

This was an eye-opener for Nordin. In one year, the inventory of beds was changed, but not in design or quality. The change, even though it broke with the concept, was to introduce queen and king sizes. One year later, sales had more than doubled.

With the change in beds, a new range of linens logically followed: blankets, mattresses, sheets and pillows, and so on. Then ready-made curtains were also introduced (a late triumph for Kamprad, who had maintained that the same should be done in Europe—now an accomplished feat). The kitchen products, so successful in Europe, created the same dilemma. The cabinets were too short, the stoves and dishwashers were sticking out when installed; it just looked crazy. Everything was redesigned, and now even the kitchen sales are booming.

Tiny factors could acquire great importance in the decision making. The dining cutlery was perfect but missing the right kind of spoon. This was corrected, resulting in an immediate increase in sales. Couches like "Aivak," with overstuffed cushions, were introduced (in Europe you sit on top of a sofa, in the United States you sink into it) and are selling very well even in Europe. A table without ample room for an overstuffed Thanksgiving turkey plus dinner plates and glasses on either side does not have the right dimensions to be sold in big America. The typical American recliner was developed in the United States and is now to be offered on the European market. Slowly but surely, the staff in both Älmhult and IKEA North America have begun to understand the potential benefits of working together. The clash of cultures, not seen in the beginning, is now examined in detail, and the resulting decisions affect IKEA in both directions across the Atlantic.

There were some American businessmen who saw the dynamics in the Ikean concept. In California a threatening copycat alternative under the name of STØR—with a line through the "O" to indicate Scandinavian ancestry—was developed. STØR was copying IKEA from products to product names, from the store layouts to the classic playroom for children with the happy, multicolored balls to tumble around in. It even reproduced the IKEA catalog (today distributed in twelve million copies in the United States) and the parade of flags outside the store. But according to Göran Carstedt, STØR was copying only the surface.

> What they could not reach and didn't understand was the dramatic trinity of price, function, and design of the IKEA concept. Another thing they missed was the intricate network that supplies all the 150 stores with the same products from suppliers with whom meaningful cooperation exists. STØR also failed to understand the importance of the concept of democratic design and the benefits of RTA [ready to assemble], an idea they simply repudiated. And they didn't comprehend the significance of the catalog as an inspiration and a magnet pulling people into the stores.

STØR started out with commercial success and ended with a crash. Carstedt bought out their stores, which have cost blood, sweat, and tears to straighten out. The one and only serious attempt to compete with IKEA on its own terms ended in fiasco. Carstedt, today working outside the IKEA sphere as an esteemed expert in "learning companies," and still a warm admirer of his former employer (but critical of some aspects: "IKEA at its worst is like a sect"), wished to mix the Swedish flag colors of blue and yellow with some stars and stripes. This logo created wonderment inside the Swedish branch of the company, which was always skeptical about new metaphors, but it resulted in the comprehension that the United States would allow itself to be conquered only by those who made an effort to understand the American buying culture.

IKEA under Carstedt also acquired a distinctive image in a cocksure marketing strategy ("It's a big country—someone's got to furnish it") that didn't shy away from being controversial. When the ad agency head, Donny Deutsch, included a gay male couple in an ad as an example of the variety of people to whom IKEA might become important, an outcry was heard from the Bible Belt. However, thousands of cheers came from minorities, who, in IKEA, suddenly recognized a company unafraid to break with taboos.

Perhaps it wasn't pure coincidence that, during this adjustment project, the head of a profitable site such as the Elizabeth store, located near Newark Airport, had been handpicked from the department store giant Macy's. Bob Kay stands, dressed casually in blue jeans and a sweater, in the glow of a Saturday sun watching the free bus from Manhattan spill out load after load of customers. The New Yorkers are a minority among his thirteen thousand customers on a Saturday like this one, but over the course of a year they represent 22 to 23 percent of two million visitors. In addition, they have more purchasing power than any other category of customer, and they influence public opinion. They look on the Swedish furniture as the "in" thing and spread the word around.

All of these factors have contributed to the Americanization of IKEA, but that concept must not be misunderstood. When a manager calls an IKEA store in California from one in Chicago, he hears the same piece of music while waiting on "hold" that he hears in his own store. The same music is distributed to many stores simultaneously by satellite. This example illustrates how the IKEA spirit works in reality. It is the company classics that are the backbone of the store—the bookcase "Billy," the chair called "Poäng," the tealights that sell more than one million packages at an unbeatable price, the selection of office furnishings (fifty million Americans work at home). In short, "the concept" is holding its own; "Americanization" is just a fine-tuning of the instrument.

You could say that the first boss of IKEA North America, Björn Bayley, laid down a foundation of down-to-earth wisdom and loyalty on which the more visionary thinking of Göran Carstedt—who built six new stores and prepared the mega-store in Chicago—could skillfully be based. Now Jan Kjellman, the latest in charge, following a tough financial and structural reorganization, can purposefully harvest the fruits from two decades of struggle and sometimes bitter lessons. His mission is to increase market share and improve profits at the speed of two new North American stores per year.

Therefore, on an early January morning in 1999, you hear the smattering of applause in the employee cafeteria of IKEA's headquarters in Philadelphia when the young accountant Jill Matherson presents the results from the first quarter. For the first time, costs have dropped below the magic mark of 30 percent of sales; the cost increase is a smaller percentage of sales than the preliminary profit; the new Chicago store (which Kjellman, in a letter to Kamprad, refers to as "the Beauty") has reached the break-even point after only forty-five days; and Elizabeth (which the same letter writer calls "the Beast") is increasing its profit by 43 percent in record fashion. "Thank you, folks, go home and enjoy yourselves during the weekend, but preferably not any longer, because we have lots more to do before we are completely satisfied," Kjellman says in his parting words, and the echo is heard of Ingvar Kamprad's "minute of silence" in 1986, when sales for the first time reached $10 billion and profit $1 billion.

"Never be cocky in the moment of triumph. Always prepare for harder times."

"If you can only rein in your kindness, you will succeed in North America," Ingvar Kamprad wrote to the newly appointed Jan Kjellman, setting the tone right away by postponing the construction of Chicago's mega-store for two years. Together with Anders Moberg, he demanded that the new boss first straighten out the finances in the poorly performing stores in California. But when that was accomplished, what would happen with the United States and Canada? How far would the expansion be pursued? The answer was once given by Anders Moberg: "Nothing contradicts the possibility," he said, "that IKEA North America will one day produce sales and make a profit as big as today's total IKEA sales in all the world combined."

At that time, the man who, in 1961, quit betting after winning eighty dollars in Las Vegas might be ready to give up his doubts about the United States. But how could this expansion be accomplished? What moves could still be made? How would IKEA increase the profit, lower the costs, and render the logistics more effective? Elizabeth's sales figures are exploding. As the first store in the United States to pass the billion-kronor mark ($155 million) in sales, the pressure is constantly mounting, and the wear and tear on the store is great. Bob Kay guesses that yet another store must be opened in the New York area to relieve the pressure. This will assuredly lower the sales for Elizabeth, but from a current incredible level.

For the headquarters in Philadelphia, it is a question of finding a strategy that, on the one hand, facilitates physical expansion and, on the other, refines every inch of floor space without jeopardizing quality or human resources. It's an obvious worry that the turnover in some instances is 80 percent among the lowest-paid employees. Constant retraining of new personnel is costly. Here U.S. managers might be able to learn again from the dynamic pair, Bayley and Berglund, in Seattle. Not only have they lowered the turnover rate rather drastically with the help of unusual strategies, but they have increased loyalty. One move that has attracted wide attention all around the state of Washington, as well as in the media, is once a year to allow the Saturday sales (minus taxes) to go in full to the personnel. Each employee receives a percentage of sales (which last time exceeded $700,000) corresponding to their length of employment in the company. Even the last one hired gets a little something. The highest payoff to employees who have been working since the opening in 1994 has been $7,000 on this single day.

It has not been announced that this specific system of reward is to be continued in the IKEA world; however, Berglund and Bayley are determined to continue on their chosen path. "It is, after all, the employees who made our success possible." The top IKEA leaders are now discussing the Seattle experience, which has been made possible because the owners themselves can make decisions without asking permission from IKEA. What the company will decide as a general policy is an open question. Developments, however, indicate that Seattle might attract imitators, but adjusted to the cultures and profit levels of their own countries and stores.

Seattle has also introduced an interesting new management concept, with the staff-oriented Berglund leading the way. There are two bosses on each level in the Seattle store—just like Bayley and Berglund at the very top. There are two "deco" managers (Aimie Triana and Kathleen McIver), for example. This feeling of total personal responsibility for the company is believed by Björn Bayley to explain the many initiatives and improvisations, as well as the excellent profit margin and strong rate of sales, that have made the generosity toward the staff possible in the first place. "I thought I was the most scrupulous of all when it comes to saving, scraping, and economizing. By now both Berglund and I know, as independent owners, that we still have some way to go regarding managing the organization and its finances."

While the experiments in Seattle show a kind of "inner expansion" that can be contagious, a colorful chart on the wall of Jan Kjellman's office paints the ambitions for "external expansion" in North America up to the year 2004. It is a scenario implying billions in investments during a short time period. Only "the Beauty" in Chicago, wonderfully light and clear and grand, will cost close to a half-billion kronor. Midway through the year 2000, a store will open in San Francisco. In that project's "war room" in Philadelphia, you can already find exciting blueprints by Nils Anckarcrona, the in-house architect for fifteen years. To follow are stores in Toronto, San Diego, Boston, Minneapolis, Detroit, and Dallas—as well as Washington, D.C., New York, and, of course, Los Angeles.

Just a lingering note.

The last Sunday bus from the Elizabeth IKEA store has emptied its passengers in Manhattan. On Fifth Avenue across from Central Park, the Guggenheim Museum is preparing a Picasso exhibit; the public gingerly steps around packing crates. This is where the young furniture dealer from Älmhult in 1961 got one of his most eccentric ideas. Imagine building a round store where the customers take an elevator to the top floor and then, in a slow spiral, descend toward the bottom past thousands of pieces of furniture and accessories! What wouldn't they have time to buy!

Ingvar Kamprad had the wrong idea. It did not work, but the inspiration from the Guggenheim yielded a thousand times in return in other ways, and America has found a quite different value in his empire than he perhaps imagined. For no one can say how any company adventure might end. The Elizabeth store happens to be constructed on top of one of those garbage dumps that for so long gave New Jersey a lot of trouble. An exhaust pipe runs from the ground through the whole building releasing the methane gas from the collected garbage of a whole century.

But the store built on top of trash is a gold mine. So it goes.

IKEA, like all other dynamic companies, presents its own contradictions. The Beauty and the Beast. Internal and external development. The bottom line and *A Furniture Dealer's Testament*. The local against the global. Humility and grandiosity. The dream to be accepted as "good" Americans but retaining the pure Småland touch. In all of this, and in the struggle between sworn values and a changeable reality, North America mirrors what Ingvar Kamprad means by the expression "a market like any other."

But no one, least of all the Småland founder, should attempt to deny the special magic exerted on a Nordic mind by the concept of America. Here's the place where, during scarcely one century, more than one million Swedes arrived, the majority recruited from just the type of unyielding moraine for which the stone fences of Småland are symbolic. A small, poor country drained of its youth and its collected dreams. Here they often transformed those dreams into reality, and just like Ingvar Kamprad, they formulated their credo of a glorious future where most remains still undone.

That wave of immigrants has swept by; the prairie has long since been conquered. But a new wave of immigration is under way—a wave of ideas, of new thinking with which to conquer new markets and tempt new talents. As the head decorator in Seattle, Kathleen McIver explains her reasons for giving up her own business to become an Ikean: "I sought out IKEA because of their different philosophy."

Right. The new immigration doesn't spring, like the old one, from a fear of persecution for faith or political conviction or to escape poverty, but out of a belief. The new immigrants are thoughts invading minds, and if everything goes well, they will build bridges between the New and the Old Worlds.

Or like the railroad builder James J. Hill might have said, if he had lived in our time: "Give me enough good Swedish ideas, and I will build a road right through cyberspace."

But that is another story.

The Next Frontier

> To create a better everyday life for the major-
> ity of people.
>
> —INGVAR KAMPRAD, *THE LIVING CONCEPT*

> We must have confidence in the masses.
>
> —CHAIRMAN MAO TSE-TUNG, 1955

It is mid-March 1998. The teeth of Asia's stock exchanges are chattering from the most profound financial malaria, and in Beijing the Ninth People's Congress has opened. The message to the one thousand increasingly individualistic members meeting in parliament in Tiananmen Square is unambiguous and harsh: development, severe rationing, industrialization, reduction of bureaucracy, increased efficiency, unemployment.

Sometime soon after the beginning of the twenty-first century, the prophecy in Mao's *Little Red Book* will be realized: China will be one of the world's leading industrial nations. Haste is required, however, and there is a price to pay for becoming one market among others.

It is on a day in the middle of such a macro-event that IKEA's forty-eight-year-old managing director, Anders Moberg, lands in the metropolis of Shanghai to meet his future staff of three hundred in China and to inaugurate the 143rd store on the corner of Long Hua West and Zhong Shan South Road, which will also be store number one behind the Great Wall of China.

On this particular day, in the sudden heat, thousands of people are swarming along the city's promenade against a horizon of skyscrapers and cranes on the opposite bank of the river. The roar of traffic in the distance is drowned by the thunder of twenty thousand building projects, for the largest city in China is in the middle of the nervous leap that, sometime at the beginning of the next century, will make it the financial center of Asia.

These are revolutionary days for the nation with the largest population in the world. Shanghai is booming, and it is also a moment of change for IKEA.

Opening a new store in itself could be compared to giving birth to a child—a revolution in miniature, a miracle. At first, the astonishment was always great each time it occurred, but as IKEA grows and expands, it's hard to keep track of each new beginning. Yet the arrival of a new store is and remains the extreme and thoroughly planned symbol of economic vigor. To give birth to many "children" each year is thus evidence of the company's high level of fertility.

Whenever a new birth occurs, it is a great event.

The decision about Shanghai was made by the board of INGKA Holdings in August 1995 but had been a vision much earlier—when Lars Göran Peterson and Ingvar Kamprad went to Canton. For a long time, it was a question of China or Japan—which country would be most suitable for a store? For Kamprad, the decision was quite simple: "The Japanese already have most of the good things in life, but to the Chinese, on the other hand, IKEA might mean something."

In the first wave, 100 million kronor ($12.5 million) was allotted (which turned out to be quite insufficient), and Kamprad bet his managing director a bottle of whisky that Moberg would not be able to start the first Chinese store before the turn of the century. But the process went faster than had been calculated. The national manager in Beijing, Birger Lund, investigated the market and visited the homes of typical middle-class Chinese families. The conclusions were obvious: a low-price investment in household furnishings would strike a chord in "the majority of people." The basis seemed astonishing. As Kamprad said, presume that in a decade or so the Chinese middle class will be 20 percent of the population; then the market will suddenly be as large as that of Europe.

In the spring of 1997, the first store manager was formally appointed—the artistic, long-haired Canadian Peter Anderson. More money was allotted, and in October the Norwegian Erik Arneberg arrived with the very first construction group.

From all of Sweden, Erik had handpicked eighteen colleagues he particularly liked working with, experts in everything from decoration to furniture and kitchens who now formed a well-knit pioneer force, or "delivery room" (in actual fact, one of the greatest task forces ever in the history of the company).

The day after the opening, they have already begun returning home. The midwives, the anesthetists, the ward assistants have done their job, and now, as usual, the indigenous employees who have been undergoing training are to take over.

Thus, the birth of a store is preceded by labor pains as well as transports of delight. It is a concentration of IKEA's collected talents and experience and energy, and it is a demonstration that the company still "can." With obvious nostalgia, builders of other days were tempted to attend the event. Just as cabinet ministers in the old days witnessed a royal birth, they came to Shanghai, remembering how they themselves were once part of bringing stores into the world in Germany, Canada, and Sweden.

As a hostess is almost trampled while she hands out gift tokens to the first lucky 188 visitors, as sofas tip over and things are snatched out of hands, a smile comes to the face of the veteran Thomas Blomkvist, a legend from the conquest of Germany. An opening without chaos or lines, without bloodshed or fights, he thinks to himself, is quite simply not a good start.

For IKEA, this "birth" in Shanghai is more charged with symbolism than any other new investment has been for a very long time. Perhaps it can be compared with the opening in Spreitenbach—the first step out onto the continent of Europe. Just as the Swiss store became the trumpet signal to conquer Europe, it is hoped that Shanghai will mark the takeoff to an even greater milestone—winning the market of over one billion Chinese. The contract with a Chinese joint interest has already been signed to open a store in Beijing, and the future manager has been appointed. In Canton another good site is lying in wait. Moberg is open to more Chinese cities, for there is a need for five, six, or seven stores for the local market to have sufficient volume and be able to function efficiently as suppliers. The truth is that China has now been "opened," and anything can begin to happen.

This day in Shanghai in March 1998 will be described in the future as the first in a new epoch for IKEA.

But everything depends, of course, on the perspective.

Where does a trend begin? When is the first step taken toward an invisible goal? How is the birth of a new thinking calculated? When does a change of paradigm occur?

How is the future born in a company? Does it not in practice happen every day, in the dynamics of small steps?

IKEA's relations with Asia are an old love affair with more future than history.

After the band clad in red, its conductor in yellow, has finished playing its Souza march outside the shiny glass store in Shanghai, and after the Swedish ambassador has cut, not a ribbon, but a board with a Swedish flag painted on it and declared the store open (although it has actually sneakily been open for several weeks), and after impatient Shanghai inhabitants have broken through the police ranks and charged the store, the IKEA veteran Lars Göran Peterson, who has been specially invited by Moberg as guest of honor, can be seen calmly watching this chaotic scene.

On this magical day, he remembers quite a different picture. On October 18, 1977, together with a brave little Småland delegation, he had gone for the first time to a poverty-stricken China. The Cultural Revolution over, the huge country wanted to open up to the world again and was in dire need of hard currency and open communication with the rest of the world.

The Swedes had traveled via Hong Kong, then by train to Canton and the great trade fair. There Lars Göran signed the first direct order from a Chinese producer. From his papers, it appears to have been a consignment of sixty-six Oriental rugs, to the tune of 70,500 kronor, and ten thousand circular rush mats.

These orders, for a total of a few hundred thousand kronor, constitute the beginning of trade today worth at least two billion. That is the beginning of the Chinese leap that, within a decade or two, is likely to shift the center of gravity in IKEA's geography and results.

Since then, direct imports from China have grown and grown, particularly in recent years. In the purchasing office in Shanghai alone, invoicing increased by 57 percent in a single year. Anders Moberg would never mention it, but in the organization there are eager people talking more and more about doubling IKEA's turnover within five years to over 100 billion kronor.

The trend in Shanghai is heading in the same direction, as it is in the other purchasing offices in China and, it should be added, all over the region. The same song can be heard in New Delhi (where IKEA buys up to five million meters of cloth per annum and indirectly employs two hundred thousand Indians), Ho Chi Minh City, and soon two new purchasing offices in China. Everywhere purchases are to double, everywhere the potential for production that will match the future scenario is being charted.

If IKEA is to double its reach, the supply of goods according to the concept must be guaranteed, and that requirement makes Asia a key factor. The whole region is being methodically fine-combed for the best quality, the lowest price, the surest delivery, as has already been done in Taiwan, South Korea, the Philippines, Malaysia, Singapore, and Hong Kong. In the latter two places, the total is five profitable stores.

In the 1990s and the 2000s, Asia is the place.

Everywhere low prices and capacity have been sought, as once was (and still is) done in Poland, in Hungary, Romania, and so on. Everywhere the concept and the straightforward *Furniture Dealer's Testament* is being sold, for the world is full of Smålanders. In China the faithful were easily able to pick up Mao's *Little Red Book* and read: "Hard work and thrift should be applied as a general principle." Simplicity is a virtue, Kamprad said in 1973.

It so happens that on January 26, 1998, when John C. Wallace, the young American industrialist and head of the furniture company RAPEXCO, made a New Year speech to his twenty-seven hundred Vietnamese workers, he sounded like a carbon copy of his idol, Ingvar Kamprad, making his Christmas speech.

RAPEXCO had produced almost half a million chairs for IKEA during 1997. In speaking to workers paid at the most eight hundred kronor ($100) a month about the importance of quality control and on-time shipping, Wallace was describing his confidence in the company and the people.

"My greatest worry is that we will become self-satisfied with what we've done," he said. In conclusion, he paid homage to IKEA—the company had given him resources and long-term orders to increase continuously the manufacture of mostly rattan furniture. Ingvar Kamprad's ideas and trust were a major contribution to Wallace's ability to build a profitable business relationship with IKEA.

Thus, the spirit of Älmhult spreads its moraine culture of making do, of thrift and simplicity, to Asia as well. Implacable contracts are signed, unconditionally prohibiting the use of child labor and preaching IKEA's eternal down-to-earth morality. On the wall of the Dong Sheng lamp factory outside Shanghai, which supplies the Swedish furniture giant with millions of table lamps, is a handwritten text in Chinese: *Quality is our life*.

This provides some idea of IKEA's future contour. It is in Asia where ancient production methods are now rapidly being replaced by modern rationality, but still at a low price. However, the founder is reluctant to count his chickens before they are hatched. He becomes clearly annoyed when he thinks that visions have been confused with reality.

However, it is not unlikely that China will, one not too distant day, be the greatest internal IKEA market, supplied by its own vast hinterland through still unexplored sources of production and unknown supplies of raw materials. It may seem a long way off in a country where transport of a few hundred miles can take as long as delivering goods from Hong Kong to Rome.

Another day in quite a different future scenario is application of the old mail-order concept, which was the cradle of everything, via the Internet. Even China, in that scenario, could become a "minor" market.

"A glorious future!"

Those words have recurred through this book. They happen to be the very last words in *A Furniture Dealer's Testament*.

Ingvar Kamprad has achieved nearly everything he set out to do. Could he have created IKEA today?

I asked him this question many years ago, and his answer then was much the same as it is today:

Yes, but with other premises.

Far too many good products are still manufactured for the few. If you go into an ordinary optician's office, there are perhaps still lenses to be bought for eight hundred kronor, but

then there is a gap between those and a pair of truly good quality, which you'll have to pay five thousand kronor for. A large black hole exists between the very good and what people can afford to buy.

So I think it would be possible to find a variation on the same theme as ours even today. But the starting points would be different. The greatest difference is perhaps that people are too well off today to dare start anything. If you are poor from the beginning but have a good idea, then you have everything to gain and nothing to lose. But people with a middling safe salary—why should they work hard and risk money of their own for a good idea?

Perhaps this is what makes the future so attractive for IKEA in Asia in particular. That is where most still remains to be done, and where there are tremendous prospects delineated by the kind of harsh columns of stone fences that once showed Ingvar Kamprad the way. Asia is like a repetition of poverty-stricken Småland. As Mao said in October 1945:

"The world moves on, the future is bright, and no one can stop this general course of development of history."

REFLECTIONS
OF A VISIONARY

Group Portrait of a Man
and His Life's Work

I am typically Swedish. I find it difficult to
laugh without alcohol.

—INGVAR KAMPRAD

Once in the early 1950s, old Marcus Wallenberg, the famous Swedish banker, and Ingvar Kamprad, the young upstart, were at a bank meeting. The doyen of Swedish business wanted to meet the number one entrepreneur.

"How nice to meet you, Engineer Kamprad," said Wallenberg, in that formal Swedish manner.

The young Kamprad let it pass—it was the first time anyone had addressed him as "Engineer." It sounded bizarre. Ingvar had no academic background at all, and he was certainly no engineer.

They met twice more, and on both occasions Wallenberg used the title "Engineer."

Who is this man we have followed through this book? What shall we call him? Engineer? Manufacturer? Innovator? Lion Tamer? The greatest small-business entrepreneur in the world? Perhaps all those rolled into one—or something else we cannot fathom, because he is a man with so many faces.

But whoever he is, what drives him? What makes him think as he does and governs his decisions? What are his longings, fears, delights?

And how does the mutual feedback between the man and his life's work function? How much of IKEA consists of Ingvar Kamprad, and how much of Kamprad is IKEA? Have we any inkling of his motives? What does his money mean to him?

There are days when he seems a prisoner in his own system, obsessed by expanding his own house while at the same time locked in it. The day he is free of IKEA, life for him will no longer be worth living. The day IKEA is "free" of him, the company will change, but in what way no one can predict.

The head-to-foot company IKEA.

He loves it, always wants to lie as close to it as possible, and never tires of improving it, never wants to go home from work. Lack-tables, shower curtains, shelving, the "Bang" mug, a new cutting board, the "Tore" drawer units, establishing Saint Petersburg, using scrap timber as raw material, the question of an internal ambassador for IKEA, plywood in furniture, apartments in Kuala Lumpur—these are the things that matter.

He asks a thousand questions, exhorts, provokes, lets go, but comes back, encourages with a single friendly word, demolishes with a random word, hugs, kisses, and irritates with his presence. He is thrifty, sometimes thoughtless and abrupt, but toward friends he is warm and generous. He bombards his people with a thousand ideas from a bottomless store, thoughts crowding in, clamoring to get out, to be realized before he says thanks and good-bye.

> A demon in me says I have so much to do. . . . I am never satisfied. Something tells me what I'm doing at the moment has to be done better tomorrow.

Images of him rise to mind.

- Ingvar in Lausanne one Saturday morning—searching in the market for a seller of picture postcards forty centimes cheaper than the ones he's already found.

- Ingvar in the woods—looking for wild mushrooms, his eagle eye honing in on the smallest chanterelle no one else is to have.

- Ingvar on the verandah of the fishing hut on the reedy lake edge—sitting at its knife-scarred table where so many perch have been gutted and so many good business contracts have been confirmed with a handshake and a drink.

- Ingvar together with the young management trainees in Älmhult—nervous and happy at the same time, an Aristotle with his students in a peripatetic school, his upper lip bulging with snuff, his cup of coffee within reach, the future in his eyes, his massive body, his restless legs.

- Ingvar in the sauna—arguing so energetically that the sweat pours off him, more from his passion than from the heat.

- Ingvar in the store in Aubonne (or any other in the world)—eager, irritable ("What have they done with the price tag?"), restlessly happy ("Can't you take a picture of me with the children in the play area? This is what it should look like").

- Ingvar on product range discussion days—a seventy-two-year-old with the right to veto among thirty-two-year-olds planning the bestsellers of the twenty-first century, the old stallion in a herd of snorting colts.

He is not easy to sum up. Like all artists, he is many things.

He is an artist, creativity personified, with the artist's obsession, refusal to compromise, ruthlessness, eagerness, and inability to say, "That's enough, I've done my bit," for the greatest work of art always remains to be created, and what he did yesterday was never really finished.

His artistry has nothing to do with art in the ordinary sense. When I asked him where he got his taste from, he replied abruptly: "I have no taste. I wouldn't be able to furnish my own room. But," he adds, "I know others who would be able to."

"Christ," he says. "I wish I was a bit cultured. Like Margaretha. She reads novels. The best I can do is to take a few catalogs and leaf through them."

He loves to contradict what has just been said. He is his own maverick. His praise always has an emergency exit for harsh criticism, his criticism containing a bleeding heart, his laughter only a nano-tear from weeping.

The tears are as close to the surface as his sense of right and wrong, his common sense, his business sense, and his self-pity.

When he talks about his sons, great tears come into his eyes. He tells how he once slapped the youngest for acting up at dinner, and how he is still seized with misery and anger at himself for losing his temper. (Mathias says he has forgotten.)

His compounded leadership has already invoked research, books, and thousands of articles all over the world—including Miriam Salzer's excellent thesis "Identity Across Borders," produced at Linköping University and concentrating on the IKEA spirit. But few have tried to capture where he found his inspiration for leadership, how his undertakings, his position as head of the firm, and his style of leadership have been formed during his life.

He has a Janus face of leadership. He is immensely strong, almost dominantly authoritarian, and at the same time listening and flexible, almost lovingly sensitive. He is in the lead and at the same time at the rear, both captain and private. He would prefer not to be an officer, but once he is, he loves the fellowship of uniform and is as proud as a peacock to be in his local infantry regiment.

He is also the all-knowing superior, delighting in spotting knowledgeable talent in the ranks and never tiring of preaching everyone's participation in success as well as adversity.

What is rarely noted is his weakness for strong personalities, some would say "strong men," a characteristic that is particularly evident looking back on his life. He unreservedly "admires" a tremendous number of people of all categories, from leading industrialists to the in-house heroes: a Bruno Winborg at Swedwood or a Göran Peterson, the veteran purchaser. But his previous overshadowing models seem to have been his intractable grandmother and his respected, authoritarian father.

There is also something submissive, a kind of "obeyer," in this leader. "I found it easy to subordinate myself at school," he once wrote to me:

At Manhem, as the boys' house was called at boarding school in Osby (the girls' house was called Solgården, Sunny Farm), without a murmur I fell in with the quite widespread bullying. My "boss" was for a while a freckled youth called Robert. I had to make his bed, clean his shoes, and run errands for him, and I was exhorted to tell tales—which I refused, however. In the end, he grew tired of me and left me alone. My roommate, Wolfgang, refused to cooperate, and he suffered a lot of beating.

His business experiences were what taught him, gradually but definitely, to loathe all kinds of elitism and bullying. In the Communist countries with which IKEA built up close business relations, he found talk of equal rights to be pure and simple chimera. Shops just for top party men contained everything denied to the people, and in this he found yet another dimension to support his message of a better everyday life for the many.

Today IKEA expounds his philosophy in Poland, Hungary, China, the Czech Republic, and soon in Russia—all totalitarian states learning to furnish democratically.

To lead people is primarily to motivate them. In that way, it is possible to make otherwise weak-willed individuals carry out great deeds. But when it comes to my own leadership, I have perhaps been too democratic, often a little too forgiving of infringements.

How can a man who has succeeded so splendidly seriously maintain that he is insecure? Is his achievement not evidence of a certainty of action and thought surpassing the potential of most of us even in our best moments?

But Ingvar does not see himself in that light; it's hard to get an idea of what it is he is after. Perhaps he has a longing for praise, the bounty that confirms that he is the best. But there also seems to be in him a kind of genuine despair that not everything has turned out exactly as he had hoped.

"I'm such a nervous person," he said. "I have to be at the airport an hour and a half early to feel safe, and I am fearfully ashamed if I arrive at a meeting a minute late." It took him years to get over his shyness and stand outside the checkouts to interview strangers in his endless attempts to make the store into the perfect marketplace. "I have to take myself by the scruff of my neck. Now, go and speak to ten customers. 'Hello, I work here. What did you think about us?' But it was tough."

He comes back again and again, with painful self-searching and an almost bitter undertone, to his "defects," a hopeless favorite expression he uses both about himself and all too often about other people when he is dissatisfied. He wishes he were someone else, then the next moment thanks God that his handicaps are balanced by a number of good qualities. At one moment, he fishes for compliments as consolation; the next he expresses genuine pride, joy, happiness, over being what he is.

"No one exaggerates as I do," he admits one day. "You have to modify what I say."

Anyone who sees IKEA's monumental progress may find it difficult to understand why Ingvar wrestles with self-doubt. Nonetheless, still in the autumn of his years and despite his astonishing life's work, there is an outsider within him who always feels threatened, a small, naive, seventeen-year-old entrepreneur fussing over a lost öre and crying when he is misunderstood. Even today, behind this multinational tycoon is a country boy with a fierce sense of being an underdog, standing on tiptoe and peering uneasily through adult eyes: Am I good enough?

He talks about his relationship with the ex-prime minister, Ingvar Carlsson, a man with whom he occasionally had good discussions and whom he admires. He found Carlsson unswervingly honest, but what he particularly remembers is Carlsson's story about his humiliation at school when he was pointed out as a pupil receiving a grant to pay for his schooling. He described the shame of hearing the headmaster call out the names of those who could not afford the fees.

Ingvar recognizes himself as an outsider, and in that way he is one of us all. He knows what it is to be odd, to fall outside of the establishment, to feel rage against injustices. Just like his wife and sons, he has had no problem resisting the temptation to become a conceited nouveau riche. He keeps coming back with delight to an old headline in a popular tabloid: "The Furniture King Who Does Not Look Like a Capitalist."

The article describes him as a "troublesome capitalist who is far too likable"—just what he wants to be. Rebel and friend of the people, patriot and capitalist, all in the same bargain box.

The tales of the simplicity and thrift of the billionaire are more than just myths—they are reality. His total lack of external finery, grand clothes and habits, smart watches, or luxury car (he drives an old Volvo estate wagon) has become so much a part of the image of himself and the company that even with the best will in the world he would not be able to be rid of it—the consequences would be catastrophic.

As a result of this economy, no one in IKEA may travel business class, for the top man flies economy and frets if he has to rebook for something more expensive. If Ingvar changed habits, the cost structure of his empire would collapse. Bemused associates see him lugging his suitcases on the local train from Copenhagen to Humlebæk—should they help? But he rejects all assistance. There's nothing special about him. He wants to know what things are like for ordinary people. No private chauffeur, no butler, no swaggering court—Ingvar melts into the crowd.

The retiring chairman of the board of this global company has an office of his own—at the store in Aubonne. It consists of the "Signatur" knee-hole desk, the "Karmila" chair, a telephone, a mobile wall, a "Billy" bookcase, and an amateurish handwritten notice leaning against the wall that says "INGVAR."

So much for a billionaire's office.

Add a wastepaper basket, for the residues of his snuff are substantial.

At a staff lunch at the head office, he pays from his own Småland purse. When I fly, he is pleased if I buy two large packs of tax-free snuff for him at Arlanda Airport; someone whispers in my ear that a Ballantine whisky at bargain price would have increased his delight.

Håkan Eriksson, a Poland veteran, tells of how he and Ingvar arrived in Warsaw, having been booked into the Forum Hotel. "Doesn't the Grand exist any longer?" asked Ingvar. "Yes, but it's run-down," said Håkan. "The water runs out in the middle of a shower, and there are cockroaches."

"Can't we try it all the same?" said Ingvar, and their hotel booking was canceled. In the morning, Eriksson saw a cockroach slinking out of his case, and because he had to repack it, he was late for their breakfast together at seven o'clock. Ingvar greeted him just as he always greets people who are late—with a brief "Good afternoon" to emphasize that they have overslept. "Cockroaches in my room," said Håkan dryly. Ingvar listened thoughtfully, then said, "Now listen, this is really a fairly good hotel—it's not often you're allowed friends in your room."

There are exceptions to this habitual simplicity.

A retired policeman and his wife live in the IKEA-owned house they rent outside Lausanne—for security reasons and for protection when Ingvar is away. He also bought a vineyard in the south of France for cash after a great return on an investment in the Cross Air Airline. Nowadays, and as a punishment for his frivolity, he constantly worries about the profitability of the vineyard and lets out rooms to keep it going.

Once or twice he wonders whether perhaps the vineyard shouldn't be mentioned in this book, for what would people in the company say?

Not allowing himself to be arrogant, he puts himself last in the line for food at certain functions, although others urge him to go first. He simply can't.

Yet he does want to shine, just like the rest of us. He longs for acknowledgment—and more than others, receives it, from his grandmother, his mother and father, his wife Margaretha. He is so used to love that he becomes confused if he catches so much as a glimpse of the opposite.

But showing satisfaction, regardless of how well everything is going, is the equivalent of boasting and indirectly the same as the beginning of failure. The peasant's distrust of a favorable destiny keeps his feet on the ground. Yes, the harvest was good this year, but no one knows what the autumn will be like, so it is best not to take anything for granted.

When asked what really drives him, he replies, with shame: "Perhaps a kind of snobbery. Something to do with the delight in shining and demonstrating something, becoming a famous person in a special way . . . a kind of pride or vanity that conceals something else inside me."

He says he is searching for an honest answer to the question of whether it is fun making money, but he does not know if he has an answer. Somehow or other he has passed that stage.

But wasn't it exciting to make that first million?

It must have been, but I don't remember. When the first hundred came in, the first thousand—yes, of course, I must have been tremendously pleased at the time, but I've forgotten.

You can't eat money. It's one thing to be wealthy, but the driving force—isn't that what you dreamed of being able to do and that you are then able to do, for Father, Mother, for yourself or someone else who means something to you?

But in the 1950s you bought a Porsche, then later another.

Now you're describing another side of my rather hopeless life. When I started at the Forest Owners' Association in Växjö, I was twenty. My contemporaries all went off dancing on Saturdays. When I was doing national service, they all went out drinking, while I, stupid idiot that I was, went down to that basement office. Business always came first. I lost a dreadfully important part of my youth just by working all the time. Long afterward, when things were going wrong with my first marriage and from a financial point of view I was all right, I seemed to pause, and I started dancing, partying, and drinking. I needed to turn around and take something back.

That was when I bought the Porsche. But I had trouble with it, and I didn't want to acknowledge that, so I bought another, just as white, with the same red leather upholstery, so no one but those nearest to me noticed how much I'd spent.

But when I read that I am worth fifty billion, I say, "Good, good that it's gone well," but then I think, "I can't sell the foundation, and what would I do with the money if I could?"

But to be called a billionaire—I do think that's good if it's meant that I can realize a whole lot of things, not for myself or the family but for the company. Then there's a pride in having succeeded—not for the money, but for the happiness that my concept has caught on.

So money no longer means anything to you?

I hope I am being honest if I answer no. I can't be any more honest than to say that I actually don't know if I'm being honest. The company's finances are one thing, my own quite another.

Ingvar Kamprad's relation to alcohol is a chapter in itself. His wife says rather wearily and resignedly, but forgivingly, that "he was in a lousy state" when they first met—a kind way of saying "alcoholic." Strong liquor habits were part of growing up in the countryside. Before going dancing, young men used to drink *blödder,* a mixture of honey, sugar, and potatoes. Ingvar remembers this fermented drink with some distaste.

He also remembers being drunk for the first time—the result of stealing the remnants from his father's bottles in the kitchen. The boy soon passed out; his mother Berta refused to have anything to do with her son for a whole week, and Feodor gave him a serious talking-to once he had emerged from his coma.

Strong drink was an early formed habit. He states quite factually how it was when he started defining himself as an alcoholic.

It must have been the early 1960s—some mornings my hands shook. In Poland they drank constantly, before, afterward, and during negotiations.

Then I found it a good way of forgetting. I'd had a few wakeful nights, my marriage at the time was heading for a bitter end, my nerves were to pieces. Without noticing, I'd started taking a drink or two before meals.

In the end, I went to my doctor. "Hans," I said, "you mustn't tell me I must stop drinking, because I don't want to." Then he gave me some good advice. Take a rest from alcohol three times a year for three weeks at a time. First of all, you'll convince yourself you can keep off it, and second, your kidneys and liver will have time to recover.

I'd decided before I got back to the office, it would be three times a year, five dry weeks each time. Later on, I also tried six weeks, sometimes even up to ten, so perhaps I'll soon add a fourth time each year.

Against all accepted definitions, he calls himself an alcoholic who is "under control."

An old associate stopped drinking because he could no longer cope with it. I wrote a four-page letter to him to say I considered him to be on leave and he was welcome to return. He was as pleased as punch and returned. But one night he drove off the road. Despite his treatment, he had started drinking again.

It would be awful if I were made to stop. My great challenge is to be moderate, to be able to take only a glass of wine a day like other people. The problem is I want more.

The anecdotes crowd in, his image already superimposed, as images do with people who have come close to you and exposed their deepest dimensions. The man I have been speaking to for nearly a year is not one, but many.

Is he satisfied with his life?

He doesn't hear the question, or perhaps shies away from it.

From a definitional point of view, neither he nor any other Ikean says he is satisfied. "I think I've shaken hands with ten thousand of my employees," he says with a kind of pride, as if that were where happiness resided. "I've probably got time for a few thousand more."

When touching his coworkers, his illusion of belonging to an extended family is still real. Perhaps the answer to the fateful question of what will happen to IKEA when the founder is gone lies there. How much does the company's soul still require his laying on of hands, his physical and mental presence, his indefatigability, his passion and knowledge?

Just take his specialty prices. He is obsessed by prices, comparing everything—the price of gherkins, of hotels, toothpaste at any bargain market, plywood, beer glasses, snuff, and spirits. He scans his wife's grocery bills with fascination. One evening at Humlebæk, he shows me a price list several hundred pages long, the total sum of all goods in IKEA's enormous range. "Once upon a time, I knew most of our prices by heart." He says it both wearily and self-appreciatively—but also with a kind of sorrow that he is no longer 100 percent up-to-date, as if it were humanly possible to remember twenty thousand articles and variations of them.

What still remains is this incomprehensible ability to remember details in all matters concerning the company—its staff, products, and finances—while at the same time maintaining an overall view. It is a part of his masterfulness as a businessman. Has this example been infectious enough, is the pattern indelible enough that the concept of IKEA will be sustained in the foreseeable future? Who is to take over such responsibilities? Must there be someone? What will it mean the day Ingvar raises his hat and finds he can no longer decide the mood of an entire store with just a word?

An infinite responsibility rests on the shoulders of whoever is to take over this heritage.

Late autumn in Småland, cold winds coming off the water. Ingvar is walking up through the damp swaying grass, past those eternal stone walls that are on posters in IKEA stores all over the world, reminding everyone of a morality, an origin. He stops in a lovely birch grove, gentle but strong white trunks bowing politely, just low enough. "This is where I'd thought of lying," he says, walking on. "I've already spoken to the parson, and it's okay."

Later that evening, he says: "What I like in most people is humility and strength of will. Caring about things, being willing to merge into fellowship. But most of all I think I value humility."

He seems to be describing the person he wants to be.

APPENDIX A
INGVAR KAMPRAD'S
CONCLUDING WORDS

How This Book Came About

From the beginning we agreed that this
would be a book about IKEA, with me as an
appendix, and it did not turn out like that.
On the other hand, I was the only one present
from the very beginning of the story of IKEA.

I am glad now, afterward, that it didn't hurt as much as I had thought it would. I, who have never allowed an "at home with" article, was faced suddenly with a well-known author in my own home, talking about the concept, ideas, and myself. I've always tried to keep a clear boundary between my work and my private life, and I have very seldom opened the door even a crack into the latter.

I admire Bertil Torekull for his picturesque way of interpreting a story of incoherent thoughts, whims, and ideas and yet finding some kind of consistency, extracting fragments of my stories and those of many others, then making them into a description of a company and the people behind it. Now, afterward, the time has also come to forgive the author for breaking his promise. From the beginning, we agreed that this would be a book about IKEA, with me as an appendix, and it did not turn out like that. On the other hand, I was the only one present from the very beginning of the story of IKEA.

How It Came About

In September 1996, I had an opportunity to spend a few days with three of my more recent ex-assistants. They know me particularly well after more than fifteen years of close cooperation marked by an openness in all matters. I can't remember any question I haven't thrashed out with them. We have also hatched out ideas together, and most of all, I have had my own ideas critically examined and complemented by them or, alternatively, rejected.

It is no exaggeration to say that the history of IKEA would have looked very different without my assistants' wisdom, their knowledge, and, most of all, their great interest in the culture of our company—what we ordinarily call the IKEA spirit. In the 1960s, I had already learned the value of collaborating with a clever assistant; overall, I think that has been my best school.

But back to September 1996 and the meeting with the three. They had worked together with me over various periods during the 1980s and 1990s, and it now seemed we were at the point of using them as advisers. Various family matters and the question of internal and external publicity were on the agenda.

It is always difficult for parents to judge the capacity of their children. Although I have the advantage of being close to my three sons, there is, of course, a great risk of my judgments being subjective. To my great delight, all three of my sons are interested in "helping" their father. One of the chapters starts with early evidence of this. It is really very easy to hug such children.

At this meeting with my assistants, I was given valuable advice on how my sons' qualities could best be nurtured as well as suggestions for their further training.

The other great question at the meeting was about internal and external publicity. Over the years, I have written a great deal on all kinds of matters, not least on our business idea and the culture of our company, but also on many other questions of varied importance. I find writing a great labor, as I both think and write very slowly.

We at the meeting soon agreed that I should try to make a summary of whatever concerned the future in the form of a booklet for internal use, with advice to future generations—advice based on the pieces of the puzzle that I have acquired over the years in conversation with thousands of associates all over the IKEA world, and that I tried to put together into a unified pattern. I very much appreciate the assignment and only hope my abilities have been sufficient.

External Publicity

For over ten years, I have often been called on by a number of writers and publishers wanting to write my biography. I have always been very reluctant to and have evaded the issue as politely as possible. Surely no wider circle is really interested in what Ingvar Kamprad got up to as a small boy—things going badly for him at school, being shy with girls, or when young, making a political blunder that he would bitterly regret.

One of the many writers suggested that the book be written so that it could be used as study material for future entrepreneurs. That was the only time I listened properly, but I turned it down for the time being. At the meeting with my assistants, they all agreed that I was wrong. Under any circumstances, a great deal would be written about IKEA, so by cooperating it would be all to the good.

By the end of the day, I had been convinced. The book would be about IKEA and me, in that order. It was easy to gain a hearing for my view that I couldn't write the book myself. All three know I need a lot of time to produce even a short piece of writing. So we discussed possible writers and eventually decided on the man who wrote this book.

I am very pleased that Bertil Torekull took up the challenge, not only because of his great descriptive abilities, but also because of his sound judgment and wide knowledge of the business world. In addition, he knew IKEA fairly well from a few previous interviews.

We didn't draw up any special time schedule but simply established that the book should come out in good time before the turn of the century. As all three had predicted, quite a lot would be written about IKEA. So it was urgent to get started more quickly than had previously been planned.

The Three Assistants

As mentioned before, I have always been spoiled by having an assistant at my side with whom to share the ups and downs of the day, someone with whom I can discuss my own ideas and who produces his own ideas on everything from major strategic plans to minor details in the daily scramble. Wisdom and great ability to accomplish things have characterized them all. They have also been in charge of clearing up the organizational disaster that is me—no easy task, I should add.

I am naming only the three who were important in the production of this book. They are good examples of my present and previous assistants. At the appointment of my successor, Anders Moberg, in 1986, we drew up a clear division of labor between us, and we also decided to share an assistant. That has turned out to be a good procedure, making communication between us easier and certainly clearing away many misunderstandings.

Hans Gydell has had a long career in IKEA and became my assistant in the early 1980s. He really does know the art of achieving good results with small means. He became the financial director and also deputy managing director of the IKEA Group, the gray eminence behind Anders Moberg—in other words, the same role he had with me. In spring 1999, he became the vice president of the Group, next in command to Anders Dahlvig.

Anders Dahlvig, "shared" with Anders Moberg, became my assistant in 1988. He has also had a long history with IKEA. He loves simplicity and keeps an eye on our cultural matters. When Anders Moberg unexpectedly decided to leave IKEA in the spring of 1999, I was glad to see Anders Dahlvig succeed him.

Staffan Jeppsson took over from Anders in 1990. He has had "only" eighteen years with IKEA and at present is in charge of the interiors of all our stores. He is clever and efficient—a skilled organizer with great feeling for the environment.

There are, of course, hundreds of other humble and strong-willed enthusiasts in the business whom I would like to name and say something about, both down the ladder and up, many of whom I've worked with from the beginning as well as in modern times. I know we need each other, and it is together that we've built our IKEA. Few of the ideas have been mine alone. Most have been hatched out together. Perhaps that is why I have learned to be skeptical about all those desks that are so far away from reality.

While working on the book, I have had many pleasant meetings with the author, who has made me search my memory hard for details. We at once agreed that honesty was to be the key word, and that is what has come to pass. A tendency to exaggerate what is positive and what is negative lies in my very nature. Few people have laughed or cried as much as I have. The author has been a good moderator, although I think he exaggerates a little here and there when it comes to my personal contribution.

The author has, of course, had free access to our archives, which house everything that has been written over the years about IKEA—and that is quite a bit.

He has carried out admirable field work and interviewed many people, made observations of his own, and traveled near and far to IKEA countries. He has had free access to the large IKEA family of thirty-seven thousand people, to our suppliers, and also to ex-IKEA employees. In most cases, he has chosen his interviewees entirely on his own.

Naturally, he has also talked to my wife, Margaretha, who through all these years has been a particularly good adviser, not least as a good judge of people. On a practical level, she has also borne the entire burden of caring for and bringing up our children. Her skill at languages was invaluable during the period of going international—I am almost an imbecile in the field of languages.

Perhaps what I've missed most in my life was never taking the time to be with the children when they were young, except extremely sporadically. The few exceptions still remain in my memory as small islands of happiness. The author has given the children a chapter of their own in the book. That feels good.

I have also talked about my many defects. Lack of self-confidence, difficulty making decisions, disastrous organizational skills, and horribly poor receptivity are all faults I fully recognize in myself. Fortunately, Our

Lord has granted me the ability to know my weaknesses, so that I have had opportunities to compensate for them, not least in my choice of associates. I have also been given a certain nose for business and a reasonable dose of peasant common sense.

Finally, I am often asked whether when I was young I was able to predict the development that IKEA has achieved. Naturally not, although my dreams early on were both great and bold. My life was to be spent demonstrating that a functional and good article *does not* have to be expensive. That is still true today. We still have a long way to go— or as I have written so many times and said at the end of hundreds of speeches:

We are just at the beginning. A glorious future!

—*Ingvar Kamprad*
Epalinges, June 1998

APPENDIX B
A FURNITURE
DEALER'S TESTAMENT

To create a better everyday life for the
many . . . by offering a wide range of
well-designed, functional home furnishing
products at prices so low that as many
people as possible will be able to afford them.

We have decided once and for all to side with the many. What is good for our customers is also, in the long run, good for us. This is an objective that carries obligations.

All nations and societies in both the East and West spend a disproportionate amount of their resources on satisfying a minority of the population. In our line of business, for example, far too many of the fine designs and new ideas are reserved for a small circle of the affluent. That situation has influenced the formulation of our objectives.

After only a couple of decades, we have achieved good results. A well-known Swedish industrialist-politician has said that IKEA has meant more for the process of democratization than many political measures put together. We believe too that our actions have inspired many of our colleagues to work along the same lines. Sweden, our "domestic market," has become a world pioneer in that many of the new concepts have been devised right from the outset for the benefit of the many—for all those with limited resources. We are in the forefront of that development.

But we have great ambitions. We know that we can be a beneficial influence on practically all markets. We know that in the future we will be able to make a valuable contribution to the process of democratization outside our own homeland too. We know that larger production runs give us new advantages on our home ground, as well as more markets to spread our risks over. That is why it is our duty to expand.

The means we use for achieving our goals are characterized by our unprejudiced approach—by "doing it a different way," if you will—and by our aim to be simple and straightforward in ourselves and in our relations with others. *Lifestyle* is a strong word, but I do not hesitate to use it. Part of creating a better everyday life for the many also consists of breaking free from status and convention—becoming freer as human beings. We aim to make our name synonymous with that concept too—for our own benefit and for the inspiration of others. We must, however, always bear in mind that freedom implies responsibility, meaning that we must demand much of ourselves.

> No method is more effective than the good
> example.

I claimed earlier that we contribute to the process of democratization. Let me add, to avoid any misunderstanding, that this does not mean that we take a position on questions of equality—such as salary issues. Though you may say that, here again, we approach these problems from a different perspective.

Our product range and price philosophy, which are the essence of our work, are described in the following sections. They also describe the rules and methods that we have worked out over the years as cornerstones of the framework of ideas that have made and will continue to make IKEA a unique company.

—*Ingvar Kamprad*
20 December 1976

1. The Product Range Is Our Identity

We shall offer a wide range of well-designed, functional home furnishing products at prices so low that as many people as possible will be able to afford them.

Range

The objective *must* be to encompass the total home environment, that is, to offer furnishings and fittings for every part of the home whether indoors or outdoors. The range *may* also include tools, utensils, and ornaments for the home as well as more or less advanced components for do-it-yourself furnishing and interior decoration. It *may* also contain a smaller number of articles for public buildings. The range must always be limited to avoid any adverse effect on the overall price picture. The main effort must always be concentrated on the essential products in each product area.

Profile

The main emphasis must always be on our basic range—on the part that is "typically IKEA." Our basic range must have its own profile. It must reflect our way of thinking by being as simple and straightforward as we are ourselves. It must be durable and easy to live with. It must reflect an easier, more natural and unconstrained way of life. It must express form and be colorful and cheerful, with a youthful accent that appeals to the young at heart of all ages.

In Scandinavia people should perceive our basic range as typically IKEA. Elsewhere, they should perceive it as typically Swedish.

Alongside the basic product range, we may have a smaller range in a more traditional style that appeals to most people and may be combined with our basic range. This part of the range must be *strictly limited* outside Scandinavia.

Function and Technical Quality

IKEA does not go in for throwaway products. Whatever the consumer purchases shall give long-term enjoyment. That is why our products must be functional and well made. But quality must never be an end in itself: it must be adjusted to the consumer's needs. A tabletop, for example, needs a more durable surface than a shelf in a bookcase. In the former case, a more expensive finish offers the consumer long-lasting utility, whereas in the latter it just hurts the customer by adding to the price. Quality must always be adapted to the consumer's interests in the long term. Our benchmarks should be the basic Swedish Möbelfakta requirements or other sensible norms.

Low Price with a Meaning

The many usually have limited financial resources. It is the many whom we aim to serve. The first rule is to maintain an extremely low level of prices. But they must be low prices with a meaning. We must not compromise either functionality or technical quality.

No effort must be spared to ensure that our prices are perceived to be low. There shall always be a substantial price difference compared to our competitors, and we shall always have the best value-for-money offers for every function. Every product area must include "breathtaking offers," and our range must never grow so large as to jeopardize our price picture. The concept of a low price with a meaning makes enormous demands on all our coworkers. That includes product developers, designers, purchasers, office and warehouse staff, salespeople, and all other cost bearers who are in a position to influence our purchase prices and *all our other costs*—in short, every single one of us! Without low costs, we can never accomplish our purpose.

Changes in Our Range Policy

Our basic policy of serving the many can never be changed. Changes in the guidelines given here concerning the composition of our product range can be made only by joint decision of the boards of Ingka Holding BV and Inter IKEA Systems BV.

2. The IKEA Spirit
Is a Strong and Living Reality

You have certainly experienced it. You may even have given it your own interpretation. Obviously it was easier to keep alive in the old days when there were not so many of us, when we were all within reach of each other and could talk to each other. It is naturally harder now that the individual has gradually been lost in the gray conformity of collective bargaining and the numbered files of the personnel department.

Things were more concrete in those days—the readiness to give each other a helping hand with everything; the art of managing on small means, of making the best with what we had; the cost consciousness to the point of being stingy; the humbleness; the unconquerable enthusiasm and the wonderful sense of community through thick and thin. But both IKEA and society have changed since then.

The spirit is still to be found, however, in every one of our workplaces, among old coworkers and new ones. Heroic efforts are still being made, daily, and there are many, many who still feel the same way. Not everybody in a large group like ours can feel the same sense of responsibility and enthusiasm. Some undoubtedly regard the job simply as a means of livelihood—a job like any other. Sometimes you and I must share the blame for failing to keep the flame alight, maybe for faltering in our own commitment at times, for simply not having the energy to infuse life and warmth into an apparently monotonous task.

The true IKEA spirit is still built from our enthusiasm, from our constant striving for renewal, from our cost consciousness, from our readiness to take responsibility and help out, from our humbleness in approaching our task, and from the simplicity of our way of doing things. We must look after each other and inspire each other. Those who cannot or will not join us are to be pitied.

A job must never be just a livelihood. If you are not enthusiastic about your job, one-third of your life goes to waste, and a magazine in your desk drawer can never make up for that.

For those of you who bear any kind of leadership responsibility, it is crucially important to motivate and develop your coworkers. A team spirit is a fine thing, but it requires that everybody on the team be dedicated to their tasks. You, as the captain, make the decisions after consulting the team. There is no time for argument afterward. Take a football team as your model!

Be thankful to those who are the pillars of our society! Those simple, quiet, taken-for-granted people who always are willing to lend a helping hand. They do their duty and shoulder their responsibility without being noticed. To them, a defined area of responsibility is a necessary but distasteful word. To them, the whole is just as self-evident as always helping and always sharing. I call them stalwarts simply because every system needs them. They are to be found everywhere—in our warehouses, in our offices, among our sales force. They are the very embodiment of the IKEA spirit.

Yes, the IKEA spirit still lives, but it too must be cultivated and developed to keep pace with the times. *Development is not always the same thing as progress.* It is often up to you, as the leader and bearer of responsibility, to make development progressive.

3. Profit Gives Us Resources

A better everyday life for the many! To achieve our aim, we must have resources—especially in the area of finance. We do not believe in waiting for ripe plums to fall into our mouths. We believe in hard, committed work that brings results.

Profit is a wonderful word! Let us start by stripping the word *profit* of its dramatic overtones. It is a word that politicians often use and abuse. Profit gives us resources. There are two ways to get resources: either through our own profit or through subsidy. All state subsidies are paid for either out of the state's profit on operations of some kind or from taxes of some kind that you and I have to pay. Let us be self-reliant in the matter of building up financial resources too.

The aim of our effort to build up financial resources is *to reach a good result in the long term*. You know what it takes to do that: we must offer the lowest prices, and we must combine them with good quality. If we charge too much, we will not be able to offer the lowest prices. If we charge too little, we will not be able to build up resources. A wonderful problem!

It forces us to develop products more economically, to purchase more efficiently, and to be relentlessly stubborn in cost savings of all kinds. That is our secret. That is the foundation of our success.

4. Reaching Good Results with Small Means

That is an old IKEA idea that is more relevant than ever. Time after time we have proved that we can get good results with small means or very limited resources. Wasting resources is a mortal sin at IKEA. It is hardly an art to reach set targets if you do not have to count the cost. Any architect can design a desk that will cost five thousand kronor. But only the most highly skilled can design a good, functional desk that will cost one hundred kronor. *Expensive solutions to any kind of problem are usually the work of mediocrity.*

We have no respect for a solution until we know what it costs. An IKEA product without a price tag is always wrong! It is just as wrong as when a government does not tell the taxpayers what a "free" school lunch costs per portion.

Before you choose a solution, look at it in relation to the cost. Only then can you fully determine its worth.

Waste of resources is one of the greatest diseases of mankind. Many modern buildings are more like monuments to human stupidity than rational answers to needs. But waste costs us even more in little everyday things: filing papers that you will never need again; spending time proving that you were right anyway; postponing a decision to the next meeting because you do not want to take the responsibility now; telephoning when you could just as easily write a note or send a fax. The list is endless.

Use your resources the IKEA way. Then you will reach good results with small means.

5. Simplicity Is a Virtue

There have to be rules to enable a lot of people to function together in a community or a company. But the more complicated the rules are, the harder they are to comply with. Complicated rules paralyze!

Historical baggage, fear, and unwillingness to take responsibility are the breeding ground for bureaucracy. Indecisiveness generates more statistics, more studies, more committees, more bureaucracy. Bureaucracy complicates and paralyzes!

Planning is often synonymous with bureaucracy. Planning is, of course, needed to lay out guidelines for your work and to enable a company to function in the long term. But do not forget that *exaggerated planning is the most common cause of corporate death.* Exaggerated planning constrains your freedom of action and leaves you less time to get things done. Complicated planning paralyzes. So let simplicity and common sense guide your planning.

Simplicity is a fine tradition among us. Simple routines have a greater impact. Simplicity in our behavior gives us strength. Simplicity and humbleness characterize us in our relations with each other, with our suppliers, and with our customers. It is not just to cut costs that we avoid luxury hotels. We do not need fancy cars, posh titles, tailor-made uniforms, or other status symbols. We rely on our own strength and our own will!

6. Doing It a Different Way

If from the start we had consulted experts about whether a little community like Älmhult could support a company like IKEA, they would have undoubtedly advised against it. Nevertheless, Älmhult is now home to one of the world's biggest facilities in the home furnishings business.

By always asking why we are doing this or that, we can find new paths. By refusing to accept a pattern simply because it is well established, we make progress. We dare to do it a different way! Not just in large matters, but in solving small everyday problems too.

It is no coincidence that our purchasers go to a window factory for table legs and a shirt factory for cushions. It is quite simply the answer to the question "Why?"

Our protest against convention is not protest for its own sake: it is a deliberate expression of our constant search for development and improvement.

Maintaining and developing the dynamic of our business is one of our most important tasks. That is why I hope, for example, that we will never have two identical stores. We know that the latest one is bound to have several things wrong with it but will nevertheless, all in all, be the best one yet. Dynamics and the desire to experiment must continually lead us forward. "Why?" will remain an important key word.

7. Concentration Is Important to Our Success

The general who divides his resources will invariably be defeated. Even a multitalented athlete has problems.

For us too, it is a matter of concentration—focusing our resources. We can never do everything, everywhere, all at the same time.

Our range cannot be allowed to overflow. We can never satisfy all tastes anyway. We must concentrate on our own profile. We can never promote the whole of our range at once. We must concentrate. We cannot conquer every market at once. We must concentrate for maximum impact, often with small means.

While we are concentrating on important areas, we must *lista* ourselves on others. *Lista* is a common term in Småland; it means doing what you have to do with an absolute minimum of resources.

When we are building up a new market, we concentrate on marketing. Concentration means that at certain vital stages we are forced to neglect otherwise important aspects, such as security systems. That is why we have to make extra special demands on the honesty and loyalty of every coworker.

Concentration—the very word means strength. Use it in your daily work. It will give you results.

8. Taking Responsibility Is a Privilege

There are people at all levels in every type of company and community who would rather make their own decisions than hide behind those made by others—people who dare to take responsibility. The fewer such responsibility-takers a company or a community has, the more bureaucratic it is. Constant meetings and group discussions are often the result of unwillingness or inability on the part of the person in charge to make decisions. Democracy or the obligation to consult are sometimes cited as excuses.

Taking responsibility has nothing to do with education, financial position, or rank. Responsibility-takers can be found in the warehouse or among the purchasers, sales force, or office staff—in short, everywhere. They are necessary in every system. They are essential for all progress. They are the ones who keep the wheels turning.

In our IKEA family, we want to keep the focus on the individual and support each other. We all have our rights, but we also have our duties. Freedom with responsibility. Your initiative and mine—our ability to take responsibility and make decisions—are decisive.

Only those who are asleep make no mistakes. Making mistakes is the privilege of the active—of those who can correct their mistakes and put them right.

Our objectives require us constantly to practice making decisions and taking responsibility, constantly to overcome our fear of making mistakes. *The fear of making mistakes is the root of bureaucracy and the enemy of development.* No decision can claim to be the only right one; it is the energy put into the decision that determines whether it is right. We must be allowed to make mistakes. It is always the mediocre people who are negative, who spend their time proving that they were not wrong. The strong person is always positive and looks forward.

It is always the positive people who win. They are always a joy to their colleagues and to themselves. But winning does not mean that someone else has to lose. The finest victories are those without losers. If somebody steals a model from us, we do not sue them, because a lawsuit is always negative. We solve the problem instead by developing a new and even better model.

Exercise your privilege—your right and your duty to make decisions and take responsibility.

9. Most Things Still Remain to Be Done— A Glorious Future!

The feeling of having finished something is an effective sleeping pill. A person who retires feeling that he has done his bit will quickly wither away. A company that feels that it has reached its goal will quickly stagnate and lose its vitality.

Happiness is not reaching your goal. Happiness is being on the way. It is our wonderful fate to be just at the beginning, in all areas. We will move ahead only by constantly asking ourselves how what we are doing today can be done better tomorrow. The positive joy of discovery must be our inspiration in the future too. The word *impossible* has been and must remain deleted from our dictionary.

Experience is a word to be handled carefully.

Experience is a brake on all development. Many people cite experience as an excuse for not trying anything new. Still, it can be wise to rely on experience at times. But if you do, you should preferably rely on your own. That is usually more valuable than lengthy investigations.

Our ambition to develop ourselves as human beings and coworkers must remain high. *Humbleness* is the key word. Being humble means so much to us in our work and in our leisure. It is even decisive for us as human beings. It means not just consideration and respect for our fellow men and women, but also kindness and generosity. Will power and strength without humbleness often lead to conflict. Together with humbleness, will power and strength are your secret weapons for development as an individual and fellow human being.

Bear in mind that *time is your most important resource*. You can do so much in ten minutes. Ten minutes, once gone, are gone for good. You can never get them back.

Ten minutes are not just one-sixth of your hourly pay. Ten minutes are a piece of yourself. Divide your life into ten-minute units and sacrifice as few of them as possible in meaningless activity.

Most of the job remains to be done. Let us continue to be a group of positive fanatics who stubbornly and persistently refuse to accept the impossible, the negative. What we want to do, we can do and will do together. A glorious future!

APPENDIX C
IMPORTANT DATES
IN THE LIFE OF
INGVAR KAMPRAD
AND IKEA

1926	Ingvar Kamprad born in the parish of Pjätteryd near Älmhult in southern Sweden
1933	His parents Feodor and Berta Kamprad move to Elmtaryd, the farm where IKEA was dreamed up
1943	IKEA (the initials stand for Ingvar Kamprad Elmtaryd Agunnaryd) is legally registered as a firm
1950	Ingvar Kamprad marries Kerstin Wadling; the marriage is dissolved in 1961
1951	First million Swedish kronor (SKR) turnover (125.000 US $)
1953	Furniture exhibition opens in Älmhult
1958	First IKEA store opens (Älmhult)
1961	First outsourcing: Polish production "rescues" IKEA
1963	Ingvar Kamprad marries Margaretha Stennert; they will have three sons
1965	"Kungens Kurva", outside Stockholm, still the company's flagship store, opens
1970	"Kungens Kurva" burns down, reopens next year marking the start of a totally new concept (cash-and-carry)

1973	Ingvar Kamprad emigrates to Denmark, due to tax reasons. First European store outside Scandinavia opens in Spreitenbach, Switzerland
1978	The Kamprad family settles in Switzerland
1982	Stichtung IKEA is formed, IKEA becomes a trust
1983	Ingvar Kamprad becomes honorary doctor at the Lund University, Sweden
1986	Ingvar Kamprad retires as director of IKEA, succeeded by longtime collaborator Anders Moberg, born not far from Älmhult. Total sale reaches ten billion SKR (1.25 billion US $)
1989	Ingvar Kamprad is named The International Swede of the Year.
1992	Ingvar Kamprad receives the prestigious Swedish Association of Engineering Science Award
1997-1998	Total sales report for fifty billion SKR (6.25 billion US $)
1998	The 137th store inaugurates in Shanghai, no. 1 in China (later followed by one store in Beijing). "The IKEA story" is first published, now translated into 13 different languages.
1999	Anders Dahlvig, former close assistant of Mr Kamprad succeeds Anders Moberg as director of the group. The 150th store opens in Budapest, Hungary. Sales reach over 60 billion SKR (7.5 billion US $)
2000	First store in Russia opens in March followed by a second Moscow store in December.

2002	The 175th store in operation. Total sale climbs to 100 billion Swedish Kronor (12.5 billion US $)
2003	Thirteen new stores open around the world
2004	Mattias Kamprad, youngest son of the founder, appointed new country director of Denmark. His brothers, Peter (eldest) and Jonas, occupy other important board posts in IKEA International, IKANO and Inter IKEA. Eighteen new stores open worldwide.
2005	First store in Portugal opens, so in Turkey too (the group's 24th franchise store). Number of employees reaches 90.000. The US organization celebrates its 20th anniversary. Total sale not far from 150 billion SKR (18.7 US $). The number of store reaches 226 (including the franchisees).
2006	First store in Japan will open among nineteen other new stores worldwide, the US, Russia and China being among IKEA's fastest-growing markets. Mr Kamprad will celebrate his 80th birthday, still working the clock around as his company's "senior advisor".

(2010 Goal set for US: 50 IKEA outlets to compare with 160 in Europe 2005... For other US figures: see the foreword and the special US chapter)

ACKNOWLEDGMENTS

Interviewing for a book of this kind is rather like picking flowers in a meadow. Some of the flowers beckon temptingly from the edge of the ditch, with others you have to go down on your knees to see their beauty, some you observe indirectly—but they are all there, representing a wealth of possibilities, the framework of a vast flora.

Now that I have completed my journey through IKEA, certain faces glow in my memory. The sight of the women frenziedly weaving in the Sheena carpet factory, a drive of an hour or two out of Delhi, merges into the picture of the young checkout clerk in Aubonne demanding to see the founder's identity card to check for his staff discount after he has bought a large pack of tealights.

I remember Shierley Bao, the Chinese purchaser, and her genuine delight as she walked through the new store in Shanghai and first saw with her own eyes the results of her work in the form of displayed articles. And Per Hahn, the business area manager, elegantly giving a quick lesson one hot "family day" in Älmhult on the art of selling the "Billy" bookcase and other storage items for several billions. And the retired employee Rolf Forsberg telling me about his previous work overseeing the Småland van park—"Oh, when all the vans were there on parade, newly washed. . . . " And Marianne Wir, all-seeing receptionist, one of the firm's "mothers"—or, as she says, "fenders."

Just as the army of anonymous people, all worthy of a monument, helped Ingvar Kamprad realize his dream of IKEA, there are innumerable individuals who, though quite unaware, provided me with important ideas while I was working on the book. I want to thank them for their generosity, their help, and their hospitality.

Of course, this project would never have been accomplished without the full support and confidence of Ingvar Kamprad and his extended family.

The journey I have had to make with this book into another person's inner being has seemed to me pure privilege. To be allowed to follow so closely a boy's wild dreams via a small company's transformation into his materialized visions has been an adventure. If the reading of these pages inspires someone to venture into the prodigious challenge of entrepreneurship, I know someone who would be happy.